STEEPED IN

Heritage

NEW ECOLOGIES FOR
THE TWENTY-FIRST CENTURY

Series Editors:
Arturo Escobar, University of North Carolina, Chapel Hill
Dianne Rocheleau, Clark University

This series addresses two trends: critical conversations in academic fields about nature, sustainability, globalization, and culture, including constructive engagements among the natural, social, and human sciences; and intellectual and political conversations among social movements and other nonacademic knowledge producers about alternative practices and socio-natural worlds. Its objective is to establish a synergy between these theoretical and political developments in both academic and nonacademic arenas. This synergy is a sine qua non for new thinking about the real promise of emergent ecologies. The series includes works that envision more lasting and just ways of being-in-place and being-in-networks with a diversity of humans and other living and nonliving beings.

New Ecologies for the Twenty-First Century aims to promote a dialogue between those who are transforming the understanding of the relationship between nature and culture. The series revisits existing fields such as environmental history, historical ecology, environmental anthropology, ecological economics, and cultural and political ecology. It addresses emerging tendencies, such as the use of complexity theory to rethink a range of questions on the nature-culture axis. It also deals with epistemological and ontological concerns, building bridges between the various forms of knowing and ways of being embedded in the multiplicity of practices of social actors worldwide. This series hopes to foster convergences among differently located actors and to provide a forum for authors and readers to widen the fields of theoretical inquiry, professional practice, and social struggles that characterize the current environmental arena.

STEEPED IN

Heritage

THE RACIAL POLITICS OF
SOUTH AFRICAN ROOIBOS TEA

Sarah Ives

Duke University Press · Durham and London · 2017

Cover design by Heather Hensley; interior designed by Courtney Leigh Baker
Typeset in Garamond Premier Pro by Copperline Books

Library of Congress Cataloging-in-Publication Data
Names: Ives, Sarah Fleming, author.
Title: Steeped in heritage : the racial politics of South African
rooibos tea / Sarah Ives.
Description: Durham : Duke University Press, 2017. | Series: New ecologies
for the twenty-first century | Includes bibliographical references and index.
Identifiers: LCCN 2017013669 (print)
LCCN 2017015471 (ebook)
ISBN 9780822372301 (ebook)
ISBN 9780822369868 (hardcover)
ISBN 9780822369936 (pbk.)
Subjects: LCSH: Rooibos tea—South Africa. |
Rooibos tea industry—South Africa.
Classification: LCC HD9198.S6 (ebook) | LCC HD9198.S6
194 2017 (print) | DDC 338.1/7372—DC23
LC record available at https://lccn.loc.gov/2017013669

Cover art: Loose tea photo: Heather Hensley.
Tea bag outline: Tatiana Popova / Shutterstock.com.

Duke University Press gratefully acknowledges
the support of Stanford University, which provided funds
toward the publication of this book.

In loving memory of
Robert James Caldwell

The greatest service which can be rendered to any country is to add a useful plant to its culture. —Thomas Jefferson

If South Africa had to name a national drink, it would certainly be Rooibos tea. This golden-red brew discovered by the Khoisan is a flavour as indigenous as licking the sweat from a Kudu's snout. —"Southafricanisms: Rooibos Tea," Why Go South Africa website

Contents

Preface

As I sit in a San Francisco coffee shop writing about rooibos tea, the plant's growing region seems even farther away than the two ten-hour flights to South Africa's Western Cape. Music blares while hipsters with tight jeans, hooded sweatshirts, and baseball caps with ironic messages such as "I ♥ Wall Street" pour specialty coffees and serve house-made baked goods. Dozens of hopeful young entrepreneurs type on their laptops, surrounding me with the energy of the "second tech boom." At the counter, the menu advertises Five Mountains Tea. Listed second, under "Nile Valley Chamomile" and above the more local "Pacific Peppermint," is "Cedarburg[1] Rooibos." One cup costs $2.50—or, at the current exchange rate, about twenty South African rands. Why the high price? The menu advertises "single origin, heirloom, sustainable" tea with flavors of "malty grains, cedar, raisins." It is "not caffeinated but high antioxidant." What does heirloom rooibos mean, I wonder? What does the company mean by "sustainable"?

Curious, I use the coffee shop's free Internet to peruse Five Mountains Tea's website. It calls rooibos the "world's first tea (tisane/herbal) from the South African Khoisan tribe." Under its certification labels (USDA Organic, Single Origin, Sustainable Harvest, and a fourth that is too blurry to read), the website provides details about the tea:

Varietal: Aspalathus Linearis. In the legume family, Rooibos (Red Bush), fine needle like leaves
Profile: malty grains, cedar, raisin
Process: Sustainably harvested legume > withered indoors > lightly rolled > fully oxidized > re-rolled > re-withered > fully dried
Attributes: Non-caffeinated, antioxidant rich, calming, low tannins. Rich in vitamins and minerals such as vitamin C, calcium and iron

Preparation: 1 Tbs. per 8 oz., 195°F, 5–7 min. For iced tea, steep tea
strongly, allow to cool, pour over ice
Region: Cedarburg Mts. Western Cape province, South Africa. Deep
sandy soil. Low rainfall. 200–500m elev.32°S, 19°E
Garden: Citrusdal

The price, the location, the description, the aura of the tea, all come together
to create feelings of desire and distinction that arise from an imagined geography celebrating the idea of both global connectedness and exotic, distanced
foreignness. An Internet search for academic work on rooibos garners more
than six thousand results, virtually all about its health benefits. The articles
are filled with scientific-sounding terms, such as bioactivity, antigen, flavonoid,
and clastogen—terms that require experts to decode. To those untrained in
the nuances of tea chemistry, clastogens and flavonoids appear as mysterious
and unfamiliar as the African wilderness.

Writing about the social world of coffee, Paige West (2012) describes a similar experience of encountering her research in a New York café. She reflects
on the effort exerted by multiple people in multiple parts of the world to get
a cup of coffee from the fields of Papua New Guinea to a shop in the United
States. This labor, she describes, is not just the physical toil in the fields or the
movement of the coffee from place to place or even the brewing of the coffee
by the local barista. Instead, she explores the multiple forms labor takes, such as
reproductive labor, alienated factory and farm labor, marketing labor, and artisanal labor, to produce value in a global economy. Sitting in the San Francisco
coffee shop, I found myself wondering: What kinds of value do descriptions
of the tea's territory, healing powers, and taste foster in the social world of
rooibos? What, in turn, are the effects—both material and symbolic—of this
value on the people in the growing region?

South Africa's rooibos region provides a dramatic example for understanding the world through a commodity. While rooibos marketing aims to enchant
the tea for global consumers, residents of the region expressed their own form
of place-based enchantment—an enchantment that celebrates rooibos's indigeneity and its unique ecosystem but could also erase the presence of nonwhite
people's labor and histories on the land. *Steeped in Heritage* ultimately takes up
residents' struggles over rooibos, its land, and its cultural ownership to understand how communities negotiate uncertain landscapes: places of imperiled
ecosystems in the face of climate change and precarious social relations in the
postapartheid era.

Acknowledgments

This book grew out of a dissertation submitted to Stanford University's Department of Anthropology, but the ideas go back further to my first trip to South Africa as an undergraduate studying geography and environmental studies at Dartmouth College. As with most research projects, *Steeped in Heritage* emerged accidentally. I had initially planned to study in Zimbabwe, but a series of political upheavals led to a last-minute switch to South Africa. My time at the University of Pretoria began a fifteen-year engagement with the country and introduced me to a key part of South African hospitality: rooibos tea. When I entered my host family's home for the first time, I was met with the words: "What tea would you like? English or rooibos?" I asked, "What is rooibos?" Ironically prescient perhaps, "What is rooibos?" ultimately became the subject of an inquiry I would return to over and over during my doctorate and beyond. After many years and research projects, the answer I uncovered was far from simple.

I could not begin to give proper thanks to all those who offered support during each stage of this project. I am deeply in debt to the people of the rooibos-growing region for their time, generosity, hospitality, and patience. They laughed with—and sometimes at—the *Amerikaanse meisie* as I negotiated the social and ecological terrain of the rooibos world.

The book would not have been possible without the help of many individuals and institutions. I thank James Ferguson, my graduate adviser at Stanford University. He provided guidance throughout the research and writing process, from grounding my ideas to pushing my theoretical engagements to commenting on numerous drafts. My dissertation committee, Liisa Malkki, Paulla Ebron, and Lynn Meskell, provided invaluable feedback and encouragement. Through her close readings during a writing seminar, Liisa helped me find my voice whenever I buried it in academic language.

In South Africa, scholars at the Institute for Poverty, Land and Agrarian Studies at the University of the Western Cape and the Department of Sociology and Social Anthropology at the University of Stellenbosch provided instrumental support and advice during my fieldwork. The Environmental Monitoring Group and Indigo Development and Change assisted with my understanding of the climate aspects of the rooibos-growing region. In addition, Alison Montgomery was a vital resource for working through the everyday negotiations of fieldwork. This project was generously funded by the Mellon/ ACLS Dissertation Completion Fellowship, the Wenner-Gren Foundation, the IIE Student Fulbright, the U.S. Department of Education, Stanford's Department of Anthropology, and Stanford's Center for African Studies. A postdoctoral position in Stanford's Program in Writing and Rhetoric provided funding during the writing stage.

I am indebted to colleagues and mentors who helped push my ideas forward. Jesse Davie-Kessler and Alexandra Kelly gave rigorous feedback on multiple iterations of this material. Steven Robins, Lisa Poggiali, Bruce O'Neill, Thomas Blom Hansen, Anna Tsing, Hannah Appel, Rosemary Coombe, Andries du Toit, and Margo Fleming also provided guidance. Katherine Ives and Katie Ives gave me support during each stage of the process by eagerly providing feedback on my writing and ideas from a nonacademic perspective. Jack Shepherd introduced me to research in South Africa as a college student and helped shape the way I engage with the country today. Mona Domosh taught me how to interrogate place and space as more than just the backdrop for human experience.

Steeped in Heritage also benefited from panel sessions at conferences, including the American Anthropological Association's annual meeting; the Association of American Geographers' annual meeting; the African Studies Association's annual meeting; "Land Divided: Land and South African Society in 2013 in Comparative Perspective" at the University of Cape Town; "Climate Change and Culture" at the University of Prince Edward Island; and "Political Ecologies of Conflict, Capitalism and Contestation" at Wageningen University and School of Oriental and African Studies, University of London. Portions of this book appeared in *American Ethnologist* (2014) and *American Anthropologist* (2014), as well as in *The Sage Handbook of Intellectual Property*. The ideas benefited greatly from the editors and anonymous reviewers of these publications. I also thank Gisela Fosado and Lydia Rose Rappoport-Hankins of Duke University Press, and the anonymous reviewers they enlisted, for their assistance in sharpening my final contribution. Several other Duke University

Press employees played key roles in the book's production (including project editors Sara Leone and Christi Stanforth and designer Heather Hensley) and will work to put it in readers' hands. I am grateful for their efforts.

Last, thank you to Mike Montgomery for his unconditional support and patience during the research and writing process, and for sharing my passion for a daily cup of rooibos tea.

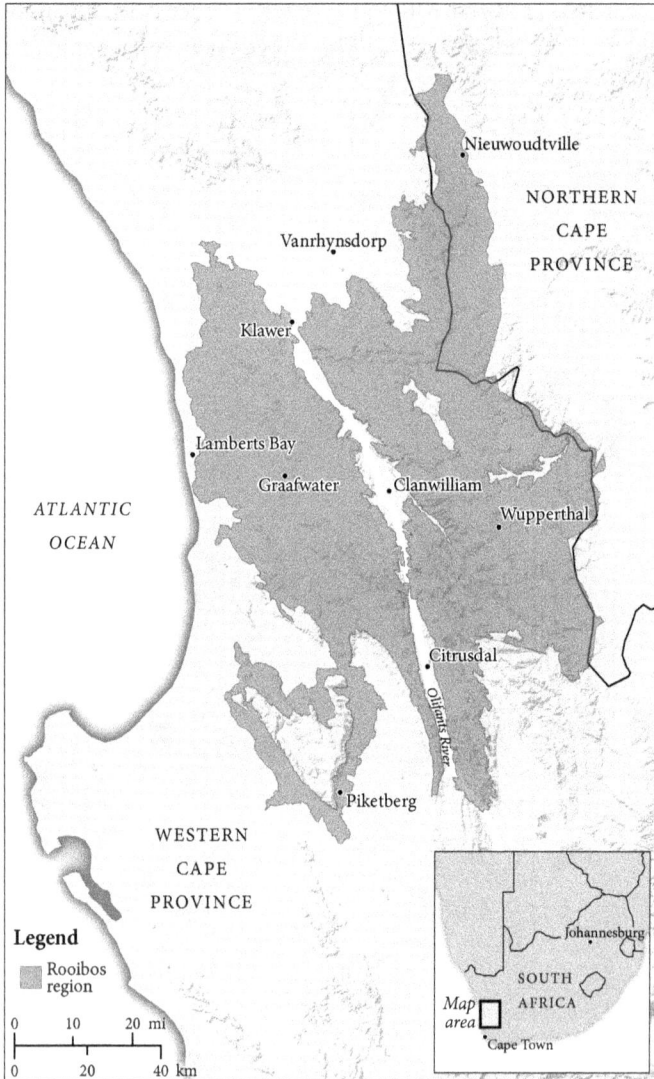

MAP FM.1. Map of the rooibos-growing region. Created by Tim Stallman based on information supplied by Mike Wallace, Western Cape Department of Agriculture, South Africa.

Introduction

THE "ROOIBOS REVOLUTION"

Deep in the heart of South Africa, in the mountains and valleys
of the Cederberg region near Cape Town, vast vistas, fields of verdant green bushes,
fill the landscape. Traveling throughout this precipitous expanse, one may
not suspect that this bright bush, which the locals refer to as "Rooibos," could be such
a versatile and remarkable herb. Rooibos tea remained virtually unheard of
for centuries, known only to the Khoisans, a tribe of South African Bushmen....
The secret of this delicious herb nearly vanished into oblivion due to the
environment and landscape, as the isolated tribe dwindled away and eventually
disappeared.... Luckily, Rooibos tea was re-discovered in 1772 by botanist
Carl Humberg, who then brought it back as a beverage.... Thus, the
Worldwide Rooibos Revolution had begun. —CHRIS CASON, "Rooibos Tea"

The Cederberg region of South Africa is a dry, seemingly marginal place, with brown-gray plants that appear to come alive with a brief surprise of color after the winter rains, only to retreat again to brown-gray when the rains fail and drought sets in. During the summers I lived in Clanwilliam, a small town that housed a tea-processing plant, the landscape seared with heat and left everyone searching the sky (or the weather forecast) for rain. Rainfall in the region was highly variable. Some areas received less than 150 millimeters per year, and surface water was limited. A sign posted next to a large dam regularly updated the water level as its capacity decreased daily through the summer—90 percent, 70 percent, 25 percent—only to rise again in the winter—30 percent, 75 percent, 98 percent. For residents of this farming region, it was a life measured by cycles.

I first visited the area in the winter of 2009. About three hours of driving separate Clanwilliam from Africa's southwestern tip. The journey takes you from Cape Town's skyscrapers through the informal settlements that surround the city to long stretches of wheat fields, punctuated by the occasional small town. Eventually, a steep road winds its way up a high pass and marks the passage from the vast open fields to the rocky shrubs of the Cederberg. The short Southern Hemisphere winter could be deceptively cool, and during my first visit the mountains were white with snow from a recent storm. When residents learned that I planned to live there from 2010 to 2011, they only hinted at the harsh conditions that were to follow. Months later, everyone seemed to delight in asking me, "How are you surviving in this heat?" Or, "I thought about you when the weather went back above 45 degrees [Celsius]," teasing smiles spreading across their faces. For more than a hundred years, farmers had battled the long summers with irrigation to produce crops that had evolved in faraway ecosystems: potatoes, grapes, and citrus. Beyond the edges of these fields, however, residents also harvested indigenous rooibos plants and used the bush's leaves to create an earthy tea.

A native plant, rooibos is adapted to the region's hot, dry summers. The narrow needle-like leaves from which the tea derives have limited surface area to minimize moisture loss. Driving to a rooibos farm in the early stages of my research, I found myself hopelessly lost in a maze of dirt roads. The vegetation all looked the same—indigenous bushes and blooming protea flowers. I couldn't tell where the farm ended and the uncultivated land began. Far from cellphone reception, I started to feel desperate until I came across a group of farmworkers walking to the pavement that I had left behind miles before. "*Waar is die plaas, asseblief?*" I called out in Afrikaans, the most commonly used local language, asking where the farm was located. One worker laughed, probably as much at my American accent as at my seemingly redundant question. "*Dit is die plaas*," he responded. As I looked around, rows of rooibos plants began to form in front of my eyes among the rocks and shrubs. I laughed—*this* was the farm. Unlike the neat rows of local grape or citrus fields, rooibos farms can blend so seamlessly into the landscape that an untrained—or panicked—eye can miss them.

This book explores how rooibos farming is entangled with political, economic, and environmental struggles over land, labor, and ideas of native belonging. Much lore surrounds the tea. The "remarkable herb" Chris Cason (2004) describes, "remained virtually unheard of for centuries, known only to the Khoisans [*sic*], a tribe of South African Bushmen." "Luckily," he continues, the tea was "re-discovered" and now serves consumers around the world. In the last hundred years, rooibos has moved from wild plant gathered for local consumption to a global commodity. Now comprising about 10 percent of the global herbal tea market, rooibos can be found in trendy cafés as far afield as Hollywood, Munich, and Beijing (Department of Agriculture, Forestry, and Fisheries 2014). By 2011, about five thousand people worked at rooibos farms and processing plants, and rooibos had become an approximately $70 million-dollar industry (Department of Agriculture, Forestry, and Fisheries 2011).

Tea marketers describe rooibos as a cure-all that will do everything from preventing cancer to thwarting the effects of aging. Advertisements alternately refer to the tea as an exotic commodity, a traditional Indigenous[1] medicine, and South Africa's national beverage. These depictions, however, are more than mere marketing flourish. Many local residents describe the tea as "Mandela-like," imbued with charismatic qualities that supposedly would heal the unhealthy body, the divided nation, and the depleted land. In this way, rooibos is rife with semiotic possibilities. Cultivating rooibos is as much about harvesting an indigenous plant as it is about producing a storied commodity. Rooibos tea packaging is nearly always accompanied by brochures, origin narratives, and images. These stories require a production of locality—a natural, indigenous, exotic locality that is either unpeopled (the African wilderness) or populated only by "natives" who are envisioned as a natural part of the Bush and not fully or securely human.

This book, then, is not just about rooibos but also about how people claim their belonging in relation to an uncertain political, economic, *and* ecological future. By exploring the ironies and surprises that surround the plant/commodity, *Steeped in Heritage* looks at how people envision themselves as attached to places and how those attachments play out in fierce contestations over nature, race, and heritage in a land where climatic shifts are pushing the indigenous ecosystem southward. How do residents grapple with their "precarious" identities, and how do they articulate their own concepts of what it means to be indigenous when their uncertain claims to belonging in place merge with the uncertainty of the rootedness of place itself? I will show how residents' relations with rooibos as a commodity, as an indigenous plant, and even as an extension of the self help to answer these questions.

Arjun Appadurai (1986) argues that we have reached a "commodity ecumene" defined by relationships that link people around the world through consumption. These relations are punctuated by connections and disconnections, productions and erasures. Consumers prefer to be ignorant about some aspects of food production, yet they are also captivated by the lore of food origins. By purchasing food from other countries, they construct a meaningful cognitive geography about the world and their place in it (Fischer and Benson 2006). Tea consumers in the United States and Europe can fantasize about preserving a wild "African Bush" or draw comfort from the idea that their purchases help "Third World" laborers earn livelihoods or maintain a particular way of life. For some consumers, the ethics of consumption centers on a self-fashioning that removes them from global inequality or complicity in environmental destruction.

Rooibos's global commodity chain brought farmers and workers into dialogue with transnational movements centered on indigenous products. By examining the industry's emphasis on the plant/commodity's indigeneity, I explore the effects of combining indigeneity and the market—in an area where both heritage and the market were hotly contested. "Rooibos tea is a fabric of society," a white farmer said as we sat in his office sipping tea and looking across his fields. In tension with effusive narratives about rooibos's nativity, the region was peopled with two groups who do not fit easily into discussions of indigeneity: "white Afrikaans" and "coloured" South Africans. Coloureds, a South African racial category, were often considered impure and denied nativity to anywhere, while Afrikaners espoused a "white African indigeneity" that was itself fiercely contested by coloured and black South Africans who stylized them as "settlers" from Europe.[2] Afrikaners could trace their history in the region as far back as the seventeenth century. They are descended primarily from Dutch Calvinists, as well as from Germans and French Huguenots, though mixing occurred among all European groups and even across racial boundaries that were porous during the early years of colonization. Often labeled an "African ethnic group," many Afrikaners did not feel a connection to Europe; rather, they believed that southern Africa was their essential homeland. Coloured South Africans, with a diverse heritage of Khoisan (or "Bushman"),[3] white settler colonists, and slaves and laborers brought from other parts of Africa and Asia, were saddled with stereotypes of inauthenticity.

The discourse of a pure, ecologically indigeneous rooibos worked alongside pathologized, deterritorialized concepts of coloured and Afrikaans identities. It is this apparent contradiction that was central to social and ecological relations in the region. Rooibos was unquestionably indigenous, its naturalness supposedly outside of politics; yet, the plant's naturalness was the source of its economic, cultural, and spiritual value and engendered its very politicization as compared to other crops. Rooibos and its ecological indigeneity brought together nature, place (as a physically and ecologically delineated region and as a geographical imaginary), race, and politics in very concrete ways. Both coloured and Afrikaans residents appeared trapped in a liminal state—neither unequivocally African nor European, yet intimately connected to the indigenous ecosystem that they cultivated and called their home. They were the people of *this* place, but also the people of *no place*. Perpetually entangled in power-laden relations of dependence and conviviality, they lived side-by-side existences marked by compromise (du Toit 1993; Mbembe 2001).

Some politicians and development workers tried to "redeem" and "explain" coloured identity by relabeling it, using the term "native Bushman." However, coloured residents often resisted attempts to be emplaced as native, a label that held both the promise of rehabilitating their supposedly pathological identities and the threat of temporally incarcerating them in a state of primitivism or even extinction. Instead, they drew on their connection to rooibos, pointing to the plant's indigeneity for evidence. In doing so, they expressed a temporally different heritage—one that is coalescing in the present and is unencumbered by a culturally indigenous identity. They showed how the object (rooibos) and not the culture (coloured or Khoisan) served as the focus of their belonging and their hopes for an economically viable future. Residents of the rooibos region undoubtedly lived in Appadurai's "commodity ecumene," as the tea linked them to packagers, companies, and consumers around the world. A global tea market searching for "new," "exotic" herbal teas affected the lives and livelihoods of workers, farm owners, and other residents. Yet the intimate negotiations of belonging through and with the indigenous plant brought together experiences of geographical precarity with economic precarity and racial—even ontological—precarity that an exploration of rooibos as a transnational commodity alone could not capture. To residents, rooibos could shift between commodity, native plant, and moral subject. In addressing residents' alternate politics of indigeneity, this book explores the kinds of activism these claims both open up and foreclose.

"WE HAVE NAMED OUR rooibos tea cooperative Ebenezer," said Theunis,[4] a coloured farmer who lived in the northernmost part of the rooibos region, straddling the Western Cape and Northern Cape provinces. "It's a biblical term that means God has carried us here. We had a lot of fights to lease this rooibos land." Theunis described how "Ebenezer" came from a passage in the Book of Samuel about an Israelite victory over the Philistines. The name literally means "the stone of help." Later, reflecting on the region's intense and personal struggles over rooibos ownership, I looked up the passage: "Then Samuel took a stone, and set it between Mizpeh and Shen, and called the name of it Ebenezer, saying, until now the Lord helped us" (Samuel 7:12). Theunis's use of "Ebenezer" seemed to encapsulate more than his fight for rooibos land in an area where white farmers owned almost all of the farm acreage. The words possessed an uncertain temporality: *Until now* God has helped us. Theunis remained unsure about the future of his tea cooperative and his own livelihood. Would he be able to compete with the agribusinesses that were increasingly involved with rooibos production? *Until now.* Would his crops survive the changing ecological climate observed in the region? *Until now.* Despite the lack of definitive answers, Theunis celebrated and gave thanks for his access to rooibos after centuries of disposession. Rooibos and its indigeneity formed an integral part of his sense of belonging and his ability to earn a living on the dry, nutrient-poor land. The rooibos he grew was a "gift from nature" and his "stone of help," memorializing his temporary victory in and with the land.

Theunis considered himself lucky. Most coloured residents did not have access to land. Today, commercial farmers—who are almost exclusively white—oversee the cultivation of approximately 93 percent of rooibos, while small-scale coloured farmers, unable to access significant amounts of land, cultivate less than 7 percent (Sandra Kruger and Associates 2009).[5] Commercial farmers expressed their own feelings of connection to—even love of—the land. "Rooibos tea started from the wild," Kobus, a white Afrikaans farmer who lived down the road from Theunis, said. He was interested in ecology and had read natural history books about the area. As we walked across his vast farmland, he stopped occasionally to point out wild rooibos plants growing at the edge of his cultivated tea fields. "Rooibos is part of the fynbos family," Kobus added. "Fynbos is the smallest of the world's six flower kingdoms. It's what makes it special, unique. It's only in South Africa, only here." He stroked the needles of a tea bush next to him. "Come, let's have a cup." As the sun went down and the escarpment faded from view, we walked back to his thatched-roofed farmhouse. Strange shadows formed when the colored lights of the rugby game showing on the television inside flashed across the open fields. Thinking that I heard baboons barking nearby, I scrambled to catch up with Kobus, who walked steadily across the dusty soil, his dog nipping at his heels.

The story of rooibos tea unfolds in the margins. Punctuated with rumors of public fights, political corruption, and corporate greed, it is a story about globalization and isolation, neoliberal economic reforms and postapartheid politics. It is about "whiteness" and "colouredness," migrants and indigeneity. Finally, it is a story of economic and ecological uncertainty and of the ways residents of a rural farming community understood and experienced these tensions. Yet significantly, it is also a story about the crop itself, an indigenous plant with particular qualities that make it valuable and intensely political. When farmers discussed price volatility in the area's other major agricultural industries—citrus, grapes, and sheep—they described currency exchange rates or trade agreements. When discussing the rooibos market, however, a farmer said, "Everything is personal." *Steeped in Heritage* explores how firm distinctions between the natural and cultural landscapes blurred and gave way to a hybrid ecology of belonging. The geography of the landscape merged with the biography of the people and informed their entangled histories.

Though deeply personal, the stories told by coloured farmers such as Theunis, by white commercial farmers such as Kobus, and by farmworkers, marketers, scientists, and politicians resonated with theories of race, globalization, and contemporary capitalism. The book specifically addresses connections between race and nature in the context of a commodity that was celebrated for its ecological indigeneity and of people who did not fall straightforwardly into the category of culturally "Indigenous." In the Cederberg region, links between race and nature formed a terrain for the exercise of power and the legitimation of political, social, and economic hierarchies and violent exclusions. Control over natural resources and knowledge of botany played a considerable role in consolidating white residents' power and in naturalizing Afrikaans belonging.

Struggles over rooibos took place in a region in which possibilities for wage labor were becoming precarious and the majority of land remained in white hands. According to the South African government, 25.5 percent of the population was unemployed.[6] With both land tenure and employment uncertain, mobilizations around cultural ownership took on growing importance as political rallying points and means of economic survival. Detailed ethnographic work in the rooibos region shows that such claims emerged in unexpected ways. Coloured people rejected a spatially incarcerating idea of cultural indigeneity, *even as they recognized the Khoisan as the original users of the rooibos plant and often acknowledged their (partial) descent from these groups.* Rather than embracing a primordial attachment to the landscape through genealogical ties to a culturally indigenous past, both coloured and Afrikaans residents found economic possibilities in and metonymic identification with rooibos. Yet these plant-human connections remained inextricably tied to the violent racial histories mapped to and still existent in the ecosystem.

As its economic value increased, rooibos's role in contestations over belonging also rose. Formerly seen as just a wild plant and local beverage, rooibos became a culturally significant commodity through which coloured and white residents measured their indigeneity and, more broadly, their belonging in South Africa and in a "globalizing" world. At stake was not the conventional scholarly concept of "indigenous"—as an enduring, even timeless, relationship between people and place. Rather, residents expressed a different kind of claim to indigeneity based on a relationship among plant, place, and person. This claim unsettled rooted, essentialized framings of indigeneity that had violently incarcerated "natives" under apartheid. Instead, it allowed for a different politics of indigeneity that was potentially more flexible, encompassing, and emancipatory.

As many scholars of anthropology, geography, and history have demonstrated, territorial governance and natural history have been linked in both colonial and postcolonial projects (Beinart and Wotshella 2011; Mukerji 2005). Political ecology studies combine "social construction of nature" literature with classic political economy tropes, such as peasant resistance against forces of capital, to argue for geographically and historically contextualized concepts of a landed, resource-based economy. Using this framework, scholars discuss issues such as environmental degradation as part of the logic of capital (Neumann 1998; Peet et al. 2011). While I draw on this literature, I also demonstrate how the rooibos landscape narrativized the region's social and ecological relations in ways that went beyond metaphor or human control: Agrarian struggles were material, symbolic, and generative. These struggles reproduced particular kinds of relations in the rooibos economy through kinship that included not only the transfer of rooibos knowledge from generation to generation but also a symbiosis between indigenous plant and person.

Despite this espoused symbiosis, relations between the human and nonhuman in the context of the rooibos region's racial landscape complicate celebratory connections between people and nature: White residents did not always consider coloured and black people to be securely or fully human. This physical and structural violence informed the region's social and ecological relations, as well as the rooibos industry's past and future. While racial thought in South Africa has long collapsed the distinction between "nature" and "native people" in an exclusionary way, I examine those same entanglements in a manner that attempts to unpack the colonialist vision of the two spheres. Can the celebration of plants as actors in the landscape also marginalize certain categories of people? To address this question, I explore how plant/commodities such as rooibos and the land on which they grow constitute a set of relationships. By examining a niche, indigenous commodity in connection with these symbolic and material struggles, I look at the tensions in the mutually fashioning dialectic between people and things, humans and nonhumans.

From its earliest history—from Marx to Malinowski to Mauss—the cultural significance of objects and exchange has been a classic concern of social science. Following Sidney Mintz (1974, 1986), scholars have used commodities such as sugar to explore articulations among production, consumption, and the social, economic, and political forces shaping the world (Appadurai 1986; Burke 1996; Chalfin 2004; Chatterjee 2001; Freidberg 2009; Paxson 2010; Taussig 1980; Tsing 2003; Wolf 1982). Most recent social science research on commodities has focused on theories of neoliberal globalization. Consumption in particular has become increasingly prevalent in theories of late capitalism as the "prime mover" of neoliberal capitalism, "a force that determines definitions of value, the construction of identities" (Comaroff and Comaroff 1999: 780). The changing agrarian landscape of the rooibos region is certainly informed by globalization and consumption; however, I see such a focus as acting only in the context of intimate relations among plant, ecosystem, farmers, and workers.

Drawing on the social relations in the tea-growing region, I argue that narratives about commodities can create their own forms of alienation. While Mintz's examination of sugar provides a critical analysis of global commodity chains, both nature and labor appear estranged. He concentrates more on the *process and the movement* of the thing through the world system than on the thing *itself.* Extending Mintz, I rethink the terms of relationality between production and consumption, white and coloured, indigenous and foreign, people and plant, labor and capital, and how this constellation of relations informs economically, politically, and ecologically significant senses of place and belonging. Through the idea of the "gift," Marcel Mauss (1990) looks at the sociality and inalienability of certain objects. For rooibos farmers such as Theunis and Kobus, love for rooibos held a symbolic meaning different from love for nonindigenous crops, because in loving rooibos, they were also loving South Africa—or, more precisely, their corner of the Western Cape. Rooibos was nature and God's gift to the region, and in turn, residents described rooibos as an inalienable part of their existence.

A Social and Natural History

The unique microclimate of the tiny geographical region allows for the best quality natural teas to be grown in the area. The harsh climate and fertile soil combine to form [a] rare herbal treasure. —DEPARTMENT OF AGRICULTURE, FORESTRY, AND FISHERIES, *A Profile of the South African Rooibos Tea Market Value Chain*

The rooibos-growing region begins about 200 kilometers north of Cape Town and extends just across the border of the Northern Cape, with the majority of land within the Western Cape's Cederberg municipality. For millennia, the area was inhabited by hunter-gatherers who are sometimes called "San." Around the beginning of the first millennium AD, herders, sometimes called

"Khoi," introduced pastoralism (Adhikari 2010a; Penn 2005). In the rooibos region, residents typically referred to the San and the Khoi, groups that were dynamic and fluid, by the merged name "Khoisan." The land had a relatively low carrying capacity, and the Khoisan were mobile, as they typically followed the seasonal rainfall. They left their mark in the thousands of paintings still visible on rocks throughout the region.

Europeans—associated predominately with the Dutch East India Company—arrived in the rooibos-growing area in the mid-seventeenth century. Colonization came slowly but violently. Colonists set up farms but often abandoned them to move back to the Cape of Good Hope, the heart of early settlement. Eventually, demographic pressure led colonial families to claim land for permanent settlement, and the region increasingly became a place of conflict among Dutch East India Company officials, white settler colonists who wanted "freedom" from the company, the Khoisan whose land they dispossessed, and escaped slaves (Mitchell 2008; Penn 2005). Dispossession occurred through various means, including violent conquest, treaty (although it is unclear whether the Khoisan entered into treaties freely or with full understanding of their consequences), and the impact of a small pox epidemic in 1713 that led to the deaths of many Khoisan. Conquest included the murder, enslavement, and rape of people and the theft of livestock by colonial marauders. By depriving pastoralists of their livestock, colonists also robbed them of their livelihoods, thereby forcing them into labor, into a hunter-gatherer subsistence, or into moving farther and farther north as the colonial frontier pushed up the continent.

In the initial years of colonization, both the Khoisan and the colonists practiced a kind of transhumance: They moved from place to place to subsist off the agriculturally marginal land. Homesteads were largely impermanent (Mitchell 2008). Like the Khoi, early colonists made their livelihoods as pastoralists, and for both groups, cattle appeared to be more important than land. Until the beginning of the nineteenth century, the colonial government and the farmers themselves did not firmly enforce property boundaries; rather, they claimed features on the land, such as the extremely important waterholes (Penn 2005). Farmers protected their newly claimed assets at gunpoint, supported by a "commando system" that acted as a semiformal militia made up primarily of white farmers, who were often supplied with gunpowder by the Dutch East India Company. They were responsible for the virtual genocide of the Khoisan—killing the men and capturing women and children to work on their farms (Adhikari 2010b).

It was not until the frontier's closure in the early nineteenth century that private land tenure became codified, as surveying, mapping, and fencing redefined the landscape and concretized the dispossession of the Khoisan that commando "extermination" had already largely carried out. As colonists moved to a more sedentary form of farming, they demanded labor in the form of chattel slaves (an amalgam of people of African and Asian origins whom settler colonists often brought from Cape Town) and indentured captive Khoisan. Through these multiple forms of violence, the Khoisan of the rooibos region eventually lost their languages (adopting Afrikaans), their access to land, and their freedom from European enslavement or indentured servitude. They came to form a highly exploitable, and almost entirely landless, laboring class that served the white farming community's shift toward rooted agricultural production. In this bonded labor, distinctions between "imported" slaves and Khoisan were fluid and largely constitutive of the region's coloured population today.

Demographic and land-use changes also permanently altered the ecosystem. Settlers' animal husbandry practices resulted in overgrazing, while their guns increased the scale of hunting to unsustainable levels. These factors led to the eventual extermination of entire species in the region, including the elephants (or *olifants* in Afrikaans) for which settlers named the river that flowed through the region and the eland that were central to San spirituality (Parkington 2003). Yet throughout this violent history, rooibos continued to grow wild in the mountains, consumed by people who would dry and ferment the needles on large, flat rocks.

While local people had consumed wild rooibos for centuries, most contemporary residents said the tea became a commercial industry around the turn of the twentieth century. Residents described an immigrant Jewish trader, Benjamin Ginsberg, who journeyed throughout the Cederberg Mountains to buy wild tea plants from coloured and white farmers. Eventually, farmers began cultivating the tea on large, white-owned commercial farms, as well as on the meager amounts of land that some coloured residents managed to retain despite their almost total dispossession. An apartheid-era marketing board formed in the 1950s, facilitating the expansion of the industry as it began processing and distributing the tea throughout the country and, eventually, the world.

Despite the industry's growth, the tea's cultivation was primarily restricted to the ecological region where it also grew wild, the fynbos biome. The biome consists of just 71,337 square kilometers of the extreme southwestern parts of South Africa (Oettle 2012). As part of the Cape Floristic Kingdom, the biome experiences long, hot, dry, and windy summers and short, wet winters. The rooibos plant, like other fynbos, is adapted to the harsh climate. Deep roots access underground water, and lateral roots absorb rainwater before it evaporates (Hawkins et al. 2011). As the tea made the passage from wild to cultivated, its genetic structure changed. Although wild and cultivated rooibos differ in terms of size and other biological attributes, they share the scientific name *Aspalathus linearis*, and despite the selection of certain rooibos genotypes for cultivation, its wild cousins remain, surrounding the cultivated rows of tea.

Climate was central not only to the growth of the plant, but also to the lives and subjectivities of the people who lived in the region. Because black Africans constituted only 5 percent of the local population, white and coloured residents often invoked a distinct *demographic exceptionalism* in which they saw themselves as part of a unique "haven" and not necessarily part of South Africa as a whole. They invoked an *ecological exceptionalism* in relation to rooibos and the fynbos ecosystem in which it thrived. Discussions of fynbos almost always centered on its endemism.[7] The Cape Floristic Kingdom supports more than seven thousand species of plants—80 percent of which are endemic—and sections of the rooibos-growing area form a global biodiversity hot spot.[8] Both coloured and Afrikaans residents repeatedly asserted that rooibos's economic and symbolic value stems in large part from its regional specificity. Rooibos is "good" because it is indigenous, and the rich plant community survived despite and through intensive agriculture. Many of the area's residents unwaveringly accepted the idea of nature as apolitical (but moral) and a realm unaffected by human interference, despite the fact that rooibos was cultivated.

Because of farmers' and marketers' emphasis on ecological endemism, even the chemistry of the plant became significant to the rooibos narrative and to the people who grew and consumed the plant. Rooibos's chemistry, explained a researcher wearing a white lab coat in a sterile Cape Town laboratory, made it "antispasmodic, anti-obesity, anti-microbial, anti-cancer." According to her, scientists have discovered approximately nine thousand flavonoids in plants. Aspalathin, however, is found only rooibos. While scientists did not yet understand exactly what role the flavonoid plays, they conjectured that it helps protect rooibos against oxidative stress caused in part by environmental factors. The plant is unique, researchers insisted, because it developed, thrived, and gained healing powers in a "difficult" environment. Residents often used similar narratives to represent their own struggles and triumphs in the region, whether it was coloured farmers describing lives informed by the timing of the rain and the coming of the harvest or Afrikaans farmers using their husbandry to justify their rightful governance over the land.

"The industry is very unique, and I am very proud to be part of an indigenous, homegrown export product," a tea marketer said. While his company exported tea to countries such as Sweden and China, we spoke in a small office located on a dusty road in the heart of rooibos country. "To think that it's a fynbos and natural and to create a brilliant, healthy product. It's 100 percent homegrown, non-invasive. . . . We have a healthy, sustainable, organic offering to the rest of the world." I had many conversations like this one with marketers, farmers, and workers. The discourse was filled with extraordinary stories of healing for people and the environment, and the tea's global commodity status began to affect local valuations of the plant's "miracle-like" qualities.

Beyond South Africa, tea has served as a power-laden sign in the fight over colonial and postcolonial representation (Besky 2014; Hung 2014; Sen 2014). The history of tea consumption, Piya Chatterjee (2001) argues, is the history of the domestication of the exotic. Tea is an alluring commodity because its distance from the familiar gradually transformed into the symbol of a quotidian, English definition of civility and taste, the measure of civilization. Hidden in this shift from the "strange" to the "familiar," Chatterjee (2001: 21) asserts, is the very history of empire: "the mappings of exoticism, the continuous struggles over symbol and sign, and the cultural cartographies of conquest."

Rooibos's miracle-like qualities seemingly left it open to any kind of signification. "Rooibos: It's More Than Just a Tea," read the headline of an article about the many wonders that rooibos contains (Skade 2012). Another article, titled "Magical Properties of Rooibos," stated, "We know about its good properties, so if we can look more into those good properties, it would not only improve our health, but the economy too" (Ndongeni 2012). Rooibos will supposedly help people lose weight, gain weight, and control diabetes; it will promote longevity, make skin more youthful, cure acne, prevent cancer and Parkinson's disease, guard vision, protect the liver, improve male fertility, soothe colicky babies, promote sleep and relaxation, provide comfort, and on and on.

"What's interesting is that in tough times, people drink more tea," a tea executive said. "It's cheap. It makes people feel comfortable. Tea and makeup, both those things go up. . . . Tea makes people feel good. . . . We're having record month after record month during the tough economic times." Another marketing narrative describes the tea with particularly dramatic language: "If

South Africa had to name a national drink, it would certainly be Rooibos tea. This golden-red brew discovered by the Khoisan and popularised by Benjamin Ginsberg is a flavour as indigenous as licking the sweat from a Kudu's snout" (Why Go South Africa 2012). Descriptions of South Africa focus not only on its ancient past and its charismatic animals but also on the role of Europeans in rediscovering and popularizing the country's assets for a modern, global audience. The world's largest flavor company, Givaudan, selected rooibos as one of the flavors "to watch" in its annual forecast for 2007, and concoctions such as Vanilla Rooibos Lattes have featured regularly in the United States as Starbucks' "Drink of the Day." Portrayals of South Africa skip from ancient history to the immediate present and future, to South Africa as a "place to watch." The marketing erases years of colonial violence, apartheid-era dispossessions, and continuing inequality. Instead, as the executive said, rooibos simply "makes people feel good."

In the triumphant discourse about rooibos, themes of land and belonging so prominent in South African history, activism, and scholarship combine with a postapartheid rainbow ideal of non-racialism and ethnically neutral calls for unity bolstered by "Proudly South African" business models. Yet in contrast to the redemptive and celebratory tales of rooibos's natural and indigenous healing power, the tea grows in a precarious place. The Cederberg was a social and ecological landscape in which many inhabitants faced uncertain futures, livelihoods, claims to belonging, and even a precarious ecosystem in the face of climate change.

After the official end of apartheid in 1994, the late 1990s marked a period of economic stagnation and changing relations of production in South Africa's agricultural sector. These combined forces led to a surfeit of unemployed people who wondered if they would ever find jobs in agriculture again. Postapartheid elation was soon met with uncertainty about the role of the new government, neoliberal economic policies, and the realization *or* desertion of the apartheid resistance movement's leftist ideology (Barchiesi 2011; Peet 2002). In this context, life for many South Africans was defined by precarity. An existence without predictability or security affected people's material and psychological welfare. South Africa remains one of the most economically unequal countries in the world, as measured by the World Bank's GINI Index.[9] According to South Africa's Department of Social Development (2012), the country ranks in the world's top ten in terms of alcohol consumption. Drug use is "extremely serious" and more than twice the global average. Violent crime statistics, while improving, still remain among the highest in the world. According to the United Nations Office on Drugs and Crime, South Africa had the tenth-highest rate of homicide in the world (out of 187 recorded countries) and the highest homicide rate of the world's forty largest countries.[10] More than a quarter of the population is unemployed,[11] but the rate of people out of work is estimated to be as high as 50 percent (du Toit and Neves 2014). This poverty is also predominately rural, with 72 percent of the poor residing in rural areas (Neves and du Toit 2013). Many poor in the rooibos region and places like it found themselves unable to find steady work on farms, obtain urban jobs, or make a living as smallholders.

In social science scholarship, themes of precarity often focus specifically on labor. In the European usage of "precarity," Franco Barchiesi (2011) writes, workers' conditions signify labor's declining centrality to people's lives. The South African context adds a racialized component to labor relations. Speaking of South Africa, Barchiesi argues that the precariousness of black workers' lives should be analyzed as a "social and existential reality akin to what Claus Offe (1997: 82) termed 'shakiness and harmful unpredictability'" (Barchiesi 2011: 9). For Offe, precariousness emerges in the contrast between the declining centrality of the "labor contract" in a social world where "jobs are insecure ('precariousness of work') and the norms that keep work central for individuals and households affected by the retrenchment of public programs and the official praise of work over welfare ('precariousness of subsistence')" (Barchiesi 2011: 9).

Barchiesi contends that South African government discourse celebrates work, production, and a morality based on personal responsibility despite enormous social disparities. The government heralded becoming a worker as the most virtuous expression of citizenship in the postapartheid nation (du Toit and Neves 2014). People from liberal commentators and social scientists to leftist critics seemed to agree that employment was the solution to the country's social problems. As a result, many political actors criticized demands that were not directly linked to labor market participation. The country's poor were turned into statistical categories, such as "disillusioned" or "active" jobseekers, "structurally unemployed," "informal microentrepreneurs," and "non-working populations" (Barchiesi 2011). But what if one could not "become a worker" because of the changing labor market? Despite politicians' rhetorical flourishes, unemployment, poverty, and disillusionment persisted in South Africa.

To Barchiesi's and Offe's idea of precarity, I add another dimension: geographical precarity. By this form of precarity, I imply that residents' uncertain claims to belonging *in place* merged with uncertainty of the *rootedness of place itself*. Farmers feared that rooibos's identity as an indigenous plant might become estranged from its territory if climate change shifted the ecosystem southward. Analyzing a classic botanical metaphor, James Clifford (1988: 338) asserts that "the idea of culture brings with it the expectation of roots, of a stable, territorialized existence." In the twenty-five years since Clifford wrote those words, social scientists have challenged ideas of territorialized existence by exploring transnational commodities and people, such as refugees, global financiers, or migrant workers, who move across space. Social scientists have not, however, paid the same kind of careful attention to the movement of eco-systems (Tsing 2015). By and large, they assume a nature that stays in place. Plants grow in their proper ecosystems, and ecosystems remain bounded in particular geographical locations. Yet current climate models predict increasing temperatures and decreasing rains in the rooibos-growing region—and farmers have already observed changes in their rooibos cultivation (Archer et al. 2008; Lötter 2015; Lötter and Maitre 2014; Oettle 2012).

Steeped in Heritage investigates how climate change unsettles not just livelihoods but also cosmologies: How does the *uprooting* of an indigenous plant affect ideas about indigeneity as *rooted* in place? What are the stakes involved for both the people and the plants? And, specifically, how do you "deterritorialize" a people—coloured people—who have never been allotted a territory in the first place, who are supposedly always alien to everywhere and whose very identities are denied cultural or place-based authenticity? The effects of precarity were magnified in a setting in which claims to belonging were becoming increasingly prominent as both sources of livelihood and foci of political mobilizations (Ives 2014b).

With this discussion of precarity, I place the concept in its historical, political, and ecological context, as well as in the context of changing labor dynamics in South African agriculture. A government study from 2013 indicated a shift away from employing large teams of permanent workers who live on the farm and toward seasonal and off-farm labor (Employment Conditions Commission 2013). Recent data indicate that nearly half of all agricultural jobs are now temporary, a percentage that is likely to increase with further casualization across the sector (Munakamwe and Jinnah 2015; Visser and Ferrer 2015). This casualization implies more than just a loss of job security. For many workers, the farm was not an impersonal place of "businesslike labour relations"; it was their home (Addison 2014: 300).

With this sense of "home," the distinction between coloured farmer and farmworker could be blurry and dynamic. Some coloured farmers worked on white commercial farms in addition to tending their own crops or had worked on commercial farms before accessing their own land. These farmers had friends, family members, and fellow church members who were workers. At the same time, many farmworkers had lived and worked for generations on the same farm and espoused a sense of ownership of the tea similar to that of coloured farmers, despite their dependence on white farm owners. They felt alienated from the fruits of their labor but not from their embodied relations with the plant and the soil.[12] In this racialized landscape of poverty, unemployment, and alienation, there emerged yet another form of precarity: the precarious subjectivities of the coloured farmers and workers who cultivated the tea.

Uprooting Indigeneity: Articulating the Indigenous in South Africa

Notions of who and what belong in certain locations have come to the forefront in discussions over cultural and biological indigeneity in a "globalizing" world. Fears of homogenization in the face of globalization have engendered obsessions not only with the idea of disappearing cultures, but also with the loss of biodiversity and ecological knowledge (Comaroff and Comaroff 2001; Gausset et al. 2011; Geschiere 2011; Nyamnjoh 2006). The contemporary movement of peoples on a worldwide scale, Sylvia Yanagisako and Carol Delany (1995: 2) argue, disrupts order and uproots people from the places where their "stories and identities make sense," challenging both identities and the hegemonic order. With the majority of private land still under white ownership, cultural identity seems primed to take a central place in political and economic mobilizations in South Africa in particular (Comaroff and Comaroff 2009).

I want to emphasize that *Steeped in Heritage* focuses on people (coloureds and Afrikaners) who challenged the idea of a culturally indigenous identity yet were deeply implicated in discussions of indigeneity through their claims to belonging with an indigeneous plant. In her discussion of indigeneity in Indonesia, Tania Murray Li (2000) points to the political risks and opportunities posed by different framings of indigeneity. She highlights the dangers of asserting that certain groups *opportunistically or artificially* adopt Indigenous identities or that they suffer from a kind of ethnic false consciousness. Academic discussions of ethnic identity framed in terms of an "invention of tradition" imply "that maximizing, goal-oriented 'actors' switch or cross boundaries in pursuit of their ends" and thus approach questions of identity in "consumer terms, as a matter of optimal selection" (Li 2000: 150; Brosius 1999; Hodgson 2002). Li's arguments are significant in that they recognize hundreds of years of oppression of people who identify as Indigenous. For most, there is far more at stake than semantics. As Li contends, a group's self-identification as Indigenous is not natural, "but neither is it simply invented, adopted, or imposed.

It is, rather, a positioning which draws upon historically sedimented practices, landscapes, and repertoires of meaning, and emerges through particular patterns of engagement and struggle" (Li 2000: 151; see also Alfred et al. 2006).

Dorothy Hodgson examines how these positionings "emerge" in Africa,[13] where the colonial history influences the "key terms of political struggle"—that is,

> the state as dominant organizing principle for governance, law, social welfare; the nation as modernist ideal embraced by African leaders; citizenship as mode of belonging; ethnicity as form of collective identification and mobilization; property as way to understand and access land; development as goal of African leaders; and modernity as aspiration of leaders and people. (Hodgson 2011: 9)

She explores how cultural minorities such as the Maasai have adopted the term "indigenous" relatively recently "as a tool for mobilization" (Hodgson 2011: 3; Igoe 2006). While few claim to be "first peoples," she argues, they do claim a "similar structural position vis-à-vis their nation-states as indigenous peoples in the Americas and Australia: the maintenance of cultural distinctiveness; a long experience of subjugation, marginalization, and dispossession by colonial and postcolonial powers; and, for some, a historical priority in terms of the occupation of their territories. . . . They argue for what scholars and advocates have termed a 'constructivist,' 'structural,' or 'relational' definition of indigenous that encompasses and reflects their situation, rather than more 'essential,' 'substantial,' or 'positivist' definitions" (Hodgson 2002: 1042).

Ideas of cultural indigeneity among white and coloured rooibos residents were problematic to the patterns of engagement and struggle described by many scholars and activists for reasons that cannot be separated from the region's profound and enduring inequities. Like the Maasai, coloured residents pushed back against "substantial" understandings of indigeneity. Unlike the Maasai, however, they did not claim a "structural" definition of indigeneity in its place; nor did they describe themselves as a sovereign people seeking decolonization.[14] Yet their claims to belonging through an indigenous plant shed light on contemporary racial dynamics that are often limited by accounts of colonialism that work with a settler/native, white/black binary.

The United Nations provides a universalizing concept of indigeneity. Its official declaration on Indigenous peoples begins as follows: "It is estimated that there are more than 370 million indigenous people spread across 70 countries worldwide. Practicing unique traditions, they retain social, cultural, economic and political characteristics that are distinct from those of the dominant societies in which they live. . . . They are the descendants according to a common definition—of those who inhabited a country or a geographical region at the time when people of different cultures or ethnic origins arrived. The new arrivals later became dominant through conquest, occupation, settlement or other means." In this description, the United Nations emphasizes "firstness," subordination, and distinction. Recognizing the difficulty of providing one, all-encompassing definition for the term "Indigenous," the United Nations instead offers an "understanding" of the word. Considering the diversity of Indigenous peoples, an official definition of "Indigenous" has not been adopted by any body in the United Nations system. In its place, the system has developed a modern understanding of this term based on the following:

- Self-identification as indigenous peoples at the individual level and accepted by the community as their member.
- Historical continuity with precolonial and/or pre-settler societies.
- Strong link to territories and surrounding natural resources.
- Distinct social, economic, or political systems.
- Distinct language, culture, and beliefs from non-dominant groups of society.
- Resolve to maintain and reproduce their ancestral environments and systems as distinctive peoples and communities.[15]

According to the United Nations, "native people" can define themselves, albeit within a framework of indigeneity that positions time (a connection to the past) and space (an uninterrupted link to a place) at the forefront. Because this concept of indigeneity is determined by the historical moment of imperialism, the term "Indigenous" appears almost meaningless outside the context of modern colonialism. It is also strikingly analogous to apartheid-era ideologies that called for maintaining and reproducing "distinctive" peoples and cultures in separate environments and through (supposedly) separate systems of governance. In a similar fashion, the anthropologists Guillermo Delgado-P and John Brown Childs (2012) define Indigenous peoples as populations who encountered Europeans for the first time five hundred years ago and who maintained their own languages, intellectual sovereignties, views of biomass, ideas about naturecultures, and diachronic notions of place-space called "homelands."

While Delgado-P and Childs, the United Nations, and other scholars and organizations attempt to be expansive in their understandings of indigeneity, undergirding these definitions are ideas of authenticity and a connection between place and culture (Igoe 2006; Lee 2006). But place is more than just a neutral, physical setting or "passive target for primordial sentiments of attachments" (Rodman 1992: 641); it is culturally and historically contextual. In apartheid South Africa, connections between people and place were infused with control and power. Legislation cemented associations between land and ethnicity, defining people as belonging to specific ethnic groups and then relegating those ethnic groups to place-based "homelands" (or Bantustans), employing the same language as Delgado-P and Childs but toward explictly violent ends. When using an ideological framework that links culture to place, coloured identity can seem unredeemable. How do you repatriate a people who supposedly have no essential home, and whose ethnogenesis many believed emerged from the shame of rape?

Lynn Meskell (2012) poses the question: How do you define "Indigenous" in South Africa? Is everyone who is not white considered Indigenous? Or are the Khoisan the lone "true," "authentic" Indigenous people? Under the United Nations definition, the only people who could be deemed Indigenous in the rooibos context would be the Khoisan, who, most residents assert, no longer "exist" in the region, having died out long ago from disease, violence, or slow incorporation into the coloured population. Even if we take the category "African" to signify indigeneity, many whites have used the term to assert that they, too, are African by birthright. The debate over "firstness" and who can and cannot be an authentic South African has profound historical and political implications. White colonists used the presumed extinction of the Khoisan and the claim of simultaneous arrival of the black or Bantu population to justify their own landownership and belonging, even though archaeological evidence has long proved otherwise (Meskell 2012; Mitchell and Whitelaw 2005).

Links between indigeneity and land are familiar themes in the humanities and social sciences. In relation to Africa and other non-Western regions, scholars often address themes of deep, organic, bodily connections to land that are assumed to be related to ancestors' presence (Lan 1985). For example, in many parts of South Africa, people buried their children's umbilical cords in the soil. Scholars such as Jacob Dlamini (2013) and Renee Sylvain (2002) have addressed the problematic nativism that essentializes this relationship in atavistic ways. Sylvain discusses how in postapartheid southern Africa, criteria for indigenous status can become "ontologically saturated with essentialist and primordialist conceptions of culture" (Sylvain 2002: 1075) For this reason, Dlamini argues, many South Africans formed a connection to the land not through their "traditional cultures" but as modern subjects who linked property ownership with civilization. Yet coloured people were given no homeland, no codified autochthony, and scarce property ownership; discursively, they did not "emerge from the soil" (Geschiere 2009). On the contrary, they supposedly came from the illegitimacy of miscegenation.

In the rooibos region, residents negotiated and narrated their belonging in ways that linked subjectivities to an indigenous plant in complex and at times unexpected ways. While Afrikaners asserted that their cultural survival hinged on a place-based identity, coloured people resisted attempts to be emplaced as "native Bushmen," a term many considered derogatory. For coloured populations, if the "native" label and its links to apartheid-era policies of control held the promise of redeeming their supposedly pathological identities, it also posed the threat of temporally incarcerating them in a state of primitivism or even extinction as "Bushmen." Instead, many coloured people in the rooibos-growing area provided a different framing of indigeneity as a relationship among people, place, and plant. Their framing allowed for fluidity in a way that redefined heritage, not only as a claim to a "traditional" past, but as a potential for the future (Ives 2014a). The intimate yet tense relationships between coloured and white communities, the object of their labor, and the potentialities of their cultural belonging were reframed by a commodity chain grounded in the sale of an indigenous plant.

Plants, Commodities, and Totems

[The social world is] produced through social relationships between organisms. These organism can be people, ancestors, spirits, animals, and plants. The social relations are not neutral and economic; they are familial and poetic. — PAIGE WEST, *From Modern Production to Imagined Primitive*

Residents often said that rooibos developed its valuable form because of its "proper" fynbos ecosystem and its "proper" local cultivators: farmers whose families had lived in the area for generations. While the tea had become a global commodity, in the growing region people and plants came together in an imagined culturally and geographically rooted world that ensured the quality and authenticity of the tea. Indeed, the sights, sounds, smells, and tastes of rooibos were everywhere in Clanwilliam, the center of rooibos processing. The sweet aroma of fermenting rooibos wafted over town when the wind blew in the right direction. The churning of the processing plant could be heard at nearby houses. Rooibos signs were scattered about the municipality, and rooibos companies sponsored local events: the arts festival, the triathlon, the flower show, school sports tournaments, and so on. Tea and other rooibos products were sold at nearly every store, and tourists could do tastings at the local factory or a rooibos café.

Rooibos, as both a "wild indigenous plant" and a "global commodity," politicized and policed the shifting and highly moralized boundaries between nature and culture, delineating who and what does and does not belong in the landscape. For many people, rooibos had the capacity to be a commodity, a native plant, and a moral subject. In *Capital, Volume One*, Karl Marx (1990 [1887]) refers to commodities as social phenomena endowed with *thing-like* status and embedded in an economic calculation. Farmers, however, rarely described rooibos cultivation and exchange as fantasized relations between "objects." Instead, they often asserted that rooibos was not an "object" at all. It was *more than a thing*; it consisted of "what is excessive in objects, as what exceeds their mere materialization as objects or their mere utilization as objects . . . ; the magic by which objects become values, fetishes, idols, and totems" (Brown 2001: 5). In anthropological scholarship, totems commonly refer to animals or plants that are thought to have a special spiritual connection with a particular group of people. Totems usually come with a specific myth (Durkheim 1982; Evans-Pritchard 1969; Malinowski 1922). Most local residents would not say that they "worshiped" rooibos, though they certainly told many totemic myths. Yet residents did ascribe a metaphysical quality to rooibos: a connection among the plant, the ritual of consumption, and the "holy act" of cultivation.

Social scientists have produced a vast literature that focuses on how examinations of commodities can "unveil" the workings of global capital and reveal "what is really going on." Many scholars have critiqued these works as decontextualized and lacking attention to the sensuousness of objects themselves. As Jane Collins (2014: 27) writes, we need to "crack open" commodities "to recover some of what neoclassical economics makes us forget: living, breathing, gendered, and raced bodies working under social relations that exploit them; bodies living in households with persons who depend on them and on whom they depend; and bodies who enter into the work of making a living with liveliness, creativity, and skill."[16]

Steeped in Heritage works alongside ethnographically informed scholarship on coffee and tea such as Paige West's (2012) exploration of the social world of coffee and Sarah Besky's (2014) and Debarati Sen's (2014) research on labor and justice on Darjeeling tea plantations.[17] In a similar way, I address how the rooibos industry uses images of primitivity to sell the product, while it simultaneously masks the structural relations that contribute to regional poverty. Like Besky, I am sensitive to the multiple forms of labor in the industry that go beyond the production of tea to include the production of feelings. However, my attention to the intertwined social and natural history of rooibos provides a different framework to think through contemporary issues of globalization, economic transition, and climatic changes. Anna Tsing (2013: 40) argues that, to understand fully the alienation in capitalist commodity production, scholars need to pay attention to the "life worlds" not just of the living, breathing bodies described by Collins, but also of nonhumans, including plants. While tea scholars such as Po-Yi Hung (2014: 374) examine how tea landscapes can become the "material form" of dilemmas around the "incompatible desires between being primitive and being modern," I focus on the intimate—and highly racialized—relations among plant, ecosystem, farmers, and workers.[18]

Throughout *Steeped in Heritage*, I am cognizant of critiques by scholars such as Ian Hodder (2012) who argue that, despite recent attention to the coproduction of humans and things, most anthropologists do not look closely at the things themselves. As a result, I attempt to explore the semiotic and material aspects of rooibos as a plant and a commodity in both its production and consumption. I address rooibos's particular ecological conditions, its smell and taste, and the biological aspects of its celebrated healing properties. However, as an anthropologist concentrating primarily on the relations between people and plant, I recognize that I remain open to Hodder's critique. I, too, predominantly focus on the human. Yet, I argue, addressing the relations between the human and nonhuman in the context of the rooibos region's racial landscape adds a profound complexity to multispecies relationships: White residents did not always consider coloured and black people fully human. This stance represented a deep physical and structural violence that informed the region's social and ecological relations, as well as the rooibos industry's past and future. Central to that future, I assert, were residents' articulations of indigeneity—not as a static, binary relationship between people and place, but as a potentially more fluid relationship among people, place, and plant.

The Cartography of Steeped in Heritage

I divide the book into five chapters. I begin by exploring the people involved in rooibos farming: How do they wrestle with their "precarious" identities, and how do they express their own concepts of what it means to be indigenous? Chapter 1, "Cultivating Indigeneity," discusses how South Africa's past made claims to indigeneity particularly complex and politicized: The country's history shows both the potentially emancipatory and troubling results of embracing an ethnic identity. In this context, many coloured people in the rooibos-growing community expressed a form of heritage that was not merely a one-to-one fixity of people to place. Instead, it was something more encompassing and flexible. Despite a rejection of a culturally indigenous heritage for themselves, coloured community members claimed a connection to rooibos, drawing on the tea's indigeneity for evidence. The manner in which they described this belonging challenges understandings of indigeneity as a form of ethnic essentialism or as a rallying cry for political activism. Their claims allowed for fluidity in a way that redefined heritage not only as a connection to a traditional past but also as a potential for the future.

Chapter 2, "Farming the Bush," continues the discussion of indigeneity and belonging through and with rooibos. By shifting attention to the cultivation of the plant itself, the chapter addresses the constellation of symbolic and material dependencies among the region's residents, rooibos, and the ecosystem as a whole. Yet the chapter also shows that the idea of this symbiosis simultaneously produced multiple erasures, including that of coloured and black workers' labor. In South Africa, ideas about race, indigeneity, and nature have been problematically intertwined in centuries of racial discourse about subhuman or nonhuman others. By examining a local history of human-nonhuman relations, the chapter explores how ecological facts become culturally meaningful and socially and politically active, in addition to being economically essential to regional livelihoods. The landscape was a physical library of the region's past and its future, embodying both its histories of violent dispossession and its narratives of belonging to a beloved ecosystem. Using detailed ethnographic examples, I articulate a theory of the Bush, or *Bos* in Afrikaans, by exploring the intertwined concepts of fyn*bos*, rooi*bos*, and *boes*man (Bushman).

Chapter 3, "Endemic Plants and Invasive People," explores the role migrants and invasive plants play in the contested landscape. As black migrants came to labor in rooibos fields alongside local coloured workers, connections between rooibos and claims to belonging unfolded in an increasingly elaborate dance. The presence of "aliens," whether they were black Africans or foreign plant species, was often—but not always—presented as a threat to the region's environmental and cultural specificity and its supposedly concomitant environmental and cultural vulnerability. This "threat" was contingent, dynamic, and entangled with politics, economics, ecology, and subjectivity. Physical geography at times gave way to postapartheid negotiations and renegotiations of spatial control, exclusion, and mobility. In this context, alien invasives emerged more as matter that was "out of control" than as matter that was "out of place" in an ecological sense (c.f Douglas 2002 [1966]). Foreign plants were not representative of the alterity of foreign people. Rather, certain assemblages of human-plant alliances and antagonisms were generative of political, social, and ecological relations—and even provided political openings.

Chapter 4, "Rumor, Conspiracy, and the Politics of Narration," explores how the stories, rumors, and cosmologies surrounding rooibos were entangled with and emerged from shifting, and at times contradictory, struggles over the plant's history, meanings, and relations. Beginning with rooibos's founding tales, narrativized histories both affected and were constitutive of people's understandings of current political, economic, and environmental trends in the region and the world. By examining a selection of rooibos rumors, the chapter considers how farm owners, workers, and community members negotiated, made sense of, and attempted to control a shifting agrarian landscape. The veracity of the stories are not the main concern, and narratives often contradict themselves and run counter to official industry histories. But I take seriously the ways in which the rumors, gossip, and cosmologies affected local residents' worldviews and had concrete effects on both the people and the plant. Through their continual retelling, the stories took on a life of their own. They became the region's daily, lived, and sedimented histories. Emphasizing the power of narration, the chapter shows how rooibos's commodity history interweaves the language of globalization, nostalgia, and class with intensely emotive ideas of ecological belonging and the changing but persistent structures of inequality in the rooibos region.

The fifth and final chapter, "Precarious Landscapes," explores how anxiety became part of daily life in South Africa, as the country saw a retreat from the hopeful and redemptive language of Nelson Mandela's Rainbow Nation to a future more uncertain and potentially threatening. In the rooibos-growing region, residents feared that something—whether it was the climate, the government, or the market—would betray them in the future. Apprehensions acquired two opposing qualities. For some, the anxiety was about constant, uncontrollable change. For others, it was about the fact that, despite the end of apartheid, little had actually changed at all: The majority of land remained in white residents' hands, and coloured residents faced seemingly insurmountable hurdles to landownership and secure livelihoods. While anxiety took different forms depending on residents' social locations, commonalities existed across social boundaries. Both coloured and white residents feared that rooibos would become a commodity and lose its miracle-like qualities. The certainty of rooibos as a stable object, anchoring uncertain lives and precarious indigeneities, seemed to be unraveling through the destabilizing economic, political, and climatic changes apparent to many residents. The final chapter specifically addresses how residents' uncertain claims to belonging in place merged with uncertainty of the rootedness of place itself. In other words, I connect fears about rooibos's commodification to the ultimate anxiety: the possibility that rooibos's identity as an indigenous crop might become uprooted from its territory if climate change shifted the ecosystem southward.

Ethnographic Ethics: Unhinging the Reasonable

A highly localized crop, rooibos grew almost exclusively in a small part of South Africa's Western Cape and Northern Cape provinces. This book is based on fieldwork in the rooibos-growing region between 2009 and 2013, as well as continued research using archives, news articles, and correspondence through 2015. Research took me from corporate headquarters to Afrikaans farmers' barbeques and from coloured farmers' remote mountain fields to informal settlements, political rallies, government offices, church services, conservationists' offices, and union headquarters. Through in-depth interviews, participant observation, and document analysis, this methodological assemblage allowed me access to the many people in the rooibos-growing community, an access that crossed the area's tightly protected racial, class, religious, and social boundaries. Researching a small, concentrated industry made it possible to interview and engage with a broad sample of people directly or indirectly involved with rooibos in the region. This comprehensive approach enabled me to examine multiple perspectives and experiences of rooibos production, processing, and distribution.

Throughout the research and writing process, I struggled with my own role in the region. Physical and structural violence became so normalized that even I—the supposedly observant anthropologist—forgot about it at times. Seeing drunken people lying face down on sidewalks or desperate unemployed men discussing suicide became as every day as the orange-red sunsets that lit up the mountains above the valley. As I formed greater ethnographic intimacies, comments about black people as "immoral" or coloured women as "sluts" were increasingly common. After months in the rural community, only extreme forms of violence seemed truly to shake me: a blood-soaked man lying in a street, a dead body at a hospital. Had the insidiousness of the mundane, everyday violence of rural South Africa become a part of my worldview? Had the banality of racism in the region made me apathetic?

While these struggles certainly bring to mind the moral and ethical implications of being a fieldworker (or a person)—and particularly a white fieldworker in a racially charged landscape—they also prompted questions about how to write someone else's "culture." *"You know, just once I'd like to read something good about my people and not just bad,"* one Afrikaans farmer's plea echoed in my mind. *"My dog killed a black"*; and *"There was a BBC reporter here, and he said to a farmer, 'How racist you are.' But the reporters should live on a farm and see. They kill you. People from Europe or the outside don't understand."* White farmers would pull me aside, talk to me for hours, wanting me to understand. "I'm not racist, but . . . ," they would say.

In her work in a South African National Park, Lynn Meskell (2012) discusses the ordinariness of racist acts. She articulates her own struggles with how to describe the men and women with whom she worked. Many professed not to see race, much like my informants' "I'm not racist, but . . ." Meskell speaks to this "lie," which she describes as a social relationship—a communicative act "founded upon a deep history of structured inequalities that many want to bury" (Meskell 2012: 127). In her research on imperial governance in the nineteenth-century Netherlands Indies, Ann Stoler (2009: 57) describes these "lies" as a form of colonial power: "the authority to designate what would count as reason and reasonable was colonialism's most insidious and effective technology of rule." While Stoler goes on to complicate and critique this claim by showing that "colonial reason" was not pervasive, I found my own understanding of the "reasonable" unhinged, challenged, and confused on a daily basis. In reflecting and writing about my time in the rooibos region, I was often disturbed and even terrified by what I had begun to accept as normal. This terror undergirds my text and my attempts to write the complex, violent, *and* loving social and ecological relations in the rooibos industry. "I love the farm," farmers told me again and again. "Why?" I would ask. "It's a natural love." The love—like the structural racism and poverty—was unquestioned, a given. I argue that this "natural" love of the land and the "natural" enduring racism were linked through the racialized landscape.

The everyday violence and quotidian racism was unavoidable, and periodically I was jarred out of my acceptance of the region's "reasonable." Coming home particularly late one night, I was reminded of the desperation and harshness of life. Earlier that evening, I had seen a man dead from a stab wound. Not shedding a tear, I walked into my room. But I couldn't sleep. I became overwhelmed by everything that I had witnessed, but I also kept thinking that there was a whole world going on late at night that I didn't usually see. I went home on Friday nights; I locked my door; I read a little and went to sleep. Meanwhile, people were abusing drugs; they were being stabbed; they were attacked by dogs; they were getting into fights; they were bleeding and dying. Babies were sick. People were being taken to jail and released from jail. And in the morning, the sun would shine and light up the mountains, a baboon would call across the flowering fynbos fields, and I would go for a morning jog and smile at my Afrikaans neighbors who power-walked every day, chatting about the latest gossip or the happenings on the Afrikaans soap opera they had watched the night before.

These stark contrasts inform the narrative in this book. Yet I also take seriously the idle gossip and politically charged rumors that circulated in moments like the morning walks, evening barbeques, rooibos industry events, and political rallies. Influenced by Janice Boddy's (1989) contemplation of spirit possession in northern Sudan, I explore how the "tea stories" that people told in the region formed their own sorts of ethnographies: They brought together disparate things, wrested concepts from their daily lives, and juxtaposed them in novel ways.

CULTIVATING

INDIGENEITY

If the Khoisan discovered rooibos, there's no record of it.
—WHITE ROOIBOS FARMER

"Rooibos is not new. For generations we have known the benefits," Johan, a coloured rooibos farmer, said, wiping the sweat from his brow as he lifted up his hat. His dusty fingerprints almost covered the hat's message: "I Love Jesus." He placed the hat back on his head, sighed, and continued, "Our forefathers, the Khoisan people . . . we didn't document; we knew for generations." We sat together in the shade of the church steeple, trying to find relief from the ever-present heat of the November sun. The town was nearly empty, with only a few children laughing and playing as their grandmothers watched them. Most of the adults had moved to the city or to surrounding farms, leaving their children behind. Those who remained tried to make a living out of remittances or government subsidies or farming the overworked soil.

Johan asserted a cultural heritage linked to the Khoisan and to their Indigenous knowledge of rooibos farming. Yet these Indigenous explanations were far from straightforward. When I spoke with adults who had left the community to work on nearby farms, many laughed and said, "We are not Khoisan." However, white Afrikaans farmers often claimed a cultural and even biological connection to the ecosystem and a personal attachment to rooibos farming so strong that they felt their blood was mingled with the soil. "People are born rooibos farmers," Kobus, an Afrikaans farmer, explained. "It is who they are." The question of *who* exactly represented the native population and *who* exactly were the original cultivators of rooibos remained contentious among the residents of the tea-growing area.

This chapter explores how residents negotiated and narrated their belonging in the rooibos region through stories that link their subjectivities to an indigenous plant in complex and at times unexpected ways. As the tea shifted from a native plant to a national beverage to a global commodity, local inhabitants—both coloured and Afrikaans—came to understand it differently. Formerly viewed as just a wild plant, rooibos became a culturally significant product against which local residents measured their sense of indigeneity and, more broadly, their claims to belonging in South Africa and the world. The manner in which people articulated this belonging challenged framings of indigeneity as a form of ethnic essentialism. While Afrikaners asserted that their cultural survival hinged upon a place-based identity, coloured residents resisted attempts to be emplaced as "native." For members of coloured populations, the native label and its links to apartheid-era policies of control held both the promise of redeeming their supposedly pathological identities and the threat of temporally incarcerating them in a state of primitivism or even extinction.

The relations between coloured and white communities were reframed by a commodity chain that seemed to necessitate autochthony to function effectively. What are the effects of combining indigeneity, the market, and local activism in an area where both heritage and the market were fiercely contested? How do celebrations of nativity account for mobility, uncertainty, and dynamism? Arjun Appadurai (1988) describes how commodities and some kinds of people move freely across space at the same time that "natives" become spatially incarcerated. A kind of "sedentarist metaphysics" can emerge in discussions of Indigenous people in which scholars and activists literally root them in place, arguing that they are so adapted to their natural environments that they are ecologically immobile (Malkki 1992). The violence of this spatial incarceration pathologizes mobility and "rootlessness" and thus can render any kind of displacement an affliction.

Following this persepective, many Indigenous debates focus on native peoples who are denied access to their ancestral homes.[1] In apartheid-era South Africa, however, the government enforced and delineated an idea of ancestral, native lands, while it restricted movement. Apartheid legislation cemented associations between land and ethnicity by defining people as belonging to specific ethnic groups and then relegating those ethnic groups to their supposedly place-based "homelands." According to the apartheid government, Zulus belonged in Zululand, Tswana belonged in Bophuthatswana, and so on. Utilizing the same rhetoric as Indigenous movements around the world, apartheid-era propaganda argued that creating ethnically based homelands "freed" the separate "nations" of South Africa. "In the world of today," a 1972 document reads, "a nation's right to determine its own identity is no longer supposed to be a disputed issue" (Information Service of South Africa 1972: 11). The government argued that apartheid was governed not by race-based discrimination and disposession but, rather, by respect for cultural differences and the need for homelands to allow people to "self-develop" in the manner of their choosing. The culturalist optic of the state replaced or masked racism as a means for controlling people and maintaining white economic and political dominance.

Yet coloured people were given no codified autochthony and no "homeland" of their own outside white South Africa. In such a context, embracing Khoisan indigeneity could serve as both a promise and a trap: It could provide a way to claim the region as their homeland, or it could leave them forever searching for some kind of authenticity. For the coloured of the rooibos region, the noose of nativity under apartheid remained powerful.

In response, coloured residents often rejected a culturally indigenous identity, even as they recognized the Khoisan as the original users of the tea. As Lionel, an unemployed farmworker described, "I want to find my parents' roots. I subscribed to Ancestry.com but I couldn't find much. . . . Our coloured people, we know our roots come from Europeans and Africans. My grandfather was an Englishman. He was one of the first settlers in the 1800s. He had a lot of land. . . . I don't feel any connection to Khoisan." Like Lionel, many coloured residents simply ignored the native identity cultivated by nongovernmental organizations (NGOs)and by national and international rooibos-marketing campaigns from companies such as Khoisan Tea and Wiedouw Tea, whose box celebrates "The process of harvesting, bruising and fermentation of Rooibos tea . . . introduced by the indigenous KHOISAN people hundreds of years ago."[2] Marketing materials packaged or repackaged rooibos in ways that were palatable for local and international consumers and investors but were also strikingly similar to the cultural essentialism that justified apartheid.

Despite the rejection of a culturally indigenous heritage for themselves, coloured community members actively claimed a connection to rooibos tea, drawing on the *tea's* indigeneity for evidence. They put forth a temporally different notion of cultural heritage. Instead of a heritage rooted in the past, they described a heritage that was ever changing and potentially still to come. When asked whether he felt that rooibos was a part of his heritage, one coloured farmer responded, "Not yet, but it will be in the future." Discussing his plans to expand his farm from small scale to commercial, the farmer asserted that the object (rooibos) and not the culture (coloured or Khoisan) acted as the focus of his belonging in the region and his hopes for an economically viable future.

"They Have No Identity or History"

Narratives of origin tell people what kind of world it is, what it consists of, and where they stand in it; they make it seem natural to them. By anchoring lives to some kind of larger, cosmic order, identities seem secured. . . . Narratives of origin incorporate classificatory schemes that describe the order of things, as well as the relations between things and different kinds of people.
—SYLVIA YANAGISAKO and CAROL DELANY, "Naturalizing Power"

[Coloured] children are born "with shame and sorrow in their blood. . . . They must inevitably be riven with hatred of their own being."
—J. M. COETZEE, *White Writing*

FIELD NOTES, APRIL 2011: *It's another hot Saturday morning, and I wake up to the booming music from the nearby market, where local people and immigrants sell goods, drink, and dance. I walk past the market and down to a local community meeting space for a demonstration presented by the Community Police Forum. I greet a few people I know, and they invite me to see the new machines the police recently received from the United States. A large circle forms around the policeman demonstrating a Breathalyzer. Everyone wants to see how it works, so they grab an intoxicated coloured man who has found his way inside the building, his torn and dusty clothes evidence of his marginal status. It is 9:30 AM. Everyone laughs heartily and encourages the policeman to have the man breathe into the machine. The man's face is blank, not registering—or perhaps not caring—that he has become a spectacle. He breathes into the machine, quietly asks people for money, and then wanders off. The Breathalyzer immediately turns green. Everyone claps and laughs. The police officer explains that the man is probably on tik, the South African slang for methamphetamine. The drugged man wanders back inside and quietly asks more people for money. They ignore him and he leaves. Later, the people inside find another apparently drunk man and continue their game.*

Intoxicated, impoverished people were such a commonplace sight in this picturesque town surrounded by high mountains and rooibos fields that no one seemed to notice them anymore. One day, walking down Main Street, I noticed blood—a big puddle and then a trail of drops. I saw a man next, his wrist and arm soaked red. He stumbled into the street. Most people ignored him. Concerned, I asked, "Is he OK? Is someone getting help?" People laughed. "He always does this when he drinks," someone said. The man stumbled and fell down, lying in the middle of the road, flat and broken, covered in blood, a red trail oozing from his body and onto his typical blue worker's uniform. I saw an official who stood with a friend, chatting. "There is a man bleeding in the street," I told him. "I know," he smiled. "He wants to kill himself. Every time he gets some *dop* in him, he tries to kill himself." In moments like this one, drunken people were no longer people, especially if they were coloured. Town residents would shake their heads at what they saw as my naïveté, giving me sociobiological explanations for alcohol use. "Sarah, the thing you need to understand about coloured people is ... ," I was told again and again by white, black, and coloured people alike, the sentence finished in various ways, such as, "they are drinking to die.... It's a social thing. It's going from generation to generation, ever since Van Riebeeck landed in Cape Town."

In historical and contemporary narratives, the coloured community has been envisioned as inauthentic, weak, and full of the shame of rape and miscegenation. According to a common South African legend, Jan Van Riebeeck, the founder of the first Dutch settlement on the Cape, was the "father of the coloured," as settlers often forced sexual relations on local women (Adhikari 2005). In the rooibos-growing area, Afrikaans farmers sometimes joked about how white people—although never *their* ancestors—would take Khoisan women into the Bush. Today, the term "coloured" refers to people from a heterogeneous combination of heritages, including those from the Khoisan community (a unifying name for the "original" inhabitants of the region, often referred to colloquially as Bushmen); people of biracial heritage;[3] and people brought as slaves or laborers from other African countries and from regions such as Southeast Asia (Jensen 2008). While initially many children who resulted from settler relations were absorbed back into their mothers' communities, "coloured" soon became its own community, codified under apartheid and either taken for granted or envisioned as a false identity by white, black, and even coloured South Africans. As an ethnic label, colouredness proved problematic to definitions of indigeneity. Their presumed placelessness emerged from an assemblage of legal, political, economic, and sociocultural exclusions.

The demographics of the rooibos region are dramatically different from those of the rest of South Africa. The region is classified as 80 percent coloured, 15 percent white, 5 percent black, and less than 1 percent Asian. The national population is classified as 79 percent black, 9 percent coloured, 9 percent white, and 2.5 percent Asian.[4] The topic of coloured identity and the terminology around labeling people "coloured" are culturally and politically fraught in South Africa. Some academics and activists prefer the term "so-called coloured," or simply "black," to describe a unified nonwhite population. Other people use the term "brown" or the Afrikaans "*bruinmense*." Or they put "coloured" into quotation marks to emphasize its colonial legacy and to deemphasize any essential qualities of the "race." However, in the rooibos region, nearly everyone I spoke with preferred the term coloured without quotation marks or the burden of a "so-called" in front of their self-identified ethnic identity. "I feel like they are denying my identity," one man replied when I asked him about the usage of "so-called." Similarly, residents felt that because the words "black" and "white" do not require quotation marks around them, neither should "coloured."[5]

"Narratives of origin tell people what kind of world it is, what it consists of, and where they stand in it," the anthropologists Sylvia Yanagisako and Carol Delany (1995: 1) argue. But what do you do if you believe that your origin narrative is rape? "Upliftment" projects and job creation organizations initiated by the state, by political parties, and by NGOs working in the rooibos-growing area attempted to explain and fix the "coloured problem" by emphasizing the population's lack of a place-based cultural identity. The Living Landscape Project, an NGO, focused on the development of school curricula that incorporate archaeological materials and the training of local people as guides, craftspeople, and heritage managers. The project aimed to reconnect residents with their surroundings through education (not through concrete land transfers).

The mission statement describes the local abundance of fossils, artifacts, and natural features that "all point to the passing of time."[6] With a focus on time, the statement continues, "it seems an obligation of archaeologists (and geologists, paleontologists) to illustrate the dimension that houses all of these records of the past. This is far from an academic exercise, as we will confront the difficult issues of global warming, the sustainable use of resources and the protection of diversity by better understanding long term environmental and human history." The project specifically emphasizes geographical dispossession in its narrative of local history: "Colonial settlement disturbed and ultimately destroyed these relationships between people and the land, though many San and Khoe were incorporated into colonial society as the labouring class. Whilst the San and Khoe languages and cultural traditions were almost lost, the Cape is alive with traces of the past in the form of rock paintings."[7]

In addition to training students and local residents, the project planned to attract tourists through rock art tours and accommodation. People in town who were involved in the project often spoke of it as a failure. "Spare us another NGO," one resident complained. They cited the lack of funds, the uncleanliness of the space, the economically unsustainable attempts to provide employment, and the dissolution of many of its programs. With their emphasis on lost heritage and animated prehistory, development workers struggled with how to repatriate a people who supposedly have no essential home.

The racial classification "coloured" often found itself mired in circular definitions that gave the population no claims to land, language, or culture. According to the government's Wilcocks Commission of 1937, colouredness—and the Cape coloured, in particular—was defined as "a person living in the Union of South Africa, who does not belong to one of its aboriginal races, but in whom the presence of Coloured blood . . . can be established with at least reasonable certainty."[8] This official document defined colouredness only by what it was not: Indigenous. With the advent of apartheid-era racial classifications, the idea of a coloured community became legally ossified yet remained culturally suspect in the eyes of white, black, and even coloured South Africans. Commissions that aimed to "understand" the coloured population, such as the Wilcocks Commission, spoke of the persistent threat that coloured men would become criminals (Badroodien and Jensen 2004).

In spite of its codification, the classification could be fluid and unstable. Before apartheid, "passing" as white was an option for coloured people who looked "white." During the apartheid era, racial categories became more rigid. Nevertheless, it was still possible to be legally reassigned a new race if you could "prove" your case. Notwithstanding the phenotypic confusion, people in the rooibos-growing area seemed to have no doubt as to who belonged to each racial group. I walked down a street with coloured rooibos farmers one day, and they stopped to talk to a woman with light skin and strikingly blue eyes. I was so surprised by their familiarity and the comfort with which they spoke, an ease that rarely accompanied cross-racial interactions, that I asked, "Is that woman coloured?" They laughed and said knowingly, "Yes, there was lots of intermixing."

Despite its fluidity, coloured identity was purportedly imbued with racially determined qualities in the rooibos region. As evidenced by the cheerful sport made of a coloured man blowing into a Breathalyzer, coloured people were often considered childlike; the women, promiscuous; the men, alcoholic and unthreatening. Because coloured people supposedly emerged out of miscegenation, they had no prelapsarian moment and no precolonial reality (Chari 2008). Apartheid legislation labeled "blacks" as "African" or "Native," and "whites" as "European," denying coloured people a geographical referent or nativity to any place. This inability to make cultural claims to land stemmed from the concept of coloured identity as placeless through apartheid's cemented homeland policy in which the government classified approximately 67 percent of South African land as "White Commercial Agriculture"; 15 percent as "Black Communal Areas" (or black homelands); 10 percent as "Other State Land"; and 8 percent as "Remainder" (note that these percentages shifted over time) (Walker 2012).

Left without a homeland during apartheid, the coloured population found itself with few options to access land in the postapartheid era. The law for making heritage-based land claims used 1913, the year of the Natives Land Act, as the cutoff date for dispossession.[9] The first major act regulating segregation before apartheid, the Natives Land Act of 1913 mandated that blacks could live only in certain parts of the country, areas that totaled about 7 percent of the country's land. Those who were dispossessed from their land before that date could not easily reclaim it. Land in the rooibos-growing region, however, had been in white hands for generations before 1913, often tracing back to the early eighteenth century. Thus, coloured people were doubly rootless: through legislation and through their identities.[10]

Coloured genealogies were so historically entangled with white South Africa that they assumed an ambiguous position in South Africa's racial hierarchies. Black migrants to the area sometimes considered coloured people dispossessors because they were genetically part white, putting coloured identity in the seemingly unredeemable status of both dispossessed and dispossessing. In this sense, John Western (2001) argues that coloured people are not analogous to Native Americans who position themselves in contrast to the European colonists who dispossessed them. Rather, he argues, coloured people are a new amalgam of local, imported, and European dispossessors. Colouredness can represent a seemingly perfect postapartheid "rainbow identity" because its heritage is European, African, and Asian, but it can also be defined as a nonidentity or a liminal identity caught between white and black and tainted from the start (Barnard 2003; Besten 2009).

With the end of apartheid, racial essentialism was still strikingly and perhaps predictably immutable. Postapartheid white nationalism couched colouredness as "leftover people"; black nationalism denied the existence of colouredness in favor of a unified black identity; and ethnonationalism groped for ethnic purity (Erasmus and Pieterse 1999). In the rooibos region, a white charity worker encapsulated this liminal position when she asked me what I thought about drinking among coloured people. "Do we seem cruel?" she asked. "I mean, I know they have trouble with their identities. They are neither white nor black and all, but do we seem cruel?" Colouredness was rejected in three directions: as not white enough, not black enough, and not pure enough to be included in a nationalist discourse, unless it could be reframed as something else.

The Violence of Pathological Belonging

In the rooibos-growing area, coloured residents felt the implications of their "rejected" identities in daily experiences of structural and physical violence. *Dop* refers to alcohol and to the *dop* system, in which white commercial farmers would pay their workers part of their salaries in a measure of cheap wine. Although it was made officially illegal in 1962, many people said that some farms still practiced it. The dop system represented just one of the many micropolitics of paternalism that characterized the intimate but highly asymmetrical white and coloured farm relations in the Western Cape (du Toit 1993). In recent years, these relations had become all the more unstable as farms turned increasingly toward seasonal employment. Many rural poor in areas such as the rooibos region found themselves unable to find steady work on farms, obtain urban jobs, or make a living as smallholders. Combined with coloured residents' uncertain claims to belonging, the precariousness of livelihoods and dependencies on white farmers formed a particular kind of dehumanizing structural violence. In such a context, scenes of despair could appear banal to many residents.

"If you want to understand coloured people," a white resident said to my friend, another American working in the area, "you need to go to the hospital on a Friday night." I hesitated about the ethics of his suggestion, but eventually decided to see what he meant. Pulling up to the hospital, we saw a truck marked "Forensic Pathology." We walked inside, and all the patients were coloured. There was blood on the floor. Something was happening behind the curtain. A coloured man standing next to me pointed and said, *"Daar, hy is dood." "Wat?"* I asked, hoping that I had not understood his Afrikaans correctly, thinking that he had said, "There, he is dead." *"Hy is dood,"* he confirmed my translation. The figure behind the curtain had been stabbed in the neck in a *shabeen*, or informal drinking house. I saw a doctor push the curtain aside and walk in. I heard crinkling and then a zip. He started wheeling the bed toward us. I looked away. The man next to me said, "I want you to look." He touched my friend's head. "You need to look." The bed wheeled past, and my friend, shaken, stepped outside. I sat there with the man still standing next to me. "My brother was also stabbed in the neck twelve years ago. That's why I am used to it," he said in a tone that seemed in the moment to be dispassionate. "That must have been really hard for you," I replied, uncertain how to respond, feeling vomit form in my throat. "No, it isn't hard. It is life. That's why I wanted your friend to look," he insisted, then returned to his brother's story. "I was trying to get to my brother. I was biking, and I saw a car coming, and they were telling me to go home. I was trying to get to my brother. I went home, and my mom was crying, and his wife wasn't understanding. I went to the hospital, but he was already dead. I said, 'Take me to the morgue. I want to see the body.'" He paused until I lifted my eyes from the floor to meet his gaze. "That's why I wanted your friend to look. Life is short. This is life."

His face was hard and calm. "That's why I take my dop at home. I have my own music, my own alcohol." He looked at his friend and asked, "Are you good enough to drink?" He nodded. As they turned to leave, he asked me where I was from. "America," I replied. "America. Wow! I didn't think I would meet someone from America." He smiled as he walked into the darkness. The white man had suggested going to the hospital as a way to affirm the supposedly inherent inadequacies of coloured people. The man at the hospital—I never learned his name—also wanted to show me what was happening. "Look," he had insisted. The structural violence and deprivation he experienced in his daily life was not just symbolic or identitarian but also literal. "Life," he said, "was short." Yet he retained a kind of hope and humor, the ability to find delight in meeting someone from far away. The humor seemed a vital part of asserting his humanity amid the violence.

This encounter with the extreme of literal violence—death—revealed something about how people negotiated daily violence that occurred in less dramatic moments. Many people laughed off or simply ignored discussions of racial identity. I met Lucas, a coloured resident, at a local café where white farmers' wives would often lunch. Unlike the men at the hospital, Lucas was considered a "respectable" coloured by many residents because he was an educated Christian. After he ordered a Coke, he began telling a story about the time he attended a meeting with people from around South Africa: "They had a 'dress your culture day.' And everyone had something to wear. I showed up in my normal street clothes. They said, 'Don't you have a culture?'" I asked Lucas what white South Africans were supposed to wear. He responded with a laugh. "Khaki," he said, referring to the safari suits popular among many Afrikaans farmers. While scholars discuss the invisibility of whiteness as an ethnic identity, Lucas described how even whites were given cultural markers (Dyer 1997; Frankenberg 1993).

"The thing about the coloured people," Le Roux, another coloured resident, said, "is they have no cultural value because they have no roots." Using a kind of self-abstraction, a "they" instead of a "we," Le Roux explained how people were always trying to place coloured people. "I've often wondered who my ancestors are. Now heritage seems so important to everyone. Well, my eyes are small, so I think I must have some Asian, maybe some Malay. And I know one of my great-grandfathers was white." We discussed how some activists prefer to include the coloured community under the umbrella term "black." "It's always about South African black versus whites. The coloureds are always in the middle. It is an identity crisis." In other parts of the country, he added, "there is a lot of debate about heritage, but not here. Here, they are exclusive to other races because they are scared. When people say, 'Where do you belong?' it's hard."

Even South Africa's Freedom Charter, a document from 1955 that lists the key principles of the main apartheid opposition groups, seems to neglect the specificity of coloured existence. The charter states: "That South Africa belongs to all who live in it, black and white, and that no government can justly claim authority unless it is based on the will of all the people; That our people have been robbed of their birthright to land, liberty and peace by a form of government founded on injustice and inequality."[11] The charter, much of which was incorporated into the postapartheid constitution, was considered notable for its discourse of non-racialism. Yet despite the fact that it was ratified by the Coloured People's Congress, a political organization formed in 1953 to support coloured franchise, it maintains the binary discourse of black and white. In this language, it is unclear whether coloured people had a "birthright to land."

The voices of those without "birthright" were often silenced, both literally and figuratively. Despite their attempts to be heard through attendance at rooibos industry meetings, coloured people were usually unacknowledged in discussions between white rooibos farmers and major rooibos corporations. "They don't care what we have to say," a coloured farmer said when I asked why he did not speak up during an industry dialogue on workers' conditions.

Coloured people also remained largely ignored in local heritage, their culture not sufficiently "authentic" for museums. One local museum included artifacts from white farmers from past centuries, with covered wagons and old farming tools. There were stories of well-known local Afrikaners, a famous writer, a doctor, a comedian, and a section about rooibos, the factory, and the benefits of the plant. Off to the side in the museum, a small exhibit about the Indigenous community featured archaeological artifacts, rock art samples, and even an old "Bushman's" skull. The nonwhite Indigenous community was displayed as though extinct, with the classic dioramas of primitive cultures, cultures so removed from present-day humans that their skulls could be displayed instead of buried in a cemetery. By denying this "Bushman" a modern humanity, Afrikaners could forge their own primacy on the land.

The picture painted by the museum was one in which precolonial people no longer exist. As one white farmer said, "Bushmen, Khoisan most of them were murdered between the whites and the blacks. They couldn't adjust to the new way of living with possessions." In other words, "Bushmen" could not own land because they quite literally could not live in a world defined by ownership; they had genetic cultural failings that kept them from moving into modern times. Instead, all that remained of the nonwhite population was the "coloured problem," a people without history, identity, or "roots," as Lucas described. If Khoisan people were extinct, then their place was in the local museum and not among the coloured community. The coloured community, instead, was merely the "bastard" offshoot of the white community.

Concrete Placelessness and Forced Nomadism

As Le Roux and others described, part of the struggle for local coloured people who wanted to understand their heritage was that they questioned, physically, where they belonged. Few coloured farmers in the region owned land, yet they still discussed rooibos as an intimate part of their heritage. Their belief in cultural ownership of rooibos did not, however, stem from concrete ownership of private property. With the exception of a small community in the northern part of the region, most small-scale coloured farmers leased their land from the Wupperthal Moravian Church. So while they felt that rooibos was central to their heritage, they lacked legal title to it or access to enough land to guarantee secure livelihoods (Surplus People Project and Legal Resources Centre 2000).[12] According to one person in the industry, hundreds of farmers worked small rooibos plots that *in total* would equal two average-size commercial farms (Keahey and Murray 2017).

Rhenish German missionaries founded Wupperthal in the 1830s. (Wupperthal and its surrounding outstations became part of the Moravian Church in 1965 after the Rhenish Missionary Society scaled back its activities in southern

Africa [Bilbe 2009].) The missionaries came to "spread the Word to among the indigenous people."[13] In Wupperthal, governance and God were one and the same. While the town had a municipal representative, the church owned the land and leased it to residents. The church also provided the majority of services, such as water and electricity, and the Church Council made most local governing decisions. Alongside its political and economic dominance, the church played a significant role in indigenous identity politics among coloured people in the area. One coloured community worker felt that the mission's success in the nineteenth century "ensured the breakdown of indigenous society." Nineteenth-century missionaries provided a list of things not permitted at the mission, including speaking Indigenous languages and dressing in Indigenous clothing.[14]

Recently, with the assistance of national and international donors, people in Wupperthal began to concentrate economically on rooibos farming and processing, as well as heritage tourism. While Wupperthal residents relied partially on farming for their livelihoods, many adults had left the area for work in the city or for seasonal work on white commercial farms. Those who remained depended heavily on remittances and pensions. Most local coloured people who did not live on church land stayed in town and did seasonal or domestic labor or resided on white commercial farms as workers. They were always on other people's land, with the possibility of eviction around every corner. Lacking secure homes, coloured anxieties about placenessness were clearly not just figurative, but real, concrete, and often desperate.

In February 2011, the local government held a public participation meeting about reforming the country's Land Tenure Security Act. The aim was to provide farmworkers with greater protection from eviction by white farmers. While waiting for the program to begin, I chatted with the person next to me. We spoke about his concerns over his home on the farm. "The farmers always try tricks. They find loopholes." He told me that farmers find any excuse to evict workers, accusing them of drunkenness or firing them just before they reach pension age. When the meeting started, a government official explained the new law and how it would give farmworkers more rights to their houses on commercial farms. Throughout, people repeatedly yelled, "*Ja!*" (Yes!) and "*Dit is reg!*" (That's right!). During the question-and-answer section, many workers began their questions by listing how long they had worked on a particular farm: twenty-seven years, sixteen years, nine years, and so on. One local coloured politician summarized, "Displacement today is now the farmworker." By using the word "displacement" rather than "dispossession," "injustice," or even "subjugation," he signaled farmworkers' lack of a rightful *place* in the landscape.

After the meeting, I talked with Riaan, a coloured worker. We discussed farm owners who complained that workers did not maintain their houses well. Riaan spoke forcefully, expressing his frustration. "But the house," he said, "it's not mine, even though my family has lived there for generations. How can I feel like I belong here?" Riaan's question encapsulated his feelings of displacement within his generational home. In her work on Australia, the anthropologist Allaine Cerwonka (2004) describes the "deterritorialization" of people who stay in place. It is not merely diasporic populations, or people forced to leave their ancestral homes, who challenge people's imagined naturalized links between identity and geography. Cerwonka instead focuses on deterritorialization experienced by people *within* their "homes," as they adapt to influxes of immigrants and the concomitant multiculturalism that unsettles feelings of cultural connections to place. Yet the link between identity and geography was far more complicated for people such as Riaan. With the majority of land in white hands, Riaan was deterritorialized in the place where his family had lived for generations. He lacked a secure home, but he also lacked the ability to claim an ancestral right to any place. *His very identity was deterritorialized.*

While the desire to reform the Land Tenure Security Act recognized a failing in the bill's ability to provide farmworkers with a stable home, a local government worker explained that implementation remained a more fundamental problem. Farm owners still dismissed workers, often leaving them with nowhere to go but the already crowded "coloured section" of town. As one former farmworker described, "The biggest challenge here is the housing. Many of the farmworkers who are dismissed come to town and look for houses. There are problems between farmworkers and the people that live in town about the housing subsidy. The waiting list for Clanwilliam—and it is a small town—is more than 1,500." I asked him what people did while they were waiting. "There is more than one family in a house. Other people are staying in shacks. In Clanwilliam there are a thousand-plus in shacks." It might come as surprise that the unemployed farmworker cited housing as a bigger challenge than finding work. Yet with more than half the population lacking formal employment, the idea of obtaining a steady job had lost its saliency for many—it was such a distant possibility that it could seem unattainable or even irrelevant.

Forced to be relatively nomadic with few job opportunities, the coloured poor of the rooibos-growing area found ways to get by, whether it was by moving to cities, staying with family members who received government subsidies, lining up each morning to wait for farmers to pick them up for temporary jobs, moving from farm to farm to ask for employment, dealing drugs, or working in the "white house," a building that allegedly offered prostitution services. Yet some white farmers attributed this waywardness to coloured people's genetic attributes, saying that they were "culturally lazy" or that they were descended from hunter-gatherers, so they were predisposed to nomadism. White farmers implied that if coloured people accepted a Khoisan indigeneity to claim a place-based heritage in the region, they would be penalized for their indigenous inadequacies. Paul, a white farmer, explained why he thought seasonal workers moved from farm to farm: "I think it's still the Bushman culture. They travel a lot." Instead of describing the increased informalization of labor and the seasonality of a crop such as rooibos, he gave coloured workers a genetic predilection toward movement. They travel, he insisted, because they did not have the same attachment to the rooibos land that he did. Or, as another farmer described, "They are descended from Bushmen or Khoisan or whatever. They roamed from place to place and didn't think about the long term."

While Paul and other white farmers denied coloured people a relationship with rooibos *land*, coloured people were not always erased from rooibos *knowledge*, albeit in problematic ways. One white farmer described how "underproduction" in the 1950s dramatically increased demand for tea. Seeds were scarce, and no one knew how to find more. One man, the story went, had a matchbox of seeds. With the money he made from selling those seeds, he was able to buy an entire farm. The story continued: "A coloured woman had seed, but she wouldn't tell anyone where she got it. So they gave her wine, and then she told them that she got the seed from the ants. Now, people follow anthills or sift the sand under bushes." According to this legend, a coloured woman guarded the secrets of rooibos, but her inability to resist alcohol unveiled the truth to white farmers. The story, though surely apocryphal, demonstrates how white farmers envisioned coloured people as weak. Like Eve, they caused the community to fall from Eden. This myth describes how coloured people can be easily controlled through alcohol, their "primal weakness," a belief perpetuated by the dop system. Today, it is still often coloured workers, and coloured women in particular, who gather rooibos seeds by hand and sell them to farmers. Sometimes they will arrive at a farmer's gate and ask whether they may collect seeds. The compensation varies from farm to farm, but often the farmer will take half of what they collect.

The story of the rooibos seeds perpetuates the stereotype that coloured people are always on the verge of falling, of losing their relative privilege over black people. Yet the story also gives coloured people some ownership, even indigenous knowledge, over the rooibos plant. It was a coloured woman who held, but then lost, the secret. Lurking in the background of this discussion, however, was the fact that most coloured people in the rooibos-growing area did not want to be naturalized as Khoisan. Being Khoisan would mean embracing an identity that was both valorized and stigmatized at the same time—valorized by marketers and stigmatized by centuries of scientific racism.

Rejecting Indigeneity

We are lucky to have our farms because apartheid took the land
from black people. We are not so black. Our heritage is white. A white
man married a brown woman. —COLOURED ROOIBOS FARMER

Scholars such as Helene Strauss (2009) argue that the end of apartheid and the extension of nonracial citizenship provided South Africans with a range of possible identities from which to choose. The idea of identity and choice reflects concepts of cultural identity in the neoliberal age, when flexibility, mobility, and consumption appear to offer people the ability to self-fashion their essences (Comaroff and Comaroff 2009). Michele Ruiters (2009) contends that many in the coloured community have undergone a kind of ethnographic refashioning as Khoisan. In recent years, activists such as Khoisan X have emerged. Recalling Malcolm X, Khoisan X was born Benny Alexander, the son of laborers in the Northern Cape province. Alexander, a former Pan-Africanist Party politician, changed his name to throw off the vestiges of domination. John Western (2001: 622) calls this self-identification with the Khoisan "an ethnocultural conjuring," a means for some coloured people to understand their heritage in a way that connects them to the land. Other South Africans have referred to people such as Khoisan X as "ethnic entrepreneurs," arguing that they are manufacturing an identity for personal or political gain.

Among the rooibos region's coloured community, cultural identity took on multiple and complex meanings. Identity could serve as a choice or an ascription, as a stigma or a shield, as a protection or a cage. Affiliating with a Khoisan heritage had multiple implications that were not always emancipatory in the way described by Khoisan X. Instead of focusing on a Khoisan indigeneity, many coloured residents imagined their redemption not through the past, not through their "culture" as such, but through their identification with an indigenous plant. While the rejection of a Khoisan identity might make sense given the stigma attached to the colonial category of Bushman, something more was at play. For some, the refusal of a Khoisan identity was a statement about their embrace of, and aspirations toward, a modern Christian respectability. Yet for most coloured residents, Christianity and indigeneity were not mutually exclusive. Instead, they attempted to redefine indigeneity in a way that they described as both aspirational and authentic to their relations with the rooibos landscape.

Marketers and community workers sometimes imagined indigenous rooibos as a commodity through which the supposedly fraught identity of coloured people could be redeemed. If the "culture of the coloured" was envisioned as problematic, hopeless, and drowned in alcohol, then reinvigorating cultural pride through connections with products such as rooibos would seem a celebration of a pre-apartheid identity with a hopeful postapartheid future. However, local coloured people's reactions to these attempts at "redemption" were decidedly mixed. Some people simply ignored the indigenous label, choosing to engage with current issues facing the area's coloured community, such as crime, unemployment, and substance abuse. Others did embrace a Khoisan identity and had done so long before community workers "told them" that they were indigenous. Still others actively rejected the heritage, asserting instead that their heritage was white. (Tellingly, few claimed a white Afrikaner identity. Instead, they more often pointed to an English or German ancestor.) Fewer still chose the label "black" to affiliate with all nonwhite South Africans in a continuing political struggle.

While coloured residents had varied responses to the label "indigenous," some tea boxes carried stories of farmworkers designed to assure consumers that their purchase would help to sustain an indigenous lifestyle. The London-based Redbush Tea Company emphasizes "Our Work with the Bushmen," with a tab on its website alongside "Our Products" and "Shop Online."[15] The website's "Welcome" page flashes images of smiling "Bushmen" interspersed with pictures of tea boxes and freshly harvested plants. While explaining that the company does not have fair trade certification, it says that it donates a percentage of its profits to the Kalahari Peoples Fund: "Redbush Tea Co. is very proud of the fact that rooibos has its historic roots as a Bushman medicine, and it is for this reason that we do, and will continue to support these truly amazing people. Redbush Tea has a long standing [sic] relationship with them."

Matt, a marketer, described Intaba brand teas. Intaba means "mountain" in Xhosa, a language spoken by black South Africans and not widely heard in the rooibos region. Matt, however, said the word "Intaba" is "nice" for consumers "because it's South African, but it's easily pronounceable." Under the lettering, Intaba's tea boxes had pictures of stick figures meant to look like rock art (figure 1.1). "The stick figure conveys heritage, and mountain is a word that is connected to tea all over," Matt explained. He linked the tea to an image of Africa and to a *general* idea of heritage not necessarily connected to the rooibos-growing region or its coloured or white populations.

Mirroring the tea box's images, some, mostly white, development organizers in the area tried to give coloured workers and their children a historical

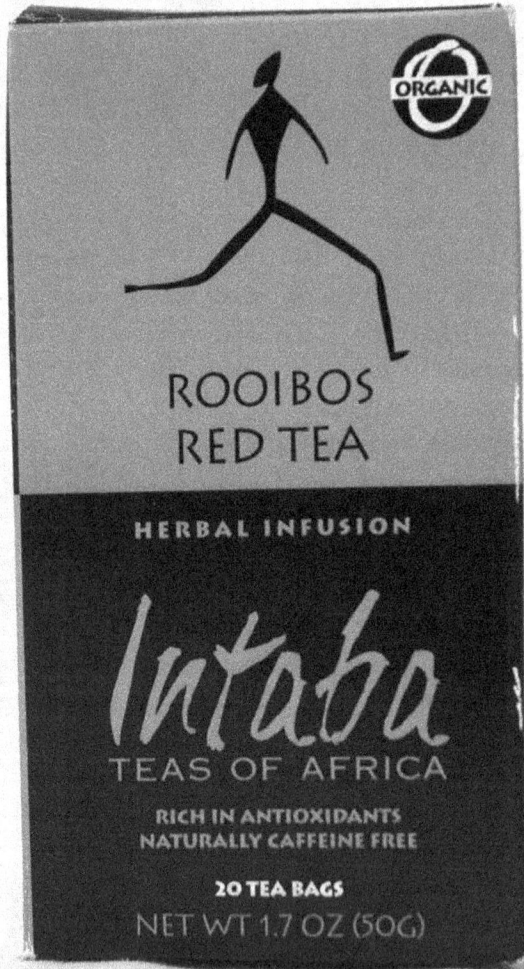

FIGURE 1.1. Intaba tea box. Photograph by the author.

narrative that might include a Khoisan heritage. As one community worker said, "The impulse of our project is to restore and bring back heritage to the community, to reinstate lost heritage, give people more a sense of who they are." There was a feeling that something, an indigenous heritage, had been forgotten and must be remembered. Yet because they employed an ideological framework that linked culture to place, they struggled with repatriating a people who supposedly have no essential home.

There have been several important critiques of NGOs and their role in the "identity business." For example, Tania Murray Li's research in Indonesia describes the violence of rendering indigeneity a mere figment of NGOs' imaginations (Li 2000). It is easy to critique a community's identity claims by saying that it is merely capitalizing on an NGO's marketing ploy. In the case of the Khoisan, Alan Barnard (2007) argues that social scientists expect a greater degree of "purity" from the Khoisan than from other South African populations. I want to emphasize that I am not denying, trivializing, or celebrating whether or not some coloured people claim a Khoisan identity. Rather, I am elucidating how people in the rooibos region challenged conventional concepts of indigeneity. Coloured residents did not merely accept a Khoisan identity rooted in the past; rather, they claimed a different and more flexible notion of indigeneity based on their connections to rooibos. This heritage was not hampered by South Africa's problematic history of a spatially incarcerating form of "nativity" that limited people's movements and their economic and political freedoms based on the apartheid government's imposed concepts of culture, tribes, and homelands.

One sunny September day, I spoke with a white university student from Cape Town who was in the rooibos-growing area to help organize the annual Lantern Festival. Associated with the Living Landscape Project, the Lantern Festival brought together drama and music groups. About four hundred, mostly coloured, children participated with art, performances, and a parade through the streets of Clanwilliam. I walked down to watch the students practice and struck up a conversation about the goals of the parade. "We take the themes from stories that Bleek and Lloyd [scholars who studied the San imprisoned on Robben Island] got from the San in the late nineteenth century. They were trying to preserve a dying culture. The idea of retelling the stories in Clanwilliam," the volunteer said, "is to capture those stories and release them to the wind." He described how the project's goal was to return the stories to the area, reinvigorating the spirit of the people and the place with an Indigenous heritage. Yet there was a subtle violence to the metaphor. Heritage was separated from the person and rendered as immaterial—and as fleeting—as the wind.

"Are you descended from the Khoisan?" I asked Willem, a coloured farmworker. "No," he replied and moved back to our conversation about working on a commercial farm. Willem explicitly and directly rejected a Khoisan heritage; he was more concerned with making a living for his family. The children involved in the Lantern Festival also often expressed a lack of interest in heritage. A development worker described her work with schoolchildren. "We go into the veld and become part of the San," she said. I asked whether she thought the children felt they were related to the San. "They are just playing a game," she said. "They are not thinking, 'Where do I come from?'" Marie, a community worker and longtime resident, helped farmworkers deal with issues such as eviction and conflicts over wages. While she heavily criticized commercial farmers for their treatment of workers, she also described rooibos tea with local pride. We discussed conversations she had had with farmworkers about rooibos and whether they felt the same pride that she did. "It depends on their loyalty to the farms," she said. "For some people, it is a family legacy that I should also fulfill. If you are loyal, you won't say something negative. Others say they are not satisfied. The relationship depends on the specific employers." In this instance, feelings about rooibos centered not on indigeneity but, rather, on a farmworker's history or relationship with a farmer.

In this vein, while some corporate tea companies named their rooibos products Intaba, Khoisan, or Bushman's Brew, small-scale coloured rooibos cooperatives looked to different sources to name their tea, many of which came from the local geography. Other coloured cooperatives used religious terms, such as Ebenezer, that honored the Old Testament. These choices signaled marketing strategies that removed indigeneity from the equation. Significantly, however, a rejection of indigeneity did not mean a rejection of land claims. A number of coloured people and organizations in the area were attempting to claim land for agricultural projects, an issue I discuss further in chapter 5. Yet these claims were not based on an idea of their history as rooted to any specific land. The claimants said that the land should be given or returned to them not because of their cultural identity but, rather, for a number of reasons: They traced their ancestry to former white and coloured landowners; they cited the large percentage of white landownership in general; they noted that their families had been living on church-owned land for generations; and so on.

"I Know I Am Khoisan Because a Professor Told Me"

On a sweltering afternoon during harvest season, I sat in a café with Paul, a local coloured man who was involved with heritage training. Paul's feelings about indigeneity were complex: He simultaneously celebrated it and dismissed its importance to his well-being. Over a pot of rooibos, we spoke at length about local rock art and how archaeologists had helped create jobs and tourism. "We learned about rooibos because Clanwilliam *is* rooibos," he said. "We connect rooibos with the Khoi because the Khoi drank it first." I asked what he enjoyed most from the training. "Well, they asked us what we wanted to learn, and we said computer training," he answered. "We also learned catering (for the ladies), entrepreneurial skills, bookkeeping, welding, plumbing, electricity. You got a certificate with these skills." He talked about how he used those skills for a different job, unrelated to heritage.

Paul became particularly animated when he described a "Cultural Walkabout" that the training group created through Clanwilliam's "coloured section." "Cederville," he began, "is the name of the coloured area." Despite the fact that I had lived in the town for months, I was surprised to learn that the area had a name. It had always been described to me as "the community" or "the other side of the road" or "that part of town," accompanied with gestures or nods of the head. Paul continued:

First, we would go the hospital, the old jail, the info center, and the church. In the info center they used to show movies, and they called it the Cederama. White people would go through the main entrance. If you look above the info desk, you will see a black door. There was a ladder there where coloured people would go up and watch at the top. Then, we would turn into the coloured area, the old part where the buildings have thatch roofs and are made with clay.... The first coloured worker at the municipality used to live in an old house there. It was about eighty-five years old. He has since died, and the building was torn down. We would take guests to the house, and he would explain how things were. In the museum there is an old clock. It had a twelve-hour bell. He would ring the bell at twelve and then the coloured people knew it was time for lunch. He would ring it again at 1 PM, and they knew it was time to go to work again. The old rugby field for coloured people was called Jubilee Park. There are now buildings there. The team was called Delicious; it still is. They played different coloured teams in other towns. Today it is still the same. Then we would go to the churches.

The trip appeared imprinted in his brain. He moved our discursive tour from the coloured part of town to the new "black section":

> Then we would go to the top where the RDP [Reconstruction and Development Programme] houses are. We would stop there because it is very dangerous. And we would point out Khayelitsha, the informal settlement. The RDP houses are coloured and Xhosa. There is high unemployment. We would tell people about the health issues, like TB. In Khayelitsha there is no water. It is mostly seasonal workers. There are illegal shabeens—that is a huge problem. All the money goes to the shabeen owners. If the people really wanted to see it, we would drive in with a Land Rover. Every weekend there are murders and rapes. Knives are a big problem. A lot of it is alcohol-related. I would never go there.

Racially partitioning each part of town in his narrative and his tour, he explained, "I know there is a lady that does a tour just in the white area." Paul's description of the Cultural Walkabout revealed his ideas about what is culturally salient to the region's heritage and to his own.

He spoke for a long time, uninterrupted by questions. He talked about how they had identified the history of their community, using words such as "we" in ways that he never used when talking about Khoisan history. He discussed the history of apartheid, the stories of his elders, and issues, such as crime and segregation, that still exist today. But tourists, he said, "they are not so much interested. They are more interested in the rock art." He said that the Cultural Walkabout tours were rarely given, unless a school group asked for one. Celebrating coloured heritage was not envisioned as palatable for international tourists because it did not fit into ideas of a pure and authentic Africa.

Finally, I interrupted. I asked Paul whether he felt a connection to the rock art, whether he felt that Khoisan heritage was his heritage. His answer surprised me. "I am related to the Khoisan," he began. "I know that because a woman, a professor, came . . . and did DNA testing. She looked at the mitochondrial DNA from the mothers and did a family tree. I was A2, which means . . . my DNA goes back thirty-five thousand years ago to the San and Khoi. . . . Everyone had the same, either A1, A2, or A3. 'A' means you are from Africa." He described the visit by a scholar, Himla Soodyall, from the University of the Witwatersrand's Human Genomic Diversity and Research Unit in the School of Pathology.

On an episode of the popular television program *Carte Blanche* titled "So Where Do We Come From?" Soodyall and South Africans of various backgrounds, including Nelson Mandela, commented on their genetic heritage.

According to the show, Mandela's DNA showed that he is distantly related to the Khoisan on his mother's side.[16] Soodyall explained, "Ultimately all lines come back with their origins in Africa, so all lineages found in peoples today have been retained by people we call Khoisan," who carry genetic signatures very similar to the "original modern human ancestor." The program emphasized how often those "who call themselves coloured" have a particularly close genetic signature to the Khoisan. One coloured panelist responded, "So I have a few brothers running around in the desert." Another cheered, "Yes! I'm from the original people."

The program highlighted how genetic testing specifically affected the coloured community, allowing its members to fill in the "gaps" in their history and to connect to heroes such as Mandela. Soodyall celebrated the fact that genetics permits South Africans an "unbiased" rewriting of history, one that acknowledges difference but not the problematic cultural differences of the apartheid government. Using a similar rationale, one self-described "liberal" Afrikaans rooibos farmer explained: "There are not a lot of indigenous brown people. . . . In South Africa, 90 percent of people, there's a connection between white, brown, and blacks, a kind of interbreeding." While we talked, his white wife prepared lunch, his white son played on the floor, and his coloured domestic worker swept the porch outside. He continued, "My father always told me—he was very outspoken against apartheid—the solution for South Africa is white and brown should just interbreed more."

In her final report for the Living History Project, sponsored primarily by the African Genome Education Institute and Ancestry24.com, Soodyall analyzed DNA results that she argues determine a person's genetic heritage. She concluded that the results "clearly demonstrate that a person's genetic ancestry *may differ from their concept of identity*. One of the major messages of this study is to drive home the point that the genetic markers used for genetic ancestry tests **cannot** reveal a person's identity or explain why they may look the way they do" (Soodyall 2008: 8; italics added). She argues, "The study also reaffirms the rich genetic diversity that exists in the southern part of Africa which is the result of different migrations from other parts of Africa to the region as well as contributions from sea-borne immigrants since mid 1600s [*sic*]." The language of the report puts forth a kind of genetic false consciousness in which an idea of genetic unity lies beneath the surface of the skin and cannot be seen by the eye.

The language of genetics can also sterilize a complex history. The report reinforced a kind of primitive fetishism in which nonwhite South Africans are linked to the distant past of human origins. The logic continues that if all humans originated in southern Africa, then we are all Khoisan. The language of the report, however, masks the often violent history of the country's "DNA legacy." Speaking of Europeans' genetic "contributions" reframes the rape and power dynamics of miscegenation through the benign phrasing of added genetic components—or, as the white farmer said, "interbreeding." The importation of slaves is collapsed into "migrations."

DNA testing becomes particularly complicated by the fact that the Khoisan were often viewed as the "first people," not only for South Africa, but also for the world. Museums frequently depicted Khoisan as lower on the evolutionary transition from humans to apes. South Africa's Origins Centre, a "world-renowned San rock art museum" in Johannesburg, displays the evolution of man through fossils of different hominids to mark the physiological changes that took place in early man. The Centre moves seamlessly from fossils to depictions of the "San people of today." The website explains, "The subject of many racist myths and misperceptions, the San people of southern Africa have often been marginalised and exploited. . . . Modern San descendants are carving niches for themselves in a modern world in which their ancient culture is out of synch."[17]

Pairing the history of humanity with the culture of the San could imply that affiliating with the San would leave a coloured person "out of synch" with the modern world, always economically disadvantaged, able to participate in the modern economy only by making crafts for tourists. San images—of ancient people phenotypically different from modern man—are reinforced in rooibos advertising such as the stick figures on the Intaba boxes. Afrikaners did not seem concerned that global marketing of rooibos with Bushman imagery would undermine their cultural ownership of the tea. Because the Bushman was "extinct," he mattered little in indigenous claims to rooibos and the rooibos landscape.[18]

Paul was clearly interested in his DNA test and later made me a copy of the certificate of his results. He was excited that the tests said he shared genetics with Mandela. "But," he added, "I didn't feel any connection to a Khoisan heritage before the DNA testing"—even, he explained, when he was learning about local rock art during his training. While some coloured people from the rooibos region may have accepted and even celebrated a genetically determined Khoisan identity, Paul's relationship with the idea of heritage was fluid, incorporating apartheid and postapartheid coloured history. He used the skills acquired during his Living Landscape training program to obtain a job at a Christian-based social service provider. People from town often said that the Living Landscape Project was a failure because so many people had left the organization. Paul felt the training was fruitful, however, because he had a different framework for successful heritage training. He had learned about the local history—rock art, rooibos, and other local flora—and gained the skills to find employment in another sector. He imagined his heritage as directed toward a future in which heritage was not a burden that linked him to the past but a resource that he could use if and when he needed it.

Some people, however, dismissed local attempts to understand indigeneous history as mere money grabs. I asked a scientist working on rooibos whether her research drew from any indigenous knowledge. She replied, "Indigenous knowledge? The sum total is that they drank the tea. Now descendants of the Khoisan, or whatever, are coming after the fact to make claims." Perhaps she saw surprise on my face, and she explained further: "It's political. Please bring me the evidence. We know they drank it, and they fermented it, but they didn't know what it did." She reached for her bookshelf, pulled out a book on medicinal plants from the 1930s, and flipped to the page on rooibos.[19] "Nowhere in the medicinal book does it say its health properties," she said. Instead, the scientist and many commercial farmers in the area credited white people with the discovery of the tea's benefits and with its transition to a cultivatable, valuable crop. According to them, even if the Khoisan drank rooibos, they could not claim indigenous ownership of it.

A more profound issue in these contested claims, however, could stem from the fact that many Afrikaans farmers did not concede indigeneity to the coloured population, claiming it for themselves instead. Yet unlike coloured residents' descriptions of a future-oriented rooibos heritage, Afrikaners described their heritage in terms of a past rooted in the rooibos landscape.

"Rooibos Is in My Blood": White African Subjectivities

Through the farms he is rooted in the past; through the farms he has substance.
—J. M. COETZEE, *Boyhood*

FIELD NOTES, NOVEMBER 2010: *It was the first rooibos meeting that I attended, and I walked into a room of Afrikaans farmers. On the one hand, it felt comically stereotypical—characters ripped from a Coetzee novel. The men stood around in khaki safari suits, large bellies protruding over belts that held up embarrassingly short shorts. Faces, many bearded, were burnt by the intense summer sun, and wrinkles formed on the parched skin of even the youngest man in the room. Boisterous laughter and conspiratorial whispers emanated from groups of farmers seeing each other outside of their usual Sunday church conversations. The noises—at once both loud and hushed—were punctuated by the distinctly rolled "r" and harsh "g" of the Afrikaans language. I was one of the only women. It was easy to see the men as mere bodies, disconnected from individual stories. I could feel how easy it is for an "inkomer" to feel unwelcome or alien from these men, generations on the same farm, generations attending the same church and playing on the same rugby fields. But then one of the men recognized me, beckoned me over, and introduced me to another farmer. "Dit is die Amerikanse meisie," he said, calling me the "American girl," accompanied by a kind-hearted joke. Later, sitting on couches in farmhouse after farmhouse, I would learn the politics, anger, and interpersonal dynamics that accompanied the different groups. Interviews would sometimes last eight hours, tea becoming lunch becoming dinner. There was an urgency, a desperation, to their stories. "This is our land; this is our culture; we are not bad people." At one farmer's home, I noticed the book* The Afrikaners: Biography of a People, *by Hermann Gilomee, in his bookshelf. I had recently purchased the book but had not yet read it. I asked him if it was good. "Not really," he replied. "You know, just once I'd like to read something good about my people and not just bad."*

The manner in which rooibos marketers, public relations officers, and development orgranizations described relations between rooibos and the Khoisan fits into the country's increasing emphasis on marketing ethnicity through the corporatization of ethnic groups and through the emphasis placed on cultural tourism. By examining Afrikaners' relations to rooibos and to the land on which it grows, I unpack ideas of whiteness and Afrikaner identity claims. Recent years have seen a marked increase in Afrikaner nationalism. Addressing the symbolic and economic role of rooibos to Afrikaners enables me to explore competing notions of indigeneity and how these ideas factor into labor relations, land claims, and continuing economic inequality in the rooibos region and in the country as a whole.

Despite their history as colonizers or "settlers" who arrived in the seventeenth, eighteenth, and nineteenth centuries, Afrikaans farmers had ideas about rootedness that cannot be ignored. The majority of the Afrikaans farmers with whom I spoke described their identity as fixed in place. "I was born a rooibos tea farmer," said Jannie, one farmer. "It's in my blood. Who would we be if we did not farm?" Jannie's cultural value and his very being stemmed from his belief in indigeneity. Scholars such as David Trigger and Cameo Dalley (2010) have explored how white people "try on words" such as "indigenous" and "autochthonous." In the rooibos region, however, many Afrikaans farmers firmly believed that they were the first rightful occupants of the landscape.

Afrikaner notions of social membership and spirituality are intimately linked to South African land. The archaeologist Michael Wilcox (2010) argues that conquests require ideologies that allow a group to imagine itself as naturally or divinely ordained to settle and improve a place. Afrikaners' "civil religion" implies that they were this Eden's chosen people. Many Afrikaners believed they were able to survive in the harsh climate and defeat the "natives" because God looked after them (Moodie 1975). From this belief, they forged a national identity that was distinctly Christian in nature. Some even wanted to name the land "Eden" (Isichei 1995). Despite the fact that their heritage was predominately Dutch, Afrikaners with whom I spoke never referred to family or a history in the Netherlands. Unlike English-speaking residents who traced their ancestry to Britain, they did not espouse any geographical affinity outside South African soil. Their ancestors' bones were buried on the farm, and one day their bones would be buried there too, their bodies going back to the land. The discourses, debates, and sentiments around this "white African indigeneity" are linked to constructions and negations of cultural value and to the value of rooibos.

"What is the history of your land?" I asked Pierrie, an Afrikaans rooibos farmer. He began his narrative by pulling out a family tree. Other farmers produced photographs of great-grandparents, and a remarkable number had typewritten family histories. Many commercial farms in the area have been in the same family for at least three generations, and some from the eighteenth century. There were strikingly few surnames in the area, and a number of people farmed next to their brothers or cousins. When I inquired about who inhabited the land before their families, they often said, "No one," or, more rarely, "I think there might have been some Bushmen."

I asked farmers about a speech given by Julius Malema, the controversial former African National Congress (ANC) Youth League leader and current leader of the Economic Freedom Fighters, a political party he founded in July 2013 after the ANC expelled him for sowing divisions, among other charges, including a conviction on charges of hate speech for singing "Dubula iBunu" (Shoot the Boer/Afrikaner). In this particular address, Malema had railed against the inadequacy of the "willing buyer, willing seller" model of postapartheid land restitution. The "willing buyer, willing seller" model is a market-based approach in which the government would not force landowners (most often white) off their land; rather, if they wanted to sell their land, they could do so. This concept became the cornerstone of the postapartheid government's land reform policy by the time the White Paper on South African Land Policy was released in 1997. Many critics within and outside the country consider the policy a failure, in part because it allows racist practices and economic inequality to masquerade under the pretense of a market economy. As Edward Lahiff (2005) argues, landowners were free to sell their land to the highest bidder or, significantly, to the buyer of their choice even if the offer was lower. As a result, landowners could avoid selling their land on "racist grounds" but still sell it on the "open market." Malema called for nationalization and land redistribution from white to black. In response, many white farmers in the rooibos region were adamant: "This is our land. *We* were the first ones here." This assertion required an imaginary either that the land was empty, *terra nullius*, or that the prior inhabitants went extinct or were not people at all, more closely linked to animals and nature than to humanity, an issue I discuss at length in chapter 2.

Many Afrikaners saw themselves as natives, not settlers. Through rituals, festivals, and origin myths, they indigenized Van Riebeeck and fostered an ethnic notion of their culture (Kuper 2003). In 1996, a group of Afrikaner nationalists went to the United Nations Working Group on Indigenous Populations and claimed indigenous status. In 2005, a group made a similar assertion to the United Nations Special Rapporteur on Indigenous Peoples during his mission to South Africa, a claim that was rejected "on the grounds that the group was neither marginalised/discriminated against, nor did it meet the other criteria 'set out in international legal standards and discourses at the present time'" (International Labour Organization and African Commission on Human and Peoples' Rights 2009: 2). This relative "foreign-ness" stems from a long history of conflicts over "first arrivals" to South Africa. While most people in the region agreed that the Khoisan were present in the area before white settlement, their alleged extinction removed them from debates over belonging. As a result, white and black populations dominated regional first-arrival narratives. In early 2012, this "arrival" imaginary created a brief scandal in South African politics. Pieter Mulder, a minister in the Department of Agriculture, Forestry, and Fisheries, was a politician in the Freedom Front Plus Party, a political party founded in 1994 by right-leaning Afrikaners with the goal of protecting Afrikaner (and thus often commercial farmer) interests. Mulder incited an uproar when he claimed that "black 'bantu-speaking' people had no historical claim" to approximately 40 percent of the country's arable land, primarily in the Western Cape and including the rooibos-growing area.

Responding to President Jacob Zuma's and Malema's comments about land redistribution during the State of the Nation address in 2012, Mulder contended that "there is sufficient proof that there were no bantu-speaking [black] people in the Western Cape and north-western Cape. . . . Africans in particular never in the past lived in the whole of South Africa." Drawing on a long tradition of apartheid archaeology in South Africa, he cited diaries of early Afrikaans settlers to argue that they did not find any black people in the region when they moved north and westward. Black people, he continued, came down the continent from Africa's equatorial regions at the same time that Europeans moved up from the south. The two groups met at the present-day Eastern Cape. In July 2014, these debates made their way into a meeting about the Rural Development and Land Reform budget. A Freedom Front Plus member argued that black people stole the country's land from the Khoi and San. He later softened his language by saying that black people did not steal the land—but that white people did not steal it either. While these comments set off a frenzy in much of South Africa, they reflected many of the conversations that I had in the rooibos region, in which Afrikaners imagined themselves as the first occupants of an empty land, inhabited only by scattered nomadic "tribes" of less-than-human "Bushmen."

The disavowal of the Khoisan gave way to an imaginary framed in terms of the mythical narrative of Afrikaner sacred history to argue that they, not black people, had arrived first in the area that would become South Africa. The beginning of apartheid marked a transformation in engagements with archaeology and history more generally. As Nick Shepherd describes, the cultivation of this myth required a South African archaeology full of suppressions and self-willed constructions of imagination. In other words, in both metaphorical and literal ways, "doing archaeology involved looking through present landscapes, with their clutter of political aspiration and cultural change, to find traces of an imagined past lying below. . . . Henceforth, the historical imagination of the South African state would creak with the ox-wagons of the Afrikaner pioneers. . . . The strange occluded twilight of prehistory, part fantasy, part brute, material artefact, was eclipsed" (Shepherd 2002: 140).

White-White Identity Politics

Despite setting themselves in opposition to coloured and black South Africans, Afrikaans rooibos farmers more often focused on white residents of British descent as their true antagonists. Countrywide, significant symbolic battles between Afrikaans and British South Africans have taken place over national anthems, holidays, postage stamps, and whether English or Afrikaans should be used in schools (Crapanzano 1985; Legassick 1980; Moodie 1975). Perhaps the greatest representation of this conflict was the Anglo-Boer War, also known as the South African War. Although the war ended more than a hundred years ago, its symbolic presence still loomed large in the rooibos region. Placemats in a local restaurant told stories of Afrikaners' suffering in concentration camps at the hands of the British. Monuments and plaques commemorated white people who had died in the war. Like much of South Africa, the region was divided at the time. According to some people, the relationships between white residents, and white farmers in particular, were still affected. As one English-speaking farmer explained, "There was a lot of bad blood left over from the Anglo-Boer War. Many people fought for the British, including my family. It was very bad because they committed atrocities against the Boers. They hung one young man publicly in town. Even growing up, people would say, '*Jy is 'n Engelsman*' [You are an Englishman]." He continued, "They think they have a God-given right to farm. They think they are holy because they are farmers."

Indeed, some Afrikaans farmers in the area did not deem English rooibos producers "farmers." English families could own farms, but they could not truly be "*boere*," the Afrikaans word for farmer. These resentments involved more than linguistic maneuvers. Class-based hostilities also informed whether or not one could be called a "farmer." In the region, white people often associated the word "farmer" with lower-class Afrikaners, whereas English people were "producers" or "farm owners." Afrikaners who celebrated the "farmer" label often did so to differentiate themselves from the image of greedy British capitalists supposedly more interested in money than in loving and belonging in the land. Coloured farmers, by contrast, were labeled "emerging farmers," which reinforced their subordinate status to both the Afrikaans and the British. It remained unclear whether they would ever fully "emerge" in the linguistic and the material sense.

A few of the newer generations of Afrikaans rooibos farmers, who perhaps wanted to emphasize a liberal attitude when talking to an American woman, complicated these straightforward labels. "I hate the word 'farmer.' I am a producer," one young man said. "The stigma in South Africa of 'farmer, Boer,' in apartheid years, they were the bad guys. Preconceived as being something. It makes it hard to get girls." Some of the younger people even seemed to refuse the regimes of racial normativity, or enacted that normativity through boasts or jokes over beer to their Afrikaans friends, only later to tell me that they felt intense guilt over their place in South Africa's racial hierarchy. Yet these confessions were rare and always spoken of hurriedly and in hushed tones.

Feelings of hostility toward the English sometimes manifested themselves in displays of loyalty toward a farm-based upbringing that disdained white-collar work. "I'm not a paper man," said Adam, an Afrikaner whose family had lived on the land for generations. "I don't know much about marketing. I like to work with my hands, not with my head." Adam asserted that he did not want to grow his business. "I don't like offices. I like nature, the outdoors.

Rooibos farming is not a job. It's who you are. I am a rooibos farmer." Arend, a young Afrikaans man, had temporarily taken a job at a rooibos plant to make extra money. He rued the fact that he was not on his family farm, working alongside his father. Throughout our conversation he spoke with a nervous stutter, but at one point he grew animated. His voice became clear and firm as he talked uninterrupted for several minutes:

> It's in your blood. We come from a generation of farmers. We will farm until they take it with force. I always thought I would do rooibos. It's in my blood. Everything I know I learned from my father. He learned from his father. I don't know how grandfather learned. He grew only for his own consumption until Rooibos Ltd. [formed]. One day I will be a farmer myself. I dream of going back to the farm. I love the farm. I don't know why, but it's where I belong. I am proud to be a farmer, proud to be a boer. I am proud to be a teamaker. . . . I will move back to my dad's farm as soon as my dad is ready to stop farming. I hope to have a son and name him after my father. Hopefully, he will take after my father.

Arend linked his subjectivity to an inseparable connection among family, land, and farming, his bloodline tied to rooibos.

Whiteness in the rooibos-growing area was often conflated with farming, and criticizing farming or distancing oneself from the farming community could be seen as a betrayal of the land and of the race. Craig, an Afrikaans farmer who considered himself politically liberal, said, "White people are traitors if they say anything bad about white farmers." A coloured municipal worker described his view of this loyalty and betrayal: "A lot of the white people that I have met send their kids away to school, but apparently some Afrikaners see that as disloyal against the local community. But classes here are all in Afrikaans, so if you want an education in English you have to go elsewhere." Afrikaners who moved to cities were seen as having lost their culture or quite simply as not being Afrikaans anymore.

Despite their condemnations of the English, most Afrikaans farmers relied on hired permanent or seasonal labor to run their farms. Some of the large-scale commercial "farmers" never worked the soil. Instead, they operated out of office buildings. However, the myth of white toil, blood, and sweat on the land remained paramount and required the erasure of coloured or black laborers, whose "toil threatens to deprive the white man of the labours that he, as Africa's new heir, must not only perform but, more important, be seen to perform" (Coetzee 1988: 5).

A few wealthier (and mostly British) people in the area used their rooibos farms as country or weekend houses and hired white managers to tend to the crops. These "weekend farmers" discussed how much they enjoyed the experience of being surrounded by quaint, nostalgic Afrikaners. One English South African described his experience at his rooibos farm, which he called a "trophy farm," as a "cultural anthropological experience. . . . Afrikaans is my second language. I am not a Calvinist, God-fearing person, but the farmers who are my neighbors have been so nice. I find it life-enriching." Although it was not economically necessary for him, the farmer liked to dabble in rooibos, playing at being a farmer to enhance his urban life.

The Afrikaner-British divisions were complicated by desires to foster business and increase tourism in the area. At a meeting of the Clanwilliam Chamber of Commerce, members decided to remove the word "Afrikaanse" from "Clanwilliam Afrikaanse Sakekamer." It was the only matter of business voted on by the chamber, and it prompted little discussion. The secretary described the reasons for changing the chamber's name, including, "The word 'Afrikaans' in the name may. . . be an obstacle for business people from other language groups to join." Only one person stood up in favor of keeping "Afrikaanse" in the name. He showed everyone a newspaper article and cited statistics about how many more Afrikaners lived in the area than English people. Another man stood up and said, "Yes, we are Afrikaners, but business today is done in English, and we must adapt." After the meeting, I spoke with the only English South African in the room. He said that it did not bother him that the group was called the "Afrikaans Chamber of Commerce," but "it might deter a Xhosa or something from joining." He added that he used to belong to Cape Town's English Chamber of Commerce but quit because it was too far away.

These discussions of belonging, of "nativeness" and one's rightful place in the region, rarely included nonwhite actors. According to this narrative, coloured people were not local; only the Khoisan were local, and the Khoisan were unable to survive in the modern world.[20] By framing these conflicts over nativity as white versus white, commercial farmers could ignore coloured claims to land or rooibos heritage, negate the role of coloured workers in the development of commercial rooibos, and deny any place-based heritage to the coloured families who had lived in the area for generations, thereby reinforcing long-standing structures of inequality. As one Afrikaans commercial farmer explained, "This whole area was not settled by black tribes until 1970. Bushmen, Khoisan, most of them were murdered." By erasing the contemporary existence of the Khoisan and negating coloured connections to land or rooibos, Afrikaners were able to cultivate their own indigeneity through their relationship with the plant.

Cerwonka (2004: 122) describes how in Australia whites used native plants in their gardens symbolically to establish a "natural" link between themselves and the landscape to show that some white people were dispossessed and injured by colonial imperialism, "a claim that stands alongside aboriginal claims." She argues that this narration of heritage provided a way for white Austrailians to connect further back than the time of colonial settlement: An environmental heritage could link white Australia to Aboriginal occupants. Cerwonka's argument, however, takes on a different nuance when placed in the rooibos context, in part because rooibos is an economically significant crop and not just a garden flower, but also because many Afrikaners felt that they were destined by God to live in the region. Their claims to ownership—to Afrikaans blood mingled with the South African soil—did not "stand alongside" Aboriginal claims. Afrikaners, and not the supposedly extinct Khoisan, had a divine right to belonging. Yet these claims to rooibos also seemed to trap them in place. "We feel for all the farmers," a wealthy rooibos farmer said. "You can't leave the farms." He was referring in part to the fact the many Afrikaans farmers did not possess the education, skills, or English-language proficiency to pursue other employment. They were able to retain their relative privilege because they were farmers. But he was also alluding to the fact that staying on the rooibos land gave their subjectivities as white South Africans an authenticity. In the rooibos-growing area, many Afrikaners felt that those who had left their farms had betrayed themselves, the Afrikaans community, and the rooibos ecosystem.

Conclusion

In the contested, complicated indigeneities of the rooibos region, locals may have forged their belonging in relation to rooibos, but their "proper" place was always uncertain, relational, and precarious—whether it was the whiteness of the Afrikaners or the liminality of the coloured people, who supposedly had no essential homeland, whose very identity was envisioned as alien to everywhere. Afrikaners believed that their blood mingled with the rooibos soil, that they were the rightful and righteous sons and daughters of the region. Coloured residents challenged the notion that one must be "culturally indigenous" to claim cultural ownership of rooibos's heritage. South Africa's history makes claims to indigeneity particularly complex and shows both the potentially emancipatory and troubling results of embracing an ethnic identity. Many coloured people in the rooibos region expressed a form of heritage that was not merely a one-to-one fixity of people to place but, rather, something more encompassing and flexible. This claim allowed for fluidity in a way that temporally redefined heritage not only as a claim to a "traditional" past but as a potential for the future.

Scholars such as Olatunde Lawuyi (1998) have discussed the increased intensity of debates involving "tradition" among those who have not benefited economically or politically since the end of apartheid. Significantly, these debates typically ignore the coloured population because it is not considered "traditional" enough. However, in a joint media statement in October 2011, the ANC Youth League and the Congress of Traditional Leaders of South Africa (CONTRALESA) referred to the Khoisan in the present tense: "The Khoi and San . . . are the first defenders of South Africa's land, natural resources and livestock from greedy and blood thirsty Settlers and Colonizers in the wars of resistance. CONTRALESA and ANC Youth League respectively work to re-assert and reclaim the Africanness of the Khoi and San people and their descendants, most of whom are referred to as Coloured" (Shivambu and Mkiva 2011). The Khoisan *are* the first defenders of South Africa's land; the ANC Youth League and CONTRALESA *will* work to "re-assert" their "Africanness." Through this statement, the organizations "redeemed" coloured identity by reasserting its indigeneity, even calling it the most indigenous form of identity in South Africa. Instead of invoking narratives of the invisibility and disappearance of the Khoisan, CONTRALESA insisted on their survival in the coloured community.

Khoisan people are not always rendered extinct in Western discourse, either. Chris Kilham, a "medicine hunter" for America's Fox News, described his encounter with indigenous rooibos and indigenous people in a dispatch from the region: "When you drive through the countryside north of Cape Town, you see rooibos everywhere. Rooibos is a traditional beverage of the native Khoi people of the Cape area, though it has become more popular in recent years due to word spreading about its high antioxidant value. Traditionally, the native people harvest the leaves."[21] Kilham used the words "tradition" and "native Khoi" people in the present tense, not in the past tense, as most coloured and white residents did. Why are these groups suddenly invoking the Khoisan? In the case of Kilham, the invocation plays into Western fantasies about exotic Africa, in which a "medicine hunter" could discover natives harvesting a wild plant (an image laughable to the residents of rooibos country). This use of indigeneity signals something about the West—a need for an exotic and primitive other against whom to measure our own "modernity" and to justify our own historical actions—or inactions—in relation to economic, structural, and physical violence in Africa. The ANC's reasons for invoking the Khoisan may speak to the increasing significance of ideas about cultural ownership in a country where more than 25 percent of the country is unemployed and the dreams of a postapartheid future remain unrealized.[22] In attempts to foster a post-racial national identity, the ANC government used the idea of the Khoisan to emphasize a pan-ethnic universal idea of humanity (Barnard 2003). South Africa's new national motto is "Diverse People Unite," written in a now extinct Khoisan (specifically, /Xam) language. By using this extinct language, the government attempted to foster national unity without favoring any of South Africa's linguistic groups. Just as the Khoisan came to represent the origins of all humanity, they also served as an empty category: admirable but extinct and seemingly apolitical in their absence.

According to many coloured residents of the rooibos-growing area, the fact that the government, marketers, and NGOs summoned a Khoisan imaginary had potentially problematic consequences. Because these groups employed an ideological framework that linked culture to place, assertions of Khoisan heritage seemed to reinforce coloured pathologies of placelessness. Many residents wanted to celebrate their coloured history and experiences, instead of erasing them or reinforcing their supposed shame by relabeling them. In this context, the concept of indigeneity had political consequences—whether coloured people claimed a Khoisan identity, rejected it, or had it imposed on them by the ANC, by white South Africans, by scholars, or by development workers. The myriad implications only served to emphasize the problematic aspects of ethnic claims in South Africa.

Parallel to discussions of *pathological* belonging, however, were adamant discussions of *charismatic* belonging. In the tea-growing region, narratives of a place-based cultural indigeneity as a solution to the so-called coloured problem ran alongside discussions of the charismatic quality of rooibos's ecological indigeneity. Both coloured and Afrikaans residents repeatedly asserted that rooibos's economic, symbolic, and affective value and its charisma stem in large part from its regional specificity. Rooibos is good *because* it is endemic. Rooibos is part of the Cape Floristic Kingdom, a biodiversity "hot spot" and World Heritage Site as designated by the United Nations Educational, Scientific and Cultural Organization (UNESCO). According to UNESCO, the area has "rich diversity, exceptional endemism, range of communities and special ecological processes." The indigenous vegetation, UNESCO continues, is "charismatic."[23] The move toward the "charismatic" by UNESCO calls to mind Max Weber's (1947 [1922]: 241) definition of charisma as "a certain quality of an individual personality by virtue of which he is set apart from ordinary men and treated as endowed with supernatural, superhuman, or at least specifically exceptional powers or qualities. These qualities are not accessible to the ordinary person, but are regarded as of divine origin or as exemplary." For Weber, charisma inspires devotion. Because of its divine aspects, charisma can also inspire particular claims to belonging. Indigeneity is what gives rooibos, and the nutrient-poor land on which it grows, economic and affective value. These concepts of value, however, both perpetuate and challenge structures of racial inequality, Afrikaans and coloured subjectivities, and traditional social science notions of cultural heritage and indigeneity as a one-to-one historical relationship between people and place.

The next chapter continues the discussion of indigeneity and belonging through and with rooibos. By shifting attention to the cultivation of the plant itself, the chapter will explore how rooibos politicized the dynamic and highly moralized boundaries between nature and culture, further delineating who and what does and does not belong in the rooibos landscape.

FARMING THE

BUSH

Apartheid divides, ecology unites.
—JANE CARRUTHERS, "Tracking in the Game Trails"

A resilient and long-standing narrative in the history of botany has
characterized its rise as coincident with and dependent on the development
of taxonomy, standardized nomenclature, and "pure" systems of classification ...
but to isolate the science of botany is to overlook the dynamic relationships
among plants, peoples, states, and economies. —LONDA L. SCHIEBINGER
and CLAUDIA SWAN, *Colonial Botany*

BOTANICAL NOTES: *The fynbos ecosystem in which rooibos grows is located
in the smallest of the world's six "floral kingdoms." Other kingdoms extend over
vast cross-border territories. The boreal, for example, represents 40 percent of the
world's land surface and includes much of North America and Eurasia. The fynbos, on the other hand, covers just 0.04 percent and exists only in the Western Cape
of South Africa (Western 2001).*

Farmers and scientists in the Cederberg region often invoked ecological exceptionalism in relation to rooibos. In this context, the story of rooibos is a
story not just about producers and consumers but also about the crop itself, a
natural, indigenous plant and global commodity with particular qualities that
make it valuable and intensely political. "Rooibos started from the wild," local
farmers, workers, and residents said repeatedly. During long hikes on dusty

mountain trails, I slowly became an expert at spotting wild rooibos plants growing among all of the other brown-green bushes with needle-like leaves, or *fynbos*, as both the Afrikaans word and botanical term describe them. When my mother visited from America, I took her on the same trails. "Is this rooibos?" she would ask, pointing to a plant between the rocks. I shook my head. "Now this one, it must be rooibos." "No," I said, laughing.

As an indigenous plant, rooibos was nearly indistinguishable from the wild plants that surrounded it. The plant was a deeply embedded part of a particular ecology, the "Bush," that allowed it to survive. On walks through this Bush, as nature is often labeled in Africa, farmers showed me centuries-old images of people and animals painted in whites and yellows on the rocks that jutted out of the sunbaked soil. According to these farmers, the "Bush paintings" were visual archives of the "extinct indigenous Bushmen" who had lived in the area prior to European arrival. With its wild rooibos, its Bush paintings, and its fenced-off farms, the landscape was a physical library of the region's past and its future, embodying both its violent racial histories of dispossession and its celebratory narratives of belonging to a beloved ecosystem. Yet this archive was not passive. The landscape did not exist merely to be raked over and remade by each new human resident. It was active, alive, and never fully controllable.

As part of this landscape, farmers and scientists said, rooibos had very specific—and "natural"—climatic needs. "What is 'healthy' soil?" the *Handbook for Implementing Rooibos Sustainability Standards* asks. "For Rooibos farmers, it means soils that closely approximate the natural soils of the Fynbos biome in terms of pH, soil structure, soil microorganisms and macrofauna (e.g., earthworms), moisture content, nutrient concentration and soil organic matter" (Pretorius et al. 2011: 65). The handbook, sponsored by the South African Rooibos Council and other local, national, and international nongovernmental organizations to create sustainability standards, goes on to specify the type of soil, precise pH, elevation, slope, and rainfall. When rooibos fields mimic the natural ecosystem, the handbook instructs, there will be more "helpful" insects and flowers in the vicinity. Central to this discussion is a symbiotic relationship among farmer, soil, plant, and indigenous insects. Working together, each participant is crucial to the health of all. Yet the idea of this symbiosis simultaneously produces multiple erasures, including that of coloured and black workers' labor.

This chapter explores how these relationships and erasures went beyond questions of ecology, economics, and politics. For many people in the rooibos region, indigeneity served as the concept through which the human, the animal, and the plant became one charismatic and moral whole. By using the idea of indigeneity to describe relations between residents and rooibos, I am not evoking "traditional knowledge" in the manner sometimes employed by scholars, such as the concept of a deeper relation between Indigenous peoples and nature (Pierotti and Wildcat 2000). Rather, I draw on the idea that Afrikaners and coloured people, groups who do not fit straightforwardly into the category of "native," made complicated *claims* to indigeneity through their relations with an indigenous plant. "Plants and humanity," one farmer explained. "I don't see ecosystems as separate."

Rooibos, as both a "wild indigenous plant" and a "cultivated global commodity," politicized and policed the highly moralized boundaries between nature and culture, delineating who and what belongs in the rooibos landscape. Through these contestations, ecological facts became culturally meaningful and socially and politically active, in addition to being economically essential to regional livelihoods. As a way into this issue, I start the chapter with two apparent paradoxes: If rooibos is "wild," how can it be cultivated? Can the celebration of plants as actors also serve to marginalize certain categories of people?

To address these questions, the chapter will examine how coloured and white residents negotiated the region's fraught history of cultural indigeneity, as well as its celebratory relation to ecological indigeneity. I articulate a theory of the Bush, or *Bos* in Afrikaans, by exploring the intertwined concepts of fyn*bos*, rooi*bos*, and *boes*man (Bushman). Both coloured and white residents expressed a love of rooibos that informed their sense of belonging in the region. At the same time, these connections were inextricably tied to the violent racial histories mapped to and still existent in the ecosystem. In South Africa, the Bush is both a racial imaginary and a multispecies ecosystem.

To understand the highly charged environment of the Bush, I use the concept of *symbiopolitics* as articulated by Stefan Helmreich (2009). By looking at the governance of entangled living things, symbiopolitics extends Michel Foucault's (2007) biopolitics (or governance that regulates populations through the application of political power to all aspects of human life) to nonhuman life.[1] In using this framework to examine the rooibos world, I emphasize how the management of populations and race undergirds the human–nonhuman interface. Residents both disrupted a human/nonhuman binary in certain moments (such as when they claimed their spiritual belonging), and concretized the distinction at other moments (such as when they denied the humanity of others). In seeing "Bushmen" as fauna, white farmers rendered them an intimate, yet never fully human, part of the landscape; they existed in rock paintings but not in the contemporary human population. As a hybrid human/

nonhuman species, they could go "extinct," no longer alive to challenge white belonging in the land. This "extinction" explains why coloured people appeared to emerge from and belong to nowhere in the white farmers' narratives. Yet these narratives did not necessarily challenge the ways that coloured farmers articulated their own affective and spiritual ideas of belonging on the land through their connections to rooibos rather than through an essentialized idea of cultural indigeneity.

With narratives of working, loving, and being part of the rooibos ecosystem, residents described a connection between the plant and their morality, spirituality, and ethics. In these connections, the notion of "cultivation" carried two different connotations: cultivation of the plant through the tending and harvesting of crops and cultivation of the composite farmer-plant moral subject through socialization to cultural norms within a much loved natural environment. Residents' ties were not solely metaphorical or metaphysical; they were also informed by a domestication and socialization of nature, in which the farmer/subject was both master and servant and God was animated in everyday experiences with the farming ecosystem. Through a spiritual ecology of belonging, farmers seemed to cherish their dependence on this indigenous plant, even as it made them vulnerable to climatic, economic, and political indeterminacies.

"Without Rooibos, We Would Be Nothing"

Seeds of domesticated plants are a literature, a hard drive and a coded record of past information. —RUTH MENDUM, "Subjectivity and Plant Domestication"

All flesh is grasse, is not onely metaphorically, but literally true, for all these creatures we behold, are but the hearbs of the field, digested into flesh in them. —SIR THOMAS BROWNE (1643), quoted in David Matless, "Bodies Made of Grass Made of Earth Made of Bodies"

Sannie, the wife of a tea farmer, described how rooibos literally permeated bodies in the area: "When I was a baby, I couldn't drink much milk, so my mother gave me rooibos. When mother sheep abandon their lambs, we give the sheep cold rooibos mixed with formula." She discussed how the tennis and rugby teams always drank cold rooibos. "I wash my dog with rooibos, my hair," she continued, listing the ways that rooibos informed her daily life. Many coloured and white farmers, workers, and town residents said that their babies drank rooibos when breastfeeding, or even drank the tea instead of breast milk. Like rooibos cultivation, people's discussions of tea consumption undermined distinctions between subjects and objects.

While gender dynamics were such that women were rarely labeled "farmers," they fed their families rooibos and produced and raised robust rooibos farmers. Consuming and serving rooibos was part of hospitality, domesticity, nutrition, and love. As a coloured farmer explained, "We grow up from babies on rooibos tea." By drinking rooibos instead of mother's milk, nonhuman nature and nurturance literally took the place of the human in ways that made Mother Nature very literal in the ideas and practices of farmers and their families. People seemingly consumed the land through the plant, and the land laid claim to the people and their labor. In this relation, "nature" seemed to enhance and infuse the human. While the charismatic nature of a consumed substance reflects common and long-standing themes in social science literature, for residents of the rooibos region, the plant itself was part of a social, ecological, and biological world that they all inhabited.

I listened intently whenever scientific researchers explained the biological aspects of rooibos and its key flavonoid (a subgroup of polyphenols): the compound *Aspalathin*. The chemistry of Aspalathin, a researcher explained, made it "anti-obesity" and "anti-cancer." She provided still more detail. Scientists have found approximately nine thousand flavonoids in plants; however, Aspalathin is found only rooibos. Scientists hypothesized that Aspalathin helps protect rooibos against oxidative stress caused in part by environmental factors. During rooibos processing, oxidation occurs and decreases the Aspalathin to about 7 percent of its original amount. However, the scientist concluded, even this small amount is absorbed into the human body, and it has been found metabolized in human blood and urine. What scientific research had discovered about rooibos chemistry was little surprise to farmers, who had professed rooibos's healing properties for generations.

On another hot afternoon, an elderly Afrikaans farmer sipped the tea his wife, Henriette, had prepared. Over the din of a televised rugby game, we talked about what it was like to grow up in the area sixty years earlier. "In the old days when there was no electricity on farms," he said, "there were wooden stoves that burned all day. They had the tea on the fire all day. That is the way it should be. We grew up drinking rooibos. My mother sent us off with a five-liter pail of water with rooibos." For many in the area, these bodily connections made rooibos continuous with the self as consumer and producer. "Without rooibos, we would be nothing," one farmer stated, a potentially telling choice of verb—not "We would *have* nothing," but "We would *be* nothing." This sentiment was echoed in his and many other farmers' descriptions of lives and livelihoods linked to and determined by the price of the tea, the timing of the rain, an infestation of undesirable insects, a connection to a family and cultural heritage, and even a healthy constitution formed by drinking rooibos instead of breast milk as a baby.

"You are only as good as your last crop. We are 100 percent dependent on weather," another Afrikaans farmer said. Through their narratives, rooibos farmers seemed to understand subjectivity and selfhood as bodily, material, relational, and dependent. My own daily bodily routines also began to include rooibos. In the mornings, I rubbed rooibos sunscreen onto my skin. In the hot afternoons, I sprayed cool rooibos moisturizing mist onto my face, and I often ended the day with a cup of rooibos to help me go to sleep. Sometimes it felt as though *I* were made of rooibos as I imagined the Aspalathin entering my bloodstream.

With these depictions of an ecologically relational subjectivity, rooibos farmers provided a challenge to theories about nature and human intervention. Metonymic identification with plants and the landscape can mask the fact that, as Bruno Latour (2008: 6) argues, "Those who wish to protect natural ecosystems, learn to their stupefaction that they have to work harder and harder—that is, to intervene even more, at always greater level of details, with ever more subtle care—to keep it 'natural enough.'" Yet because rooibos is indigenous, farming it became a narrative of living harmoniously with, in, and of nature. Rooibos, a major processor declares in its marketing materials, is a "gift from nature" and not a human creation. Farmers did not speak of taming a wild landscape, despite the fact that rooibos farming often involved the use of pesticides and the clearing of other native fynbos plants and even wild rooibos (Raimondo et al. 2009).

Because many farmers did not see these practices as contradictory, farming rooibos helped inform their images of themselves as ethical beings. At a rooibos-related meeting in 2010, one farmer raised his hand to clarify that the other participants should be sure to define "natural" as "native." In his eyes, a crop could be natural only if it was indigenous to *this* soil; an orange, even if farmed organically, could never be "natural." The distinction between natural and native, wild and cultivated—and the question of when wild rooibos historically transformed into domesticated rooibos—emerged as contingent and varied depending on the context of the conversation.

As rooibos made the passage from wild to cultivated, its genetic structure changed, and wild and cultivated rooibos differ in terms of size, mechanisms of germination, and other biological attributes (Malgas and Oettle 2007). Despite the modification of cultivated rooibos plants, their wild cousins remained, sometimes growing side by side. In contrast to rooibos farmers' slippages between wild and cultivated, Anna Tsing (2012) describes how ideas about domestication tend to be seen as "hard line: You are either in the human fold or you are out in the wild." Such views of domestication, she writes, support fantasies of domestic control and wild species' self-making. Yet, Ruth Mendum (2009) argues, plant domestication is always a negotiation during which both plants and humans are transformed in their relationality.

With rooibos, the lines between domestic and wild were even further blurred by the harvesting of wild plants for processing and sale. While wild rooibos's seed germination represented an action outside of the human, wild bush harvesting and pruning and the intentional setting and suppressing of fires represented direct human interaction with the wild. The book known as the *Right Rooibos Handbook* (Pretorius et al. 2011) even contains specific requirements for harvesting that imply a kind of cultivation: Wild rooibos should be harvested only between January and April; it should include only plants older than three years; and it should be cut only 50–70 percent down the bush. Through this kind of pruning, wild rooibos bushes were seemingly farmed, even if they were not actually planted. Indeed, projects undertaken in southern Africa often championed the idea that human effort could help or enhance nature. In the rooibos-growing area, many farmers believed that the application of chemicals and the cultivation of domesticated rooibos could improve nature by expanding the growth of indigenous plants. Through this belief, the figure of the farmer—or even of the human—was left implicit.

Drawing on and contextualizing theories of domestication, I argue that in very concrete terms rooibos, both wild and cultivated, served as an intermediary that challenges distinctions between ecological belonging and human creation. The dance of wild indigeneity and cultivation gave rooibos a quality and a tension that lent it to projects of heritage, subjectivity, and place making in this socially, economically, and agriculturally marginal land. Rooibos occupied a liminal and problematic space similar to that of Afrikaners and coloured people, a space between naturalized ideas of belonging in a landscape and culturally fraught notions of never belonging anywhere. Yet this liminality manifested itself in decidedly different ways for rooibos's identity than for coloured people's identity. Rooibos's wild/cultivated identity was celebrated, its affective value for residents deeply rooted in its natural place in a particular landscape. Coloured people's white/nonwhite identity was pathologized as unnatural.

While discussions of nature and race often focus on animals and not plants, the overall discourse of nonwhites as natural and naturalized "others" places them in a wider arena of nature, in which noncultivated plants and nonwhites exist in a realm outside of civilization. In this rhetoric, the coloured, like garden plants or cultivated rooibos, might be tamed or civilized and rescued from their barbarity. However, white and even black South Africans often did not provide that option for the Khoisan. They were "Bushmen" and as such were an inextricable part of the Bush. As relics of a prehuman past, they were doomed to extinction or to having their genetic remnants "swallowed in with mixed breeding," as one Afrikaans farmer said. In his mind, any traces of Khoisan heritage were left with nothing but coloured alcoholism and a cultureless existence. The sections that follow explore some of the stakes and the potentialities of this pathologized heritage.

"Bushmen Relics" and Rooibos Seeds: Fynbos, Rooibos, and Boesman

Making the acquaintance of a pure breed of bushman was like gaining
the confidence of a wild thing. We baited them like we would bait an animal.
— *The Bushmen: An Epic of Wild Beasts and Wilder Men*, quoted in
ALAN BARNARD, *Anthropology and the Bushman*

Race and nature work together. And it is their recombinant mutations that
so often haunt the cultural politics of identity and difference. —DONALD S. MOORE,
ANAND PANDIAN, and JAKE KOSEK, "Terrains of Power and Practice"

Shortly after I arrived in the Cederberg, I took a "Rooibos Tour" with a group of British tourists, many of whom were wearing khaki safari suits and carrying binoculars. We packed into open safari trucks to look at cultivated fields. The tourists had just finished a trip through Kruger National Park and regaled me with harrowing stories of encounters with lions and elephants. As we drove through the farm, we snapped photographs, learned about rooibos's ecology and history, and watched workers "clean" the fields. During the "rooibos safari," the farm became the wild landscape; the workers, the exotic animals; and the white farm owners, invisible. In this section, I describe the problematic conflations between race and botany that haunt ideas of ecological belonging for coloured and white rooibos farmers and workers. Yet I also argue that these conflations did not always map easily onto discussions of racial division. Instead, some tentatively hopeful discussions emerged of cross-racial love for this indigenous plant and national beverage.

While theories about ecological belonging and multispecies dependencies have helped scholars to unsettle human-nonhuman relations, nature and culture have hardly been binary when it comes to discussions of indigeneity. Rather, connections between race and nature have formed a terrain for the exercise of power and the legitimation of political, social, and economic hierarchies, authorizing violent exclusions (Moore et al. 2003). Decoupling nature from Indigenous people is difficult to this day because Indigenous people are sometimes considered exotic fauna to observe and protect—or root out (Meskell 2012). Under colonial, apartheid, and even postapartheid governance, biopolitical practices often linked nature and race unproblematically—both "nature" as the nonhuman environment and "nature" as the biological attributes of the human. According to Saul Dubow's (1995) history of racism in South Africa, popular beliefs and traditions naturalized the idea of race, rendering difference incontestable.

In the rooibos context, I stretch the concept of biopolitics to include nonhuman life *and* to complicate the politicized distinction between human and nonhuman (Arendt 1958; Foucault 2008 [2004]). In cases of extreme violence, humans do not just become "symbolic animals so that they can be extra-juridical, immoral, and killable." Rather, they are rendered actual, physical animals (Kosek 2011). Accordingly, Helmreich's (2009) "symbiopolitics" offers the beginnings of a term that is more fitting than "biopolitics" to describe rooibos's racial and botanical relations because the concept foregrounds the governance of entangled living things. Drawing on Helmreich, I define "symbiopolitics" in a manner that includes not only the entanglement of human and nonhuman organisms, but also the entanglement of human *as nonhuman*. The concept of "nonhuman" simultaneously undermines and re-centers the human by conceptualizing other species and things as lacking, while the term "nonwhite" describes people who are not categorized "white" as lacking (Kirksey and Helmreich 2010).

Rooibos seeds exemplify the region's complicated symbiopolitics through the supposed animality of its nonwhite residents. On its website, the South African Rooibos Council connects rooibos with archeological finds in the area. The council celebrates the area's rock art, geology, and biodiversity, all features that it says attract scientists from around the world. By alluding to archaeologists, the council appears to authenticate scientifically the area's naturalness and its links to ancient, pure, and extinct human cultures. According to the council, the rock art in the area is up to six thousand years old. Perhaps, it contends, "drinking rooibos tea inspired [the artists]."[2] Similar uses of language occur in the council's description of rooibos: "Early Rooibos farmers got hold of the local wisdom that ants harvested the seeds and that they could collect Rooibos seeds from anthills. Today, most farmers collect the seeds by sifting the sand around the plants." Invoking the image of a Noble Savage, the language connects rooibos to the Khoisan, giving the tea a culturally and environmentally indigenous heritage; local animals and people worked together, using each other's wisdom to uncover rooibos's secret origins. The story links the Khoisan more to nature than to culture, part of the environment and thus divorced from human conflict over land and resources in past and contemporary contexts.

While seemingly benign, the discourse draws from years of depicting the Khoisan as less than human in popular discourse, schools, and museums. Frantz Fanon's classic *The Wretched of the Earth* (2004 [1965]) shows how colonists spoke of the native in zoological terms. He argues that this use of language saddled the native with the racial violence of "exclusionary humanism." In books such as the *Natural History of the Negro Race* (Guenebault 1837), plant collecting and plant taxonomy often worked side by side with histories of racial classifications. The concept of breeds of nonhuman animals, for example, spilled over into pseudoscientific theories involving different human typologies (Anderson 2000). These ideas form a distinct continuity with early botanists, such as Georges-Louis Leclerc, who in *Buffon's Natural History: General and Particular* (1749) argued that certain climates produced inferior and superior people and plants.

In the eyes of early white settler colonists, the Khoisan were human–nonhuman hybrids. As a hybrid human species, a species separate from *Homo sapiens*, they could go "extinct." "Khoisan" was initially considered a biological, or species-based, label (Barnard 1992; Lane 1996). In making his great classificatory schemes in the eighteenth century, Carl Linnaeus said he had trouble persuading himself that Europeans and Hottentots derived from the same origin. Jan Smuts, prime minister during the pre-apartheid Union of South Africa (1919–24, 1939–48) and prominent Afrikaans philosopher, attributed climatic and evolutionary reasons for the supposedly animal-like nature of Bushmen. The Bushman, he argued, "has been physically dwarfed and shriveled and mentally stunted by nature. . . . He has become a desert animal, carved and moulded by the desert, just as much as the rest of our desert animals and plants" (Dubow 1995: 51). Bushmen, then, represented a dying branch of the evolutionary tree.

People like Smuts linked the San with South Africa's national history. The Bushman Relics Protection Act of 1911 was the first *conservation* act of the Union of South Africa. Through these "conservation" measures, the Bushmen became a remnant race or evolutionary holdover, literally a "living" prehistory (Shepherd 2002). In the 1930s and 1940s, South African National Parks allowed the San to stay on park land because it classified them as part of the natural, animal landscape. Deneys Reitz, the minister of Native Affairs in 1941, declared that "the San were a part of South Africa's fauna, they killed fewer antelopes than lions and it was 'a crime to let them die out'" (Meskell 2012: 132–33). Connections between the Khoisan and nature, however, were not always violent and did not come exclusively from white people's depictions. The rock art of the Cederberg contains *therianthropes*, or half-animal and half-human mythical figures. Through *therianthropes*, the precolonial people of the rooibos region left their own traces of human-nonhuman connections.

Notably, Afrikaners also had shifting and contingent value in local and national imaginaries. Before the South African War at the turn of the twentieth century, race science was used to show Afrikaners' degeneracy. Their time in Africa had supposedly led to their genetic decline. In part to foster shared white national unity after the war, science eventually rehabilitated the Afrikaner by showing that he was connected to the British in a chain of civilized progress because of their shared Teutonic roots (Pooley 2010).

Race, Botany, and White Naturalized Belonging

While close connections between "Bushman" and nature, or "Bushman" as nature, might seem to complicate Afrikaner claims to naturalized belonging on the land, Smuts countered this idea: "And now that desert conditions are being ameliorated by the ironic touch of civilisation, there is nothing left for him but to disappear" (Dubow 1995: 51). In the rooibos-growing area, Khoisan "extinction" supposedly occurred centuries ago, allegedly leaving no one behind but the coloured, a people who did not necessarily express an ancestral link to the Khoisan and whom the Afrikaans population saddled with uncertain claims to local heritage and to knowledge about rooibos and its cultivation. Instead, Afrikaners used their own connections to the landscape—and to rooibos in particular—to validate their essential belonging.

It was around the time of Smuts's early years that South African botany became professionalized. Afrikaners had a long history with conservation in South Africa that emerged from a belief that they knew the African landscape better than anyone else. Informal botanical knowledge often served to justify white landownership in the name of conservation or through the discourse of agricultural improvement. As botanical knowledge became more formalized, it underpinned imperial practices (Schiebinger and Swan 2005). Smuts explicitly used botany as a means to foster national unity by closely intertwining concepts of plants, patriotism, and the nation in much the same way that South Africans discuss fynbos plants today (Pooley 2010).

Significantly, Smuts and other white South Africans described a closeness to nature typically attributed to "uncivilized natives" as a positive force of *white* naturalized belonging. As Kay Anderson (2000: 14) describes, the "call of the wild" can have a mythic power in part because of the contradictory aspects of freedom and control that exist in the "discursive borderland" between the human and the nonhuman. Terms such as "Noble Savage" purportedly celebrate premodern children of nature. For Smuts, however, celebrating fynbos implied honoring white national unity to the specific exclusion of nonwhite people. Fynbos might represent the idea of a Noble Savage, but it did not represent the actual people (the coloured and black populations) whom Smuts needed to erase to claim naturalized and purified white belonging. For this reason, the Khoisan extinction story was necessary to discourses of white indigeneity—and because of this "extinction," the coloured seem to arise from nowhere.

In the postapartheid nation, however, rooibos marketing often depicted a nonracial, or racially unifed, country. Rooibos was particularly salient to the nation's image in that it is both an indigenous plant and a cultural product, the country's "patriotic national beverage" and "unique heritage." Identifications among people, the nation, and nature occur frequently in discussions of cultural heritage, as heritage management often uncritically employs models developed for natural resources, by using terms such as eco-ethnotourism and biocultural community protocols (Meskell 2012). In these forms of heritage management, the "biocultural community" can emerge as the new "stakeholder" in ways that are not necessarily emancipatory or agentive for the human part of the human–nonhuman community. These kinds of management efforts were clear in the rooibos-growing area's attempt to use the tea as a tourist attraction, such as the "Rooibos Safari" described earlier.

Bearing in mind white South Africans' history of using connections with nature to claim landownership and to render the Khoisan (and coloured and black people) nonhuman, reinforcing connections between humans and nature can be fraught in South Africa. However, I will highlight how people *naturalize themselves, naturalize others, and naturalize "nature"* in different ways according to their needs. As I discussed in chapter 1, lurking in the background of these discussions was the fact that most coloured people in the rooibos-growing area did not want to be naturalized as Khoisan. Being Khoisan meant embracing an identity that was simultaneously both valorized and stigmatized—valorized by marketers and development groups and stigmatized by centuries of scientific racism that rendered them nonhuman. Yet despite the problematic associations between human and nonhuman in South Africa, residents of the rooibos region shaped and were shaped by their intimacy with the tea, a connection that necessitates closer examinations of the plant, its cultivation, and its surrounding discourse. Residents of the region articulated their own concept of environmental determinism, a concept that was redemptive for plants but far more complex for people.

Stories of Working, Loving, and Belonging in the Rooibos Ecosystem

The landscape remains alien, impenetrable, until a language is found in which to win it, speak it, represent it. —J. M. COETZEE, *White Writing*

"Rooibos is *maklik*," Piet, a white farmer said, using the Afrikaans word for "easy." As we drove across his farm in a rusty pickup truck, he continued: "Rooibos is indigenous, so it doesn't need much work. The citrus and grapes, they take so much water and labor. You can just plant the rooibos and then leave it until harvest time." Piet employed large teams of black and coloured workers for his other commercial ventures: grapes, oranges, and sheep. We steered past workers spraying orange trees and walking among the grapevines. He boasted about the latest technology that he used to ensure that the oranges would achieve the "correct" color and shape. The rooibos sat alone at the high edge of his farm below a rocky hill, the bushes blending into the vegetation behind it and its cultivated quality perceptible to the untrained eye solely by the neat rows in which it grew (see figure 2.1).

Only during harvest and planting seasons did rooibos require much work outside of the occasional "cleaning," or weeding and pest management. In both coloured and white farmers' eyes, rooibos fields were living social spaces in which the relationship between people and plants was dialectical and generative. Farmers expressed interrelated concepts of working, loving, and belonging with the land. Many described rooibos cultivation not only as an economic activity, but also as a moral and caring act that forged their belonging with the indigenous ecosystem, even as the violence of this exclusionary belonging served to justify white ownership and coloured dispossession.

Despite the fact that scientists described rooibos's precise climatic needs, Piet said that rooibos is grown in a much less scientific way than non-native crops. Farmers heavily controlled the conditions under which citrus and grapes grew, making the sale of the fruit less dependent on its place-based specificity and ecological conditions than on local and international market conditions and currency valuations. As farmers and retailers explained, the quality of the fruit in the rooibos-growing area is virtually the same as that grown in Chile or Florida because international standards demand uniformity. Oranges and table grapes arrive in grocery stores around the world without any visible connection to the South African lands on which they grow, save for the occasional "Grown in South Africa" label.

"The difference between sheep and rooibos is that rooibos is more dependent on nature," Piet explained, comparing the tea with his other income

FIGURE 2.1. Rooibos tea field. Photograph by the author.

sources. Unlike sheep, rooibos relies far more on the coming of the seasons. Few farmers irrigate their rooibos, a fact that is remarkable, given the low rainfall the region receives. "You can't control the rain," Piet continued. "It's what makes the product special." Danie, an Afrikaans farmer who lived in a part of the rooibos-growing area that was even more water-scarce than Piet's farm, insisted that the amount of rain could actually be inversely related to the tea's quality. "Too much rain makes [it] less good," he said. Yet the lack of irrigation also made the tea's growth more vulnerable to the occasional drought years the region experienced.

It would be easy to conclude that living in a hot, dry place necessitated a struggle against a harsh and even violent landscape. Rooibos farmers, however, espoused a different concept: they worked with—and loved—the ecosystem. A few weeks after I met Piet, I sat on a worn leather couch in a farmhouse living room waiting for Frans, an Afrikaans farmer, to return from overseeing his workers. The farmhouses had started to blur together—the same dogs barking at my arrival; the same wooden floors, whitewashed walls, and biblical quotations framed next to family portraits. Frans's wife, Riana, poked her head in the door and asked whether I would like tea. "Rooibos or English?" she asked in the same phrasing that other Afrikaans wives had asked me in other farmhouses down other long dirt roads. "Rooibos, please," I responded, and a coloured domestic worker soon returned with a tray of tea, milk, sugar, and cookies. Shortly after, Frans opened the door and wiped his dusty boots on the mat. Removing his wide-brimmed hat, he walked over to shake my hand. I could smell the sweat that had seeped into his tan button-down shirt and khaki shorts. The domestic worker opened the door quietly, *"Net 'n bietjie water, Sannie,"* he called out cheerfully, asking her for some water.

He settled into his well-worn chair. "So, rooibos?" he asked. "What do you want to know?" Before I had a chance to ask any questions, he started giving me a brief tutorial on rooibos's necessary climatic conditions: "Do you know why rooibos only grows here? With any fynbos, the bacterial composition is very important. If that's not just right, it can't grow." After pausing to take a sip of water, he continued. "In Stellenbosch and Paarl, the soil has been adulterated. The Chinese have tried to grow it, the Australians too." Stellenbosch and Paarl, towns located to the south of the rooibos-growing area, are part of South Africa's wine country, and people have been cultivating wine there for centuries. An article explaining rooibos tea to U.S.-based consumers states that "numerous attempts to recreate this natural habitat" and grow the plant in other areas have failed (Van Den Berg 2012). Rooibos, Frans asserted, needs natural *South African* soil, uncorrupted by the outside world.

He explained the problems faced by farmers who violate the soil's "balance" by planting non-native crops: "The first thing you do is to adjust the pH of the soil to increase the alkalinity for grapes." He told me how fynbos soil is different from the 7 pH that typical European plants require. "With the adjusting, the natural bacteria die, and to get back to the acidity is next to impossible. It doesn't wash out easily compared to virgin soil." If the soil becomes adulterated, he insisted, it can never return to its former, pure state. According to Frans, rooibos land contained this special "virginal" quality (despite pesticide use) and therefore must be protected to retain its economic, affective, and moral value. "That's the advantage we have," he said, "one of the reasons it only grows here. The farmers, they are very protective. Once they decide to do citrus on the soil, that's it. You can't go back to rooibos."

Themes of morality and cultural ownership emerge in Frans's discussion of rooibos soil. *European* plants destroy what is indigenous and truly South African. Rooibos land is valuable because it is one of the few remaining pure parts of the country, untouched by corruption. Farmers' discourse, like Frans's explanation, often took on a righteous undertone in which the plant operated as a moral grammar linked to the crop's indigeneity. Because of the minimal use of fertilizers and irrigation, rooibos could be easier and cheaper to grow than other crops on nutrient-poor farms located in the hot, dry mountains, far from the lush valleys of wine country. While other crops might suffer in these conditions, "the plant *needs* the harsh conditions of the region, where temperatures drop to zero degrees Celsius during winter and rise to a blistering 48 degrees Celsius at the height of summer" (Palitza 2011; emphasis added). One rooibos farmer even stated that "the moment the soil gets fertile, the quality of the tea goes." The ease of cultivation gave rooibos farmers a financial incentive to grow the crop, while their ability to love and nurture the harsh, virginal land gave them a righteous means to assert their belonging.

Farming rooibos was not a neutral matter of efficiency and profit margins. For many coloured and white farmers, it also involved a deep love for the land and the plants. This "moral vision" implied an ethic. Yet the ethics were different from notions of corporate responsibility or national or international fair trade certifications. Instead, they were informed by affective relations. I intentionally use the word "affect" as opposed to "emotion" in the rooibos context because of affect's nonhuman characteristics. Affect is beyond language; it is inadvertent. Gilles Deleuze specifically addresses the affective relations between individuals and the environment in which they interact. These relations reanimate both people and the landscape: "The environment is not just a reservation of information whose circuits await mapping, but also a field of forces whose actions await experiencing" (Deleuze 1988 [1970]: ii). Jane Bennett attributes affect's power to the sublime forces of nature, sound, and the "imperceptible" presence of other beings (Bennett 2001). This sacralization of affect, the rendering of emotion and aesthetics into mysterious vital forces, in many ways parallels the sacralization of nature and ecology in the utopianism of American Transcendentalism. Bennett (2010) draws specifically on Thoreau to articulate an idea of "thing-power." She evokes Thoreau's notion of the Wild, or the idea that "things" (lakes, birds, people, and so on) have an existence that is distinguishable from human subjectivity. This otherness—or wildness—is what gives things the power to reorient human thoughts and sensibilities. Connecting affect specifically to emotion, Brian Massumi argues that affect is an autonomous set of forces that flow through the body and then *materialize* as emotion. Emotion, he continues, "is a contamination of empirical space by affect which belongs to the body without an image" (Massumi 2002: 61). As opposed to affect, emotion is identifiable and nameable, and in its naming it becomes domesticated. Because of its deeply felt and sacralized aspects, the affective becomes a charged political and—for rooibos farmers—ethical domain.

Following this moral reasoning, many commercial farmers explained rooibos cultivation not as commodity production but as preservation of a beloved natural landscape. Bertie, another Afrikaans farmer, cited protecting indigenous species as an important aspect of his farming: "I just farm rooibos and I keep the rest [of my land] natural to protect the endemic species." He criticized other farmers, particularly those who cultivated citrus: "The farmers are not very good with the environment. They see themselves as macho land tamers." His language is particularly interesting given the reputation of Afrikaans men, and farmers in particular, as being "macho" and patriarchal. However, when reframed in relation to the environment, the idea of being sensitive and caring of the landscape became acceptable. Similarly, the *Right Rooibos Handbook* uses strong language to condemn any farmer who does not act sensitively, whose fields "have fallen foul of injudicious practices such as land clearing, poor site selection, poor tilling practices and overfertilisation." These lands lose "their ability to function properly" (Pretorius et al. 2011: 57).

Noticing my interest in indigenous species, Bertie recommended that I speak with his friend, Albie, whose family had lived down the road for generations. I drove from Bertie's house and soon came across the typical setting of local white-owned farms: a whitewashed house surrounded by Australian eucalyptus trees, a small dam, and the inevitable white pickup truck. I found Albie talking with a coloured domestic worker. It was not harvest season, so his farm was relatively unpeopled and absent of any seasonal workers. He excused the worker, and we sat together and discussed his farming methods. I asked him why he cultivates rooibos. "Because it is a crop that is indigenous, endemic. It doesn't need much maintenance," he explained. Like many rooibos farmers, Albie used to farm primarily with animals, but he had issues with predators and maintaining fences. He described a kind of moral awakening and not just a way to save money on maintenance: "I was becoming more and more aware of the diversity of plant life. I started learning more and becoming entranced by the . . . fynbos. I wanted to protect the indigenous plant life. I decided to just focus on rooibos because of its history as an indigenous plant. I didn't exploit all the land, just enough to keep an income." In words that appeared contradictory, Albie pronounced the practice of rooibos farming to be a way to protect the natural landscape from human intervention.

Other coloured and white farmers described seed collection as particularly free from human interference. Typically, workers—often coloured women— would walk through fields searching for seeds that they gathered by hand. One such woman, Cheryl, explained that she located seeds "by sifting through the soil like panning for gold. It is very natural." Seeds, she said, are found, not harvested. Cheryl showed me how she picked up the sandy soil and placed it in a handmade sifter. She shook the sifter and the sand flowed out, leaving behind light-brown seeds that I found hard to decipher from small pebbles. Looking at the seeds, I tried to understand how valuable they were to Cheryl, who pieced together a living from odd jobs, seasonal work, seed collecting, and social grants. She stroked her wrinkled hand over the seeds and smiled a toothless smile.

Cheryl's care for the seeds she collected likely stemmed from a variety of reasons: their importance to her livelihood, an apparently affectionate sense of protection, and the seeds' sensitivity to physical harm such as cracking that would render them useless for farming. This sensitivity, a number of farmers explained, derived from the fact that rooibos emerged from wild seed and is therefore not uniform, unlike the highly altered oranges that grow in the valleys. As one farmer said, "There has been no human intervention in the seeds yet." The farmer added a temporal notion to his claims about rooibos's wildness. Perhaps, he continued, farmers would find a way to control seeds in the future, but the consequences of that control were still unknown—it could give farmers greater freedom to plant more bushes or it could disrupt the existing delicate balance.

Koos, an Afrikaans farmer who lived high in the mountains, also spoke reverently about rooibos seeds. He described a childhood spent surrounded by wild rooibos plants. Like all fynbos, he began, "rooibos has a protective mechanism against the cycle of life. If there is no fire, only the soft seeds germinate. The hard seeds need fire, and in fires the hardest seeds still do not germinate. It's nature protecting itself." The plant's history weaved into his own history: "I remember as kids we used to use rocks to crack the shells, but it's a sensitive process, and sometimes you wouldn't do it right and hurt the seed." When people interfered with the natural process, they got in the way of nature's delicate system, Koos explained. Yet for centuries humans and rooibos plants had lived and interacted side by side, co-constituting each other in the process. The cultivation of rooibos—and the harvesting of wild tea—challenges ideas of rooibos as a purely natural, indigenous plant, rendering it instead a crop altered by years of human-nonhuman interaction. Humans breed plants; they select; they intervene at the genetic level of reproduction; they alter the climate in which plants grow.

To treat rooibos as strictly "wild" is to erase this history and potentially naturalize agribusiness. When farmers felt that agricultural sciences remained out of financial reach, or out of their control, they often pushed back against large corporations. For example, Rooibos Ltd., the largest rooibos company, developed a relatively inexpensive—but technical and, I was told, "unnatural"—process to treat rooibos seeds, giving the company significant power over cultivation, a power and knowledge that helped it control commodity prices. To the farmers who framed rooibos cultivation as an economic and moral choice, this kind of technical power and knowledge undermined another aspect of their connections with the plant: the role of God in farming.

Rooibos Farming as a "Holy Act"

I farm with rooibos because it's just easier, less costly, and it's seen as the right thing to do.... We try to do as little as possible. The less we have to do the better.... It's easier with rooibos. You just let it grow. God takes care of it. —ROOIBOS FARMER

Cultivation and culture have a common origin in a Latin verb with dual meaning; *colere* means both to till and to worship. Men can look upwards the more steadfastly when their feet are firmly planted in their native soil. —JORIAN JENKS, quoted in Matless, "Bodies Made of Grass Made of Earth Made of Bodies"

FIELD NOTES, MARCH 2011: *I drove with a local minister along a dirt road deep in the mountains. We stopped periodically to pick up coloured laborers from different pockets of tightly packed workers' quarters. They piled silently into the back of the minister's old white truck. We were on his "farm rounds," during which he would drive to preach to workers who lived too far [away] to make the journey to the town's church. We arrived at the metal storage barn owned by a large-scale rooibos farmer. The farmer was nowhere in sight, as he was likely attending services at the "white" church in town. The storage barn became our church, the rooibos sacks our pews. The minister handed out well-worn pieces of paper with the lyrics to religious songs printed on them. With no instruments to guide our melody, we began to sing a strange, tuneless song, the smell of rooibos surrounding us, rooibos dust stuck to our shoes and clothes.*

A rooibos farmer once told me that farming was a "holy act." Through conversations that invoked God and nature's sublime presence, many farmers added another dimension to the morality of cultivating an indigenous plant. On a day so hot that even local residents commented about temperatures that inched above 117 degrees Fahrenheit, I walked through rooibos fields with Jano, a middle-aged farmer with a face wrinkled beyond his years by the intense sun. It had been months since the last rainfall, and I asked what the drought would do to his crop. "The rooibos business is by God first," he said as he looked to the sky and pointed up, "in terms of rainfall." Often devoutly Christian, farmers such as Jano expressed a connection with the plant that included not just the material or the symbolic, but also the spiritual. Farming rooibos was one way to be a good Christian and an ethical person.

God was a constant part of interactions with residents, whether they attended the Dutch Reformed Church, the Moravian Church, the Anglican Church, one of the new Evangelical churches, or no church at all. They invoked Him in casual conversations or in the prayers that often initiated rooibos-related meetings. They praised Him through song at musical performances and celebrated Him with the crosses or embroidered Bible passages that hung on farmhouse walls. Each Sunday, cars would line the road in front of the Dutch Reformed Church, and coloured and white people would walk through the streets on the way to their respective (and almost entirely separate) churches. "There is something about the farming community and religion. It's living on the land. It's in God's hands every day with the weather and the seasons," a minister said. Rooibos companies and churches were often the main forces behind local festivals and town events.

Through this emphasis on spirituality, rooibos farmers provided what seemed to be their own critique of human exceptionalism: plant, human, and God were all interrelated. This interrelation was reminiscent of the Aristotelian trinity of animal, human, and deity, a relationship that Aristotle described as hierarchical: God had power over man, and man had power over animals (Fuentes 2006). In the rooibos region, these hierarchies were complicated by ideas of modernity and Afrikaner cultural mythologies, by coloured invocations of God and rooibos, and by Afrikaans-coloured interactions. Modernity purportedly marked the human divorce from both the earth and God. In his critique of a modernist view of nature, Latour (2008) argues that "everything happens as if modernists were unable to reconcile their idea of Science and Nature—which, remember, according to their narrative, is supposed to be farther and farther removed, as time passes, from law, subjectivity, politics and religion." Core to the Afrikaner myth, however, was the idea that once the Afrikaner (man) had found a land free from human interference, he could at last be his own master, left in peace to serve the land and to live as God intended (Moodie 1975; Shepherd 2002). Many early settler colonists left Europe because they felt the continent had become too modern and had therefore lost touch with God (Adams and McShane 1992). Some, such as the missionaries in Wupperthal, came to Africa to bring religion to this "untouched" world, even using botany to help facilitate their conversions (Bravo 2005). In the remoteness of the Bush, settlers often learned and understood their history through sermons.

Rooibos farmers connected subjectivity and nature with Christianity in an intimate manner that challenges narratives that frame Christianity's view of the nonhuman world as strictly about domination and stewardship. Often devoutly religious, farmers related to the plant in ways that included material, spiritual, political, economic, and affective dimensions. Unlike narratives of Christian Enlightenment control over nature, Afrikaner lore in the rooibos region described the farmer/subject as both master and servant. According to an oft-invoked myth, agriculture served as a means for Afrikaners to interact with nature in a manner that was sanctified by religious, economic, and ecological tenets.[3] Clearly, however, a land free of human interference necessitated an erasure of those who already lived in the landscape or a re-signifying of them *as landscape or animal.* When I asked people about the history of their farms, most coloured and white farmers never articulated a history that preceded their own families, in a kind of forgetting that excluded any belonging on the land that was not distinctly personal. They described a sedentarism beyond memory.

Drawing on these overlapping sanctifications and erasures, Afrikaans and coloured narratives about land tended to value both pristine nature and human industry without focusing on any ostensible contradiction. In this context, one could accuse Afrikaans and coloured residents of not being "modern." Their attachments to land and their farming methods represented residual practices, elsewhere swept aside by urbanization, industrialization, and the transition to a finance-, information-, and service-based global society. Their connections between God and the natural world might at first appear to have more in common with "primitive" animisms than with monotheistic "modern" forms of Christianity. Yet the spirituality that infused coloured and white residents' practice of Christianity challenged this division, as their experiences with God were distinctly animated. Christian coloured and Afrikaans residents of the region included God in their descriptions of interdependencies between themselves and nature. Farmers did not necessarily see stewardship over, dependence on, and bodily, economic, and affective relations with the rooibos ecosystem as incompatible.

These spiritual connections were linked to the idea of tilling the soil of the unique ecosystem and sowing indigenous rooibos seeds (even if the actual tilling on white-owned farms was predominately undertaken by workers). Despite their focus on the naturalness of the indigenous ecosystem, Afrikaans and coloured farmers were not opposed to using whatever technology was available to them. Yet people were also future-affirming in ways that involved not just beliefs in technology and progress per se but also a continued spiritual and material relation between farmer and plant.

In her work on technoscience, Tracey Heatherington describes a Frozen Ark, or Global Seed Bank, created deep beneath the Arctic ice on a Norwegian island. This Frozen Ark preserves samples of genetic diversity so that "we may one day renew the abundance of Earth in a future graced by better knowledge and moral understanding of both ecological systems and the foundations of life itself. . . . Here at the frontier of imaginary futures, the moral and symbolic worlds of the Old Testament, environmentalism, and genomic science *awkwardly* converge" (Heatherington 2012: 40; emphasis added). In the context of Afrikaners' understandings of people, God, and nature, this convergence may not seem so "awkward." South Africa as an Eden drew on the idea of creating a new and better moral world in which man (and I use the gendered pronoun intentionally) would live with the environment, improving it through his sweat, just as his work with the land improved him. For many rooibos farmers, no contradiction existed among nature, God, and agricultural science in this Eden. Indeed, their sense of earthly paradise hinged on these convergences. The co-constitutive improvements discursively positioned the farmer as morally and spiritually superior to "weekend farmers" and even to coloured laborers who supposedly worked for money and not "for love" and "for God."

The book of Genesis (1:29, 2:15–19) decries, "And God said, Behold, I have given you every herb bearing seed, which is upon the face of the earth, and every tree, in which is the fruit of a tree yielding seed. . . . And the Lord God took man and put him in the Garden of Eden to dress it and keep it." Unlike the Garden of Eden, the historian Richard Drayton (2000) explains, the human garden is a fallen garden, destroyed by human disobedience and temptation. Yet the elements of Eden's perfect garden are supposedly still concealed in the world's now imperfect order. If man followed God's will, encoded in nature, these elements could be discovered. Drayton's description reflects common colonial and postcolonial discourses about Africa as an Eden that needs conservation or as a fallen land that needs intervention—whether humanitarian or developmental—to save it.

Again and again, rooibos farmers emphasized that they were not trying to exploit the land; rather, they were trying to live with it as stewards for future generations, to dress and to keep it according to God's will. In *White Writing*, his work on South African literature and its relation to the myth of the Cape Colony as an Edenic garden, J. M. Coetzee describes the centrality of this stewardship to Afrikaans identity in particular: "Besides farming the land in a spirit of piety toward *voorgeslagte* and *nageslagte* (past and future generations), besides being a good steward, the farmer must also love the farm, love this one patch of earth above all others, so that his proprietorship comes to embody a marriage not so much between himself and the farm as between his lineage (*familie*) and the farm" [Coetzee 1988: 89].

Coetzee articulates the same love that many Afrikaans farmers expressed to me. For rooibos farmers, however, love for rooibos land held a symbolic meaning that was different from that of love for a citrus or grape farm, because in loving their rooibos, they were also loving their corner of South Africa.

The marriage of land, farmer, and rooibos plant signified a marriage to the fynbos ecosystem, and future generations were literally born to the land. Coetzee asserts that it is not an easy marriage. An Afrikaans farmer must stay faithful and prove himself on the land: "Such a marriage must be exclusive (monogamous) and more than merely proprietorial, it will entail that in good years the farm will respond to this love by bringing forth bountifully, while in bad years he will have to stand by it, nursing it through its trials. . . . The farmer becomes *vergroeid* (inter-grown, fused) with the farm: 'Never before had he felt such a bond with the earth. It was now as if the life within it were streaming up into his body . . . as if he and the earth were living in a silent understanding" (Coetzee 1988: 89).

Rooibos farmers used similar language. "I love the farm," I was told again and again. "Why?" I would ask. "I don't know why," I was told. Or, "It's a natural love." The love was unquestioned, a given. It exists because "I am farmer," a claim that seemed a distinctly ethical statement—a bit like "I'm married" or

"I'm a husband." Many farmers spoke of "standing by their land" even in times of drought or low rooibos prices. "Why protect the land?" I asked Jonas, an Afrikaans farmer. He replied decisively, "It's our heritage, no more, no less. . . . The specialness of the town is ruined by newcomers." His language seamlessly moved between natural preservation and cultural preservation.

Perhaps tellingly, many of the region's English-speaking South Africans did not speak with the same intensity that Albie, Piet, Danie, Cheryl, and other Afrikaans and coloured residents did. Even some Afrikaners from other parts of the country seemed to mock these farmers' powerful declarations of love for rooibos. As one such *"inkomer"* explained, "The farm I bought was a farm I liked that happens to be rooibos, a product that I like. It's not a mystical pursuit for me. It's an accident for me. I like the area, the beauty of the area and the proudest product comes from there." For this farmer, farming was central to his identity, but rooibos was not. He was not born of the Cederberg soil. He did not measure his belonging against connections to the indigenous plant and its ecological region. Rather, he appreciated the "accident" of farming with a "Proudly South African" product.

Afrikaans farmers who had lived in the rooibos region for generations, by contrast, used their connections to land and belonging to describe themselves as protectors who fulfilled a moral and religious duty to God, to their families, to the ecosystem, and even, for some, to their workers. They imagined themselves as good shepherds to their workers and as good servants to God and ecosystem. Yet this connection to landscape and nature could also be seen as a blindness that denied the presence of nonwhites. Describing themselves as the natural protectors of the land helped to obscure the history of settlement and the violence of appropriation.

David McDermott Hughes (2010) describes how white settlers' romance with nature and agriculture allowed them to claim mastery and belonging in an alien land (and I would argue render that alien land a homeland), while avoiding meaningful engagement with the nonwhite population. In many contexts, nongovernmental organizations and governments assume that "Indigenous people" (however they define them) have a deeper knowledge and closer attachment to the land, even if they are deprived stakeholder positions because the organizations assume that they have no economic needs or desires. What is interesting in the case of Afrikaner stewardship is that white colonizers envisioned themselves as the proper stewards—and thus justified their landownership—because of their own autochthonous connections to the land.

For Afrikaans rooibos farmers, coloured people faded into the background as potential—or rightful—landowners, as community members, and as political voices. Discussions about the need to protect rooibos land often vindicated the continuing lack of coloured or black landownership. In South Africa, protecting biodiversity was held up as a moral and ethical mandate that could legitimately transcend local needs and rights (Meskell 2012). Protecting nature could make the lack of nonwhite landownership apolitical or even morally and religiously correct. Farming with rooibos—the national beverage and an indigenous species—could allow white farmers to cash in literally and symbolically on popular associations between native plants and contemporary citizenship.

Jon, an English-speaking conservationist working in the area, explained that rooibos farmers often dismissed his efforts to get them to enact what he described as more environmentally sustainable practices. "They say they will only preserve what they love," he stated. "The farmers say, 'No farmer will degrade our land because it's ours.'" But Jon seemed to draw from a different understanding of environmental values from that of many farmers. Rooibos farmers saw the environment as a *humanized* landscape, a nature-society hybrid. Their environmental values stemmed from the "love" that Jon described, a love informed by belonging, by livelihoods, and by a desperation to preserve a way of life linked both to income and cultural identity.

"We Are Getting Our Dignity Back"

In conversations about loving rooibos, laborers' work was unspoken, yet their presence was everywhere on the farm: harvesting, pruning, or tilling the land. Rooibos's "natural" quality, supposedly controlled by God, made labor even more invisible. As one Afrikaans farmer said, "There is no labor into rooibos. The plant is growing wild in the veld." Coloured workers' connections to the land were erased—or unheard—in these conversations. Almost always walking and hardly ever driving, coloured people moved from farm to farm across paths and dirt roads or hitched rides in the backs of trucks, largely hidden from view unless you happened to catch a glimpse through an opening in the truck's covering.

Coloured people were one with the landscape in distinctly different ways from the affective relations white farmers espoused for themselves; the coloured were ever present but unseeable. If white farmers recognized workers' presence in the fields at all, it was as labor units, while farmers possessed the skill and the heart. This easy divide between skill and labor, however, was not always straightforward. White farmers sometimes downplayed the skill involved in cultivating rooibos because the plant belonged in this soil, with this rainfall and these insects. Ideas of morality emerged not from *working* the land but, rather, from *harnessing* what was indigenous instead of planting crops, such as citrus or grapes, that might require more "skill." According to these farmers, rooibos's growth was an act of God and the white farmer, not an act of coloured labor. Yet coloured residents expressed affective relations that both paralleled and challenged white belonging with rooibos, even if they did not legally own the land they worked. As small-scale farmers and farmworkers, they connected their labor—and their bodies—with rooibos. While white farmers may have owned most of the land, some coloured farmers and laborers believed that their manual labor made them closer to the tea. Afrikaners asserted that their blood was mingled with the soil, but it was predominately coloureds who had the rooibos soil under their fingernails.

The erasure of coloured skill with rooibos did not erase their presence in white notions of morality. Like the land and the plants, coloured workers were often described by white farmers as requiring stewardship and care. Yet Afrikaners made workers part of the landscape in a way that was far less agentive than that of the plants. Afrikaans farmers repeatedly called coloured people "children" who needed protection by white farm owners, church leaders, or charity organizations. Koos discussed these relations while his coloured domestic worker washed dishes in the nearby sink, never once looking up from her task. "According to religion," Koos said, "the races shouldn't mix. It's in the Bible. But they can be friends. All my children grew up playing with black kids. They all had a little black kid." Koos and others in the region told me that the English—and presumably visiting American researchers—could never understand the relationship between the coloured worker and the Afrikaans farmer. "When the farmers are better off, everyone is [including] farmworkers," Koos explained. "There is a better relationship between the farmers and the labor here than anywhere else in the country . . . because they are intimate, no, that is not the right word, because they are closely related. They have the same language, same humor, same hardships, so the understanding is better."

In his discussion of pastoral power, Michel Foucault (2000) talks about connections between care and control in regard to a shepherd and his sheep. Incapable of acting on their own, sheep would starve or lose their way without the help of a shepherd. Anand Pandian (2008) argues that Foucault's theory reduces this relationship to a metaphor. Yet I often had difficulty deciphering metaphor from many white farmers' perceptions of reality. They talked about coloureds as children or sheep. When they described coloured people as Khoisan, they were animal-like: nomadic, wandering from place to place, and in need of tending. In this context, the relative humanization of plants in the landscape also served to dehumanize certain categories of people.

Other white residents took a different view: They argued that coloured farmworkers felt no connection to the region, that they claimed no ownership over rooibos. One white farm owner asserted that coloured workers just want "a BMW, a flat-screen TV, and a city job," while a white farm schoolteacher said, "Because of the history, coloured people are farmworkers. For them, a farmer is a bad thing . . . so they normally don't want to go into that kind of thing. They want white-collar jobs." Certainly, many coloured youth did not aspire to work on the land and instead hoped to leave for the city or move into the middle class—a dream that was often blocked by poor access to resources, lack of education, or the need to earn an immediate living. A number of coloured farmworkers emphasized that they wanted their children to graduate from high school, go to university, or "maybe work as police." The desire to leave the land differed from that of many young Afrikaans men, who typically hoped to take over the family farm. Young white women were almost entirely overlooked in inheriting farms, so their remaining in the region often depended on whom they married. Clearly, socioeconomic and political issues informed racial and gendered differences. While most white sons believed that they could earn a living from the farm, a number of coloured sons and daughters described the farm—and rural areas in general—as something to escape for an imagined better, more egalitarian urban future. More often than not, coloured teachers, ministers, and activists in the area said that the children of farmworkers remained on the farm not because they wanted to, but because they just "ended up there." One coloured activist explained, "The farms move forward, but the farmworkers don't always." Being on land and working with crops that they did not own could be more of a trap than a form spiritual belonging.

Yet white farmers' insistence that workers did not care about farms or rooibos could serve to justify white belonging on the land: They felt that white farmers truly cared for the plant and the soil, while workers were merely looking for a wage and a way out. These statements silenced workers such as Hendrik, who challenged that notion. He told me that he dreamed of having his own farm by the time he turned fifty. When I asked him whether he felt rooibos was a part of his heritage, he paused briefly before he replied: "I am not ashamed of being brown or my father being a farmworker and that my mother worked in the kitchen of a commercial farm. . . . If it don't go back to something, you weren't there. If your father was not a farmer, you don't farm. It runs in your blood. Because farming is a hard business. If you do it, you are either mad, or it is in your blood."

Like Hendrik, many coloured farmers who had managed to access rooibos land expressed a strong sense of belonging and moral stewardship. They argued, however, that their ability to break free from white commercial farms solidified their connections to rooibos. As Martin, a coloured farmer (and former farmworker) explained, "To workers, it doesn't matter what industry they are in—citrus, rooibos, it is all the same. It is just a job. But it is different for small-scale farmers. There is more of a feeling that rooibos is their heritage." Martin now worked for a small-scale farmers' cooperative that sold its tea at a premium to high-end consumers using a marketing strategy that emphasized coloured farmers' long history with the land and the plant. He expressed enormous gratitude that the cooperative's earnings had allowed him to stop taking seasonal work and instead harvest his own tea. He also critiqued the role of Christianity in relation to his rooibos heritage. Referring to Afrikaans farmers, he said vehemently, "They started the industry with the knowledge from us. . . . The whole business is built on this knowledge." While Martin himself was devoutly Christian and even belonged to a former mission church, he cursed the church's historical role in the rooibos industry. In his mind, missionaries both brought the "word" of God and stole the "word" of rooibos.

After a long conversation, Martin suggested that I speak with one of his neighbors who was also involved with a cooperative. Later that week, I followed his advice and contacted Marina. To find her house, I drove for miles on a mountain road, full of deep ruts and potholes. Dust billowed from the back of my car, its remnants hanging in the air like smoke signaling my path. I finally reached a small cluster of white houses with thatched roofs. The yipping of a small dog and the squawking of fleeing chickens greeted me as I walked along the path to Marina's farm. Among coloured farming cooperatives, women were sometimes called farmers and not just "farmers' wives." Marina greeted me and escorted me through the small patch of rooibos that grew in front of her home.

As we walked, she explained that people in her community started as farmers, but not rooibos farmers. Rooibos, she explained was not farmed; it just grew wild. "But we all drank the *veld* [wild] tea." Since it was not harvest time, she used her hands to mime how she cut the tea. "We just did it on a small scale, and we wet it and then dried it on the rocks. It's just how they do it at the big tea [processors] today," she laughed. I asked her how she learned to make the tea. "I just watched the elders. It's very, very easy. It's organic." Marina's description of her heritage with rooibos echoed the sentiments of many coloured farmers: Because they farmed the tea "more naturally," they felt they were more connected to the land than white farmers were.

Albertus, a coloured farmer from a different part of the rooibos-growing region, expressed similar sentiments. He repeatedly emphasized how natural his farming practices were. He demonstrated how he spread the tea across a drying surface with sticks instead of a machine. "Commercial farmers use petrol to do it," he said. "When we plant, our tea is wild tea mixed with planted tea, mixed with other natural bushes—because this is nature." As we walked back from his tea fields to his home, he pointed out different local plants and animals. We watched the sun set on the mountains and listened to the barking baboons. He turned to me and said, firmly, "I belong here."

Like Albertus, Nigel spoke at length about what farming with rooibos, as opposed to a nonindigenous crop, meant to him. He talked about the ease and low cost of working with rooibos. Since the plant requires few expensive inputs such as water or fertilizer, it helped resource-poor farmers such as Nigel earn a small living from the land, instead of (or in addition to) working for white farmers. Yet more important to Nigel, he described, was the connection between the plant's indigeneity and his heritage and his belonging on the land. He explained: "We are slowly starting to get our dignity because we are working with our heritage, our own rooibos. We reap the benefits of rooibos. Before, rooibos was only in the hands of white guys. This helps us become independent and proud again."

Rooibos's indigeneity provided coloured farmers with a financially feasible way to farm and, concurrently, to claim their heritage. For Afrikaans farmers, the plant's indigeneity allowed for a kind of belonging to the land that foreign plants such as citrus and grapes did not. Many coloured and white rooibos farmers saw themselves as simply harnessing, controlling, caring for, and living with that which was God's gift to the region—no matter the amount of pesticides used, land ploughed, or wild rooibos habitat destroyed. The idea of harnessing nature reflects similar discussions about bees in North America, but with a subtle difference. As Anna Tsing (1995: 123) describes, "Bees have become a part of nature that could be technologically grasped and controlled—but only by recognizing nature's inherent resistance to capture." Rooibos farmers, however, never discussed resistance from the wild; they talked about a vital and inherent interrelation among human, God, the cultivated, and the wild that became central to claims of belonging. Given the moral framework of indigeneity, many farmers expressed that stewardship was important to their senses of self (even if environmentalists condemned some of their practices, such as mono-cropping with rooibos). The economic possibilities afforded by rooibos, however, also made protecting it—not just from environmental hazards but also from "theft" by nonlocal farmers and processers—imperative.

Linking people and their development to geographical and climatic constraints can easily fall into the trap of environmental and cultural determinism. Despite these often violent and ideologically motivated determinisms, residents discussed rooibos's and farmers' interrelated *ecological belonging* in ways that could be potentially emancipatory while still radically distinct from essentialized notions of "native traditional knowledge." Incorporating the history of race and botany in South Africa, I used the framework of symbiopolitics to show how coloured and white residents articulated a complicated kind of ecological belonging in which both their livelihoods and their senses of self were formed through their spiritual connections to the rooibos landscape. People involved with rooibos farming linked subjectivity, nature, and religion in ways that were not just metaphorical but also informed by a deification of nature and by a need for economic livelihoods in the nutrient-poor, low-rainfall region in which rooibos thrives.

Connections to rooibos had implications for Afrikaans farmers that were different from those for coloured farmers in terms of livelihoods but also in terms of situating their precarious claims to autochthonous belonging. In discussing British settlers in Zimbabwe, David McDermott Hughes (2010) describes how, by loving the land, settlers ignored the social exile in which they lived. They became assimilated to the landscape around them. For Afrikaners, however, the claim was stronger than for the British. They did not just *love* the land, they believed they were *of* the land. As the Afrikaans poet Breyten Breytenbach (1996: 108) writes: "Their frontier became a heaven and the continent consumed them. . . . And they can never write the landscapes out of their system." But not only was the claim stronger; the consequences were also different: Unlike British settlers, Afrikaners had no England to which to return. The farmers I spoke with felt no connection to the Netherlands or to France, where their ancestors might have come from hundreds of years earlier. They did not speak the languages of these European countries, and they had no family stories or relatives that linked them there. While some Afrikaans rooibos farmers talked about moving to Australia if "things got bad," they did not envision Australia becoming their "real home." Cultural ownership of rooibos was in one sense a way to "own" indigeneity and make themselves autochthonous.

The stakes for coloured people in the rooibos region were greater. The majority did not have the financial means, education, or ability to speak a language other than Afrikaans to move elsewhere. Coloured people's supposedly deficient, placeless identities denied them nativity to anywhere, and white people's landownership denied them tenure or the ability to set down secure roots even in the rooibos-growing area. In her work on refugees, Liisa Malkki (1995) describes the discursive constitution of refugees and other displaced people as "bare humanity." Those providing the displaced with care and control worried that their culture had been lost or distorted when they crossed a border. In the context of the rooibos region, whites and black migrants—even the Zimbabwean refugees who had fled violence and economic uncertainty in their home country—were given a "culture," while coloured people were not.

Were coloured people, then, the representatives of bare humanity: local, yet never culturally rooted to place? Could the relative humanization—or anthropomorphizing—of plants as actors in the landscape also serve to dehumanize certain categories of people? Or did the *cross-race* love of rooibos expressed by coloured and white residents put forth more hopeful possibilities than those often articulated in narratives of South African political ecology? The South African scholars Andries du Toit and David Neves (2014: 837) argue that dichotomies such as "bare life" and "political life," "precarity" and "security," and "inclusion" and "exclusion" flatten the uneven, dynamic terrain of what might better be understood as "differential inclusion" (Mezzadra and Neilson 2012). I explore these questions and ideas of "differential inclusion" over the next three chapters.

{ 3 }

ENDEMIC PLANTS

AND INVASIVE PEOPLE

> The pioneers of every colony set in motion machinery beyond their
> ultimate control; no legislation can regulate the dissemination of seeds. As the sun
> shines and the rain falls alike on the just and the unjust, so fleets, railroads,
> and highways convey seeds good and bad to a common destination.
> —HERBERT GUTHRIE-SMITH, *Tutira*

"The aliens is killing us," Jan, a coloured rooibos farmer, said as he walked across the small plot of land that he leased from his church. He pointed to the Australian Port Jackson trees and other invasive species spilling into his crop land. While Jan was speaking of plants, he might just as easily have been discussing people—referring to the wave of migration that had increased in the area since the end of apartheid-era pass laws. The migration had altered local demographics, which previously included few black South Africans. We started talking about rooibos and his desire to have a farm of his own. He looked me in the eye and said firmly, "Sarah, I don't want to be racist, but the Zulus, the Xhosa, they had their land, and the white people had their land too."

Most of the area's residents, whether they identified as white or coloured, agreed that rooibos was indigenous and that black people, whether Zulu, Xhosa, or Zimbabwean, were "alien." In discussing how the Zulus and Xhosa "had their land," Jan was referring to the Bantustan system and the creation of fictitious ethnic homelands that was a central pillar of apartheid control. The apartheid government labeled these homelands—overcrowded, imposed, and confining though they were—"nations," in which each group would "develop" according to its supposed "cultural needs." But the government gave coloured people no homeland; they supposedly did not belong to any land outside white South Africa.

With few exceptions, coloured people in the rooibos region lived as laborers on white-owned farms, in the "coloured section" of towns, or on church land. In the postapartheid country, Jan hoped finally to gain access to his own land. Yet he saw the increasing migration of black workers as undermining that possibility, as postapartheid policies attempted to deracialize the concept of territory. If Zulus were no longer confined to Zululand, Jan commented, could he attain access to the region's scarce available land?

Chapter 2 examined how claims about rooibos, as both a "wild indigenous plant" and a "cultivated global commodity," politicized the shifting boundaries between nature and culture. Through material and affective dependencies between people and plant, rooibos fulfilled its role as symbolic unifier and economic hope, but in incomplete ways. As migrants came to labor in rooibos fields alongside local coloured residents, the connections between rooibos and claims to belonging unfolded in an ever more complex and elaborate dance. The presence of "aliens," whether they were black Africans or foreign plant species, was often—but not always—presented as a threat to the area's environmental and cultural specificity and its supposedly concomitant environmental and cultural vulnerability.

While the Khoisan might have represented the "extinct" in contestations over rooibos, land, and belonging, black people were considered so exotic that for years they were more of a spectacle than a demographic. Bertie, an Afrikaans farmer, explained, "Until about the 1980s there wasn't any blacks. There was an old guy staying on the farm from Lesotho. He came here in 1947. He told me about how he was in a shop once, and a boy came in and said that his father was dying and he wanted to see a black man before he died, so he went to the man and he rubbed his skin and all that." In recent years, the presence of black migrants had increased rapidly, and their arrival has affected labor dynamics, politics, and the ways in which coloured and white residents negotiate their precarious positions.

This chapter explores how people in the region imagined and articulated an alien invasion and risk to indigeneity posed by "alien" plants and people. In the parallels between residents' depictions of black migrants and nonindigenous plant species, it was not so much the fact of being an outsider as their capacity to live beyond attempts at control that rendered certain people and plants problematic. Their significance for white and coloured residents therefore depended on the relationships in which they were embedded. Physical geography at times gave way to postapartheid negotiations and renegotiations of spatial rule, exclusion, and mobility. In this context, alien invasives emerged more as matter that was "out of control" than as matter that was "out of place" in an ecological sense (cf. Douglas 2002 [1966]).

In many ways, residents' definitions of the "alien" represented a farmer's view of the world: Their fears and values emerged in the distinction between the cultivated and the uncultivated and the blurry line that marked that boundary. In other ways, they were reflective of discussions about foreignness and migrations in other parts of the South Africa and around the world, such as concerns that migrants would promote the casualization of labor and undermine job security. Yet in the rooibos region, alien plants were not representative of the alterity of migrants. The threat of migrants was contingent, even as it tapped into long-standing and still powerful formations of race and difference. With farming and the cultivation of rooibos, white farmers sometimes viewed migrants as desirable because of their perceived superior mental, moral, and physical strength compared with coloured workers and because of their willingness to work for lower wages. At other times, farmers envisioned migrants as socially dangerous. When white farmers themselves "introduced" black workers to cultivate their land, black people were not invasive. It was only when the same workers "broke free" of their control through affiliations with the coloured community in acts such as labor organizing and voting that they became a threat. Through this lens, danger stemmed from people and plants escaping human control and overstepping their "place" in two definitions of the word: locality and social station. Plants acted like moral subjects in white narratives while black laborers, conversely, appeared as mere units of labor power or units of risk for criminality.

Because of this mobility, ecosystems work differently from nation-states as scales of analysis. They are living and active; they are not anchored in place. In examining both the parallels and the particularities of the rooibos ecosystem and broader contestations over politics, ecology, and the economy, I reframe tensions over what constitutes "foreignness." Both the political and the scholarly focus on nationhood stems in part from postcolonial histories. In their struggles against colonialism, many liberation movements strove to produce a national people that would legitimize the existence and power of a postcolonial state. Yet these nationally based collective identities are troubled by the impermanence of this new group, "citizens," that excludes as much as it includes. Drawing on anti-colonial ideologies, many postcolonial nations' claims to sovereignty have been rooted in the supposed autochthony of colonized people. Consequently, the expulsion, and even murder, of nonautochthonous aliens has often "haunted" postcolonial nations (Hansen and Stepputat 2005: 27).

With its fragmented history as a nation-state, South Africa has emerged as a particularly prominent place through which to engage with themes of the foreign as dangerous. The territory of South Africa was first unified in the early twentieth century under British control, when former Afrikaans re-publics merged into one self-governing country named the Union of South Africa. (The country declared independence from Britain in 1960 and formed the Republic of South Africa.) However, the "unity" of the country never in-cluded the nonwhite population, who were confined to the separate "nations" of the Bantustans. In response, postapartheid reconstruction included depict-ing South Africa as one country—the Rainbow Nation—in which all people lived together in a united, nonracial nation-state.

Shortly after the emergence of this "Rainbow Nation," the spread of xeno-phobia against non–South Africans received attention from scholars and other cultural commentators, with articles about it regularly appearing in jour-nals and local newspapers (Geschiere 2011; Hickel 2014; Worby et al. 2008).[1] Yet for years immigrants had made their way to the rooibos region—the mi-grations visible in the ancient rock art that dots the landscape, the tales of colonists moving in and out in the seventeenth and eighteenth centuries, and the gravestones that bore witness to English settlers who came and went in the nineteenth century.

Throughout the colonial era, migrants had flocked to South Africa's mines and farms to search for labor, and since the end of apartheid, people from southern African countries such as Mozambique, Zimbabwe, Lesotho, and Malawi have steadily crossed the border, searching for work or asylum from precarious political and economic situations in their home countries. In the early 2000s, however, increased violence and instability in Zimbabwe led to Zimbabweans' coming to South Africa in greater numbers. At the same time, frustration over a lack of jobs and the unfulfilled promises of the postapartheid transition began to boil over. These tensions, among other factors such as the "New" South Africa's nation-building attempts, culminated in an outbreak of heavily publicized xenophobic violence in 2008 and again in 2015, during which immigrants' homes and businesses were destroyed across the nation. Yet immigrants were not the only ones rendered "alien": The violence often included black South Africans, as well. In the years since 2008, the word "xenophobia" has taken on a life of its own, migrating from its original meaning to imply racism, regionalism, or any kind of violence against difference.

In the rooibos region, the alien was regional, even ecological, in scale. It was rooted far more in relations among farmers, plants, and soil than in ideas of citizenship. Philip Mirowski (1989) describes how theories of the social have been patterned historically after our understandings of the physical world. When talking about plants, ecologists often unselfconsciously adopt such culturally loaded terms as "invaders," "invasives," "colonizers," and "fast-breeders" (Beinart and Wotshella 2011; Robbins 2004; Subramaniam 2001). Scholars, conservationists, and residents of the rooibos-growing area often used scientific terminology to describe societies as "ecologically balanced" and foreign people as "invasive to the natural state of things" or as "breeding" more rapidly and successfully than locals. Against this background, plants such as rooibos reside in a shifting biopolitical landscape in which ideas of nature and culture, race and ethnicity, indigenous and invasive were made and remade through a dynamic assemblage of discursive and material practices.

Like the proliferation of invasive Port Jackson trees, there was an anxiety that black people would physically overcome the coloured and white populations. According to the racism taught in many South African schools and embedded in popular culture in the apartheid era, coloured people were weak and degraded, while black people were "virile" and "vigorous," their fertility and fecundity posing a serious threat (Dubow 1995: 66). White and coloured residents of the rooibos-growing area often seemed to collude silently in negative perceptions of black others. They were frequently described as "invading" the landscape and altering a fragile equilibrium of long-established race and labor relations. As one white farmer declared, "Black workers are a problem. They stay and kick out the coloured people." These fears led in part to violent conflict against black South Africans in the region in 2005.

Using the violence of 2005 as a starting point, this chapter examines the shifting and layered notions of the foreign in the rooibos region. At times, foreign "threats" were mapped nationally; at times, racially or ethnically; at times, provincially; and at still other times, ecologically. Yet I also problematize the social imagination of "threat" by describing the contextual aspects of "bad" plants and "bad" people and by emphasizing the subtle moral questions implied in the discourse of foreign invasion. In many ways, connections between the foreign and the alien and the concomitant valuations of people and plants reflect the categories that postcolonial critiques would predict: Foreign plants and people are spoken of in the same language, and this language articulates fears about "others" and about the unknown future of a globalizing world in which goods and people move rapidly across borders. Yet the contingent and dynamic forms of these valuations combined to form unanticipated categories and took on meanings outside the metaphorical to include material, spiritual, and affective relations in the ecosystem, the nation, and the world. Through my examination of these categories, I follow scholarly attempts to look past reifications *while simultaneously listening to the complex—and cross-species— reifications expressed by my informants.* Even rooibos, the very symbol of indigeneity, could move in and out of these moral certainties: Rooibos is good because it is endemic; cultivated rooibos is bad because it leads to plowing in the fragile fynbos ecosystem. The cultivation of an indigenous plant for the marketplace could reconfigure it into a globalized commodity that commits violence against the landscape.

The chapter's discussion of the parallel discourses used to describe "foreign" people and plants draws from a scholarly tradition that links ecology, race, and the nation-state. In her work on refugees, Liisa Malkki (1992) describes how the "nation," as a linguistic term and a geographical imaginary, has its roots in concepts of soil and land. In phrases such as "the land rose up" and "people of a country," Malkki argues, territory is rendered strikingly human, and the connections between people and place take on both biological and metaphysical meanings. In German romantic nationalism, for example, philosophers such as Johann Herder and Immanuel Kant critiqued an Enlightenment universalism that separated the social and natural world. Instead, they asserted that the nation-state itself was a product of nature and not a human invention (Olsen 1999). Like the conflations between race and nature discussed in chapter 2, these romantic, essentialist, and organicist notions of the nation-state could have violent consequences. In the rooibos region, however, the boundaries of human and plant belonging appeared measured—and sometimes brutally policed—by standards that were decidedly more ecological than they were national. Residents feared a rogue organicism.

Remapping the Foreign

We're outsiders. We'll die as outsiders. The Afrikaner has this terrible tribal . . .
you either belong or you don't belong, even though we sent our kids to the schools and
we're involved in the church and rugby. —AFRIKAANS FARMER from the Eastern Cape

Jacobus and I sat at a picnic table outside a gas station café on the edge of the N7, the main road that connects Cape Town and Namibia. It was citrus harvest season, and we had to pause our conversation from time to time as trucks roared past carrying loads of oranges down to Cape Town's international port or up to Namibia. Wiping the sweat from his forehead, Jacobus described the nightlife in a local (white) bar. "They don't mix with you when you are new," he said. "They live in such a closed little environment. They always look at people that aren't from here as different. If I drink or if I drive too fast, they call my boss to tell him. People always comment and make other people uncomfortable and gossip and stare." What was striking about his claims was that Jacobus was not coloured, black, or English but, rather, an Afrikaner who had moved to the area from another part of South Africa a few years earlier.

When I asked Jacobus how his feeling like an outsider compared with the experiences of English-speaking people in the area, however, he immediately labeled them "less native" than himself, even though many English families had lived in the region for generations. "That's a whole other kettle of fish," he said. "The English are Cape Townians. They are weekend guests. They get seen as tourists. They are not seen as locals. . . . If you put the Cape Townians [in the local bar], the locals get rowdy and the *inkomers* and the locals get together, and it's like, 'This is our town.'" But, he still lamented, "I want to know how long I must live in this town before I'm a local. . . . It's like a school yard, the tension in the air." I asked whether coloured people were welcome in the bar. "They are tolerated for dinner, but not for drinking," he replied. "Black people don't come at all."

In many ways, Jacobus's story is not unusual. It represents a constellation of localness, racism, and fear of outsiders reflected in small towns around the world. Jacobus spoke to the shifting notions of belonging he experienced in a local bar: Black people did not figure into the dynamics because they were so foreign that they were removed from social life; coloured people played a nominal role in battles over local claims to territory; English-speaking people could go to the bar, but they were "just tourists" and therefore always passing through, even if they had been passing through for generations. Nonlocal Afrikaners had some claims to nativity by virtue of their cultural heritage, yet they could never truly belong; their blood had not mingled with the soil. As our conversation shifted to other topics, such as farmworkers and local politics, Jacobus repeatedly brought up the alterity of non-Afrikaners. Coloured people "for some reason are just different" and "don't want to be uplifted," he said, but he found himself an "other," too, with no claim to belonging in the fynbos ecosystem.

In contrast to Jacobus's depiction of "natives" versus "foreigners," discussions of xenophobia typically begin from the standpoint of the modern nation-state (Nyamnjoh 2006). Using this framework, the concept of alien people stems first and foremost from the idea of naturalized borders. John Comaroff and

Jean Comaroff (2001) argue that the politicized connection between foreign people and plants has become increasingly prominent in South Africa's Western Cape, where rooibos grows. Focusing on an outbreak of fires near Cape Town, they describe how public dialogue assigned blame to the presence of invasive plant species, a dialogue tied to the increased presence of non–South Africans in the city. Could this attention, Comaroff and Comaroff (2001: 6) ask, reflect "an existential problem presently making itself felt at the very heart of nation-states everywhere: in what does national integrity consist, what might nationhood and belonging *mean* . . . at a time when global capitalism seems everywhere to be threatening sovereign borders?" While aspects of these ideas of belonging in the context of global capitalism resonated among rooibos farmers, the growing area also reflected a more complex attitude about borders. How do we understand belonging in a region and among a people who do not necessarily see themselves as connected to a national, sovereign body politic?

In the rhetoric of the postapartheid nation, everyone was supposed to be South African, united by shared cultural referents such as rooibos and part of one Rainbow Nation, in which being Zulu or Sotho no longer meant belonging to a different homeland. After the legalized segregation of apartheid, constructing a "national people" posed the seemingly intractable problem of unifying white, black, coloured, and Indian, not to mention Zulu, Xhosa, Sotho, and so on. Media campaigns, and even the descriptions of rooibos as a national beverage, mirrored other projects aimed at uniting South Africa's population into the Rainbow Nation (Ives 2007). However, the cultivation of a diverse yet united national identity has always been precarious, at best.

Some rooibos marketing materials and farmers' narratives directly reflected efforts geared toward building national unity. People referred to the tea as "Mandela-like," implying that, like Nelson Mandela, the tea could bring hope, prosperity, and reconciliation to the country. Numerous marketing materials anointed rooibos South Africa's "national beverage," and a number of people with whom I spoke called it a "national icon." A journalist from a prominent Afrikaans newspaper described rooibos news coverage: "Rooibos is a small industry in agriculture, so we are not going to publish something every week, but in the national psyche it is a big thing." Consequently, the newspaper followed rooibos-related events closely for newsworthy moments.

Rooibos is certified as "Proudly South African," a campaign launched by the national government in 2001 to encourage citizens to buy South African–made products. If they pass periodic inspections by a compliance unit, members of the campaign can place a logo on their products. The impetus of the campaign is to sell the "South African brand" and therefore to improve the country's economy by simultaneously fostering unity. According to the website, "By buying Proudly South African, both consumers and businesses are making a personal contribution to nation-building."[2] A number of farmers expressed how important it was to them that rooibos was "Proudly South African." However, I heard the "Proudly South African" refrain far more from people involved in the industry who did not hail from the rooibos-growing region. Some South Africans who had left the country after 1994 started their own rooibos companies or served as rooibos distributors in their new homes as a way to feel connected to the country that they missed. One farmer and marketer who lived in Cape Town and oversaw his farm from afar described rooibos as a "patriotic healthy product. . . . What I am doing is adding value to South African raw materials." He wanted to create the final tea product within South Africa rather than merely exporting raw tea overseas. He linked this desire to both nationalism and capitalism: "With capitalism, you don't export raw materials that are unique to your zone. You want to create the most wealth at home. This is a nationalist principle."

The discourse of unity, however, seldom translated to the rooibos region. More often, farmers spoke of wanting to protect the tea's regional quality. Residents rarely expressed national solidarity aside from the occasional children's performance of the national anthem. At farm schools, teachers instructed students about the "proud history" of South Africa. "We teach the children to love the country's symbols," one teacher said. "We want them to be proud." Because the vast majority of these students have never left the region—or some even the farm—it was hard to tell what being proud of the country meant to them. In fact, the legitimation of the national government was far from clear in the area. Most residents felt disconnected from the "black politics" of the ruling African National Congress (ANC) and spoke repeatedly of President Jacob Zuma's corruption. As one black migrant said, "White people believe the Western Cape is their place." An Afrikaans farmer confirmed this idea to me: "We think of this as our own little country. We are not very worried about what's going on in the rest of the country." Some coloured and white residents of the province even explored a "Quebec option," through which they would work toward independence (Western 2001).

Many farmers saw the rooibos-growing area as one of the last refuges against an uncertain, "black-controlled" state. They decreased the scale of what they considered their "nation" and thus who counted as an insider and who was an outsider. When much of South Africa was embroiled in violence against people from other countries, the "xenophobia" of the rooibos region and who could claim to be autochthonous took on a different discursive tone and spatial scale. While linked to issues of labor and land claims that resonated across the country, local "xenophobia" was rooted far more in notions of belonging with the soil than in the nation. Although residents were concerned about the presence of immigrants from other African countries, their primary anxieties centered on other South Africans, black people from areas outside the ecologically and demographically unique region of rooibos country. "I miss growing up on the farm," a coloured woman reminisced about the commercial farm where her father had worked. "Now there are Xhosa people there." This constellation of anxiety and nostalgia expressed itself in discussions of violence.

The timing and the specifics of the incident residents described most often varied depending on who told the story, but most people agreed that conflict occurred in 2005 between the Sotho and the Xhosa, two groups from different parts of South Africa. A Xhosa migrant explained: "It was a communication issue. One Xhosa boy was in love with a Sotho girl. There was an argument between the girl and the boy. The brothers of the boy came over and got mad. It was really just a language issue. The conflict started there. The Sotho people assaulted the boy. The Xhosa people came back, and the violence started from there. We were forced to segregate the community by means of Xhosa on one side and Sotho on the other side in Khayelitsha. Houses were burned." Whether the narrative was retold as a love story or a labor issue, a struggle among different black migrants or between the coloured and black communities, the story had salience in the region. I heard a number of different versions of the violence, in which the ethnic groups involved and the cause and outcome of the fighting varied. I never learned what happened to the couple in question—or even whether they actually existed—but the story had an afterlife in continued rumors of xenophobia between migrants and local coloured people and between different migrant groups. Significantly, local residents, whether white or coloured, described the xenophobia as between fellow citizens, where one group was stylized as more foreign than the other.

The relative foreignness drew on contested claims to "first arrivals" that I discussed in previous chapters, in which many Afrikaans historiographies justified their naturalized belonging by citing their arrival in the Western Cape before black South Africans. It also drew on the codification of cultural separateness through Bantustans based on often arbitrary decisions of regional bureaucrats. Under apartheid, black people's presence in the rooibos-growing area would have been "unnatural" because it would likely have been illegal. One black migrant to the region shared an anecdote about his experiences with tribal homelands. When the Group Areas Act went into effect in the 1950s, he said, "We were in the Free State, but they say to my dad, 'Your name sounds Zulu, it doesn't sound Sotho,' so they sent us to Zululand. I had to learn a new language, a new culture. So now I'm Zulu." The power of the apartheid state was so great that it could literally reassign a family's heritage in a way that had a lasting impact on future generations' subjectivities. "Now," he said, "I'm a Zulu."

Aliens and "Plant Imperialism"

In recent decades, fynbos has become the prime incarnation of the fragile, wealth-producing beauties of the region; and, as it has, local environmentalists have become ever more convinced that it is caught up in a mortal struggle with alien interlopers that threaten to reduce its riches to "impenetrable monotony."
—JOHN COMAROFF and JEAN COMAROFF, "Naturing the Nation"

A group of rooibos "stakeholders" sat in the meeting room of the Clanwilliam Bowling Club, a small building on the edge of the "white section" of town. Plaques—many of them sponsored by the area's largest rooibos company—covered the walls to celebrate this or that lawn-bowling champion. Pictures showed smiling white men dressed in pure white clothes, with long white socks pulled up to their knees. Often when I drove past the Bowling Club, I saw men and women wearing wide-brimmed hats and tossing balls across the neatly trimmed grass. On that day, industry representatives and about a dozen farmers gathered around tables formed into a circle to discuss the 2011 draft of the *Handbook for Implementing Rooibos Sustainability Standards*.

I turned to Section 2.5, "Alien Plants." The booklet spelled out the danger of the plants and what farmers should do to fight them: "Invasive alien plants (IAP) are a major threat to the environment and agricultural resources. . . . They also displace habitat for indigenous and agricultural plants and animals. There are alien invasive plants on almost every farm and it is every landowner's duty, and that of the government, to combat them" (Pretorius et al. 2011: 82). The handbook emphasized the idea of duty in combating the alien threat, using rhetoric similar to war propaganda designed to mobilize citizens to fulfill their responsibilities in a joint public and private effort. The handbook called for farmers to make an IAP "control plan" that would prioritize eradicating "category one" plants, or those considered most dangerous. Maintaining this eradication, the handbook warned, "will have to continue for years to come! Prepare for this and don't waste time" (Pretorius et al. 2011: 84). The handbook, as well as many local experts, emphasized urgency. "The aliens are choking our water," a coloured farmer said. Some scientists considered alien plants and animals the greatest threat to the area's endemic plants and agricultural sustainability.

When they settled in the area, early colonizers often re-created a European ideal of a farmhouse surrounded by trees while simultaneously cutting down the few indigenous trees, such as the Clanwilliam cedar tree (*Widdringtonia cedarbergensis*) for which the Cederberg is named, to build furniture or make telephone poles. By 2010, the Clanwilliam cedar had become critically endangered, with only a few scraggily trees remaining high in the mountains. Ecologists undertook efforts to save the indigenous cedar that were as urgent and desperate as their efforts to eradicate the invasives: trees and shrubs from other Mediterranean climates, such as southern Australia. Yet the introduced trees thrived. Today, virtually every farmhouse I visited stood under the shade of a giant, non-native, tree.

William Beinart and Karen Middleton (2004: 14) call the persistence of introduced species a kind of "plant imperialism," arguing that colonization through gardening was an everyday settler activity. The rooibos region's farms and towns often had small gardens with non-native plants. Despite their tender care for the tulips growing by their doorsteps, most everyone spoke of the urgency of eliminating invasive plants, fighting against plant imperialism—or, at least, the imperialism that had escaped their control. Local residents and conservation workers renamed the out-of-control plants "alien" or "invasive," while garden flowers, bushes, and the neat, green lawn of the Clanwilliam Bowling Club were not. Instead, they focused on the formerly benign shade trees whose seeds had broken away from the garden and started demanding the area's limited environmental resources with their ever-expanding root systems, stealing water from both native plants and agricultural crops.

The Western Cape province and the fynbos ecosystem in which rooibos grows were considered particularly vulnerable—or, conversely, "hospitable"—to this infestation (Beinart and Middleton 2004). An ecological "puzzle" emerges in the fynbos biome: In its natural state, it is virtually treeless, but the biome is bioclimatically suited to tree growth. The capacity of invasive trees and shrubs to exploit the brief windows caused by fires that kill native shrubs enables them to thrive (Pooley 2012). To combat these aliens, the National Department of Water Affairs launched the Working for Water program in 1995. The program unleashed large forces of unemployed people to cut down trees and remove their roots. Residents often described the Working for Water program as a "campaign." The website explains that alien invasive species cause billions of rands of damage to South Africa's economy every year, as invasive plants, animals, and microbes "out-compete" indigenous species. Other nongovernmental organizations in the area added IAP control to their management plans, and white and coloured farmers worked to clear invasives from their farms (Department of Environmental Affairs 2015b). But as soon as they stopped, the invasives came back in what residents described as a seemingly ceaseless onslaught.

"Our forefathers didn't have a policy of keeping the land clean from aliens," a coloured farmer said. "Now, they are killing us. We just keep pulling them." The alien plants possessed a seemingly excessive vitality, a vitality accompanied by the ability to kill. Farmers had to make up for their ancestors' lack of attention to, and undervaluing of, indigeneity. At a local school, children who took agricultural classes learned which pesticides and herbicides were appropriate for protecting rooibos plants from invaders, and most commercial farmers waged chemical warfare against the aliens, despite claims that rooibos is so natural it is "basically" organic. Farmers did tend to use considerably fewer chemicals for rooibos than for most agricultural products in the area, usually spraying during the planting season and leaving the bushes alone the rest of the year. "I like farming with rooibos. Rooibos is a part of the nature," Dawid, an Afrikaans farmer, said. "When we plant, we just spray the whole field with herbicide. Then we use two pesticides for leafhoppers and worms." As he looked across the mountains beyond the fields where he used to play as boy, he described invasive insects that fed on rooibos plants and interfered with the pollination efforts of endemic bees and wasps.

Unlike Dawid, many coloured farmers used organic but highly labor-intensive methods to attempt to eradicate alien invasive species.[3] Hentie, a coloured farmer and member of a certified organic cooperative, walked through her crop. Because she had access to only a small portion of land, rows of two-year-old rooibos plants flanked the path that led to her front door. Whenever she came or went to her house, she passed the bushes and checked on their health. She pointed out bugs that ate the plants and killed them if left on the needles. In the cool of the early evening, we moved through the plants together, removing the red beetle-like insects—she did not know their names—and placing them in a jar to burn over the fire. Hentie described the economic harm that losing a rooibos bush to alien insects would do to her, but she also discussed the cost in emotional terms. The bugs were spoiling the pristine ecosystem (never mind the orange tree that grew beside her house). They did not belong there. They sucked the rooibos bushes brown. The insects' bright red color stood out against the muted greens of the fynbos plants that surrounded her fields and covered the mountains above them. Whether through chemical or mechanical means, the "infestation" had to be stopped.

Nigel Clark (2002: 5) describes how the "ecologically undesirable" is "viewed with blatant repulsion" and construed as "creeping," "insidious," "inexorable," and "explosive." The ecologically undesirable can easily merge into the demographically undesirable when people's claims to belonging are rooted in the soil. In her research on South African parks and heritage programs, Lynn Meskell (2012) explores the slippage between the language of nature and the language of culture. She recalls a conversation with a scientist about the invasive species proliferating in a national park. "Couched in the language of alien invasion," she begins, "one scientist said the unsayable: 'these migrating and threatening organisms were like Mozambicans illegally crossing into South Africa'" (Meskell 2012: 113). The scientist used the words "migration" and "threat" interchangeably, a parallel made often—but not always—in the rooibos region. The presence of aliens—whether plants or people—allowed residents to proclaim their own natural autochthony as stewards of endemic plants and protectors against threats.

Simon Pooley (2010) connects this search for autochthony to the search for white unity, particularly after the English and Afrikaans communities were torn apart by the South African War in the early twentieth century. During that time, he asserts, Western Cape botanists began urgently trying to protect the region's fynbos from imported plants. The effort hinged on popularizing fynbos as something worth saving. After the war, indigenous plants became a symbolic opportunity for whites to unify in a fight against exotic species that might harm the emerging nation's "natural wealth." One of the reasons early twentieth-century authorities gave for encouraging whites to grow indigenous plants was "because they *are* South African" (Pooley 2010: 602). The only people that white authorities labeled "South African" were, predictably, white. Yet as stated previously, the people most often tasked with the actual labor of planting were black or coloured workers, rendered invisible in the discourse.

In the rooibos-growing area, indigenous stewardship was also frequently and unapologetically racialized, with Afrikaans farmers stylizing themselves as the proper autochthonous stewards. Coloured people, whites frequently expressed, did not know how to take care of their land. Pietre, an Afrikaans farmer, discussed the abundance of weeds that grew when a white farmer left his land to work in the city. He described how the coloured tenants allowed invasives to reenter the farming landscape. Protecting the ecosystem from alien plants became another way to justify continued white landownership.

If the Western Cape's unique ecosystem made it more vulnerable to invasive species, its unique demographic composition also made it more vulnerable to alien people, many residents argued. Clark reframes the dialogue around invasives, weeds, and migrants in ways that resonate with the rooibos region. He links negative attitudes and even repulsion toward invasive plants to the uproar over "foreign" people. He echoes Mary Douglas's seminal work, *Purity and Danger* (2002 [1966]), in which "matter-out-of-place" becomes an abomination, representing pollution and dirt. Yet significantly, the presence of aliens allowed white farmers to frame themselves as the protectors of "weaker coloured people" from the influx of black migrants while simultaneously exploiting the newly available black labor forces. As Ulrich Beck (2000: 71) describes, it is aliens' "very capacity to produce '*moral outcry*' that is their paradoxical virtue."

Waiting for the Barbarians

There is no woman living along the frontier who has not dreamed of a dark
barbarian hand coming from under the bed to grip her ankle, no man who has
not frightened himself with visions of barbarians carousing in his home.
—J. M. COETZEE, *Waiting for the Barbarians*

The Stranger, threatens. . . . the proper order and healthy movement of goods,
the lawful prescription of its controlled, classed, measured, labeled products, rigorously
divided into remedies and poisons, seeds of life and seeds of death.
—JACQUES DERRIDA, *Dissemination*

"You must be extra careful on the weekends, Sarah," a coloured farmer said as I waved goodbye after a Friday interview. "Outsiders come on the weekends, and we don't know them." Throughout our conversation, he kept talking about the "strange people" who had started appearing in the rooibos region: black workers, "weird" tourists, unknown coloured workers with tattoos, and dark-skinned people selling homemade reed brooms on the streets. While most people agreed that Xhosa and Sotho made up the largest percentage of migrants and that Zimbabweans made up the largest numbers of immigrants, no official statistics existed because many of the migrants were undocumented and many of the immigrants were in the area illegally.[4] The visual and aural presence of black people was undeniable. During harvest seasons and weekends, towns swelled with people speaking languages that neither I nor the local people with whom I spoke could understand. I was alternately told that in addition to the Xhosa and the Sotho, there were Zulu- and Tswana-speaking people. Other local residents spoke of people from Lesotho, Swaziland, Nigeria, Somalia, Namibia, Angola, Mozambique, and Malawi. While I talked with immigrants from many of these places, the uncertainty expressed by residents and the listing of country after country seemed to reinforce ideas that an undefined black horde was descending on the region.

Afrikaans and coloured residents described black migrants as both a concrete and an existential threat to their livelihoods and their senses of belonging in the region, the country, and the "globalizing" world. If coloured people were neither white enough nor black enough, the presence of black people threatened their job security and their heritage-based attempts to gain access to land for cultivation. The Western Cape is filled with parables about "Africanizing." In his article "Africa Is Coming to the Western Cape," John Western (2001: 617) captures this language: "At the southern tip of Africa, culmination of one of the world's great population shifts is there for the witnessing: a southward movement of Bantu-speaking Black Africans, previously stalled in South Africa's Eastern Cape first by climatic factors and later by European-imposed racial segregation. Cape Town, throughout its demographic history a 'Coloured' and 'White' city, is now Africanizing." Discourse about black, or Bantu, movement was and still is common in whites' popular imaginations. Saul Dubow (1995: 74) describes how "constantly repeated images of Bantu 'hordes' and 'invaders' reinforce the impression of their transience and barbarity." Themes of uncontrolled movement worked alongside images of barbarism.

Certainly, most of the migrants with whom I spoke did not feel welcome or that the region was their natural home. Many longed to be somewhere else but could not afford transport home or could not find jobs elsewhere. Daniel, a black South African who shared a shack in an informal settlement with a few other migrants, spoke of the racism he experienced from white and coloured residents. "They see you as different. They assume you are from Zimbabwe or Malawi, but not South Africa," he said. In local discourse, it was the black people who were not allowed to be South African; they were the ones denied a place in the country. They were from "Africa," the "Dark Continent" with which the country, and the region in particular, did not necessarily affiliate.

Many local Afrikaners' comments about migrants reflected a natural and exclusive belonging to the soil earned not only by toil in the fields, but also, as I described in the previous chapter, by a God-given right to tend the Edenic terrain and to exist as part of the landscape. Ideas of exclusive belonging were not universally accepted in South Africa and were not shared by black migrants such as Daniel. David Lan describes the meaning of autochthons among black Zimbabweans. Similar to the ideas expressed by Afrikaners, autochthons were literally "'those who came out of the ground,' [implying] that they are thought by themselves and others to have a special ritual intimacy with the territory they occupy because they are thought of as the earliest ever to have lived there" (Lan 1985: 14). Yet Lan's informants also allowed for incorporation. If a person lived in an area for a long time, he might be adopted into the clan of that territory and treated as such by others in the clan. However, Lan argues that living in a territory is not enough to become a part of it. The person must work the land and take part in the rituals of the agricultural cycle. Territory, then, may be overcome by duration. Because of the increased turn toward informal and part-time labor, most black migrants to the rooibos region, however, never obtained stable work or access to their own land. Instead, moving from farm to farm and from informal settlement to farm, they could not take part in the rituals of the agricultural cycle or sleep in permanent homes.

"Two Zimbabweans for the Price of Zero"

When not staying in the dormitories provided by some farmers for seasonal workers, migrants were mostly confined to an informal settlement above the "coloured section" of town, an area almost completely hidden from view from any road or white person's home. The informal settlement was a jumble of metal shacks, many of which looked too small for one person to sleep, let alone the two, three, or four who often lived in each one. Unlike the rest of town, which was mostly clean and well-manicured, garbage filled the streets and empty land. The area, I was told, had become a "no-go zone" for "respectable" coloured people and unsafe for white people unless they were driving through in their trucks, scanning the streets for black migrants hoping to get work for a day, a week, or longer. It was also highly gendered, as male migrants far outnumbered female migrants. Thus, the figure of the black man loomed large in the local imaginary.

The literal and linguistic separation of white, coloured, and black led to rumors about what, exactly, might be happening in the informal settlement. Prostitution? Religious rituals? Political plots? Each new migration prompted new rumors and new uncertainties. Black migrants reputedly disrupted the politics, labor relations, and safety of the rooibos region. I asked one coloured resident about crime and rumored gangs. "This is in the informal settlements, not here in the middle where we are," she replied. A coloured activist explained her version of xenophobic conflict as surges that followed waves of different migrants: "First it was between the coloureds and the Xhosa; then it was between the Sotho and the Xhosa, and on and on." Her explanation was strikingly different from that of the love story that others had described: "The reason is the farmers. . . . Capital says that [labor] is still too expensive. What is a Zimbabwean working for? . . . Zimbabweans are cheaper labor, better educated, higher skilled. You get two for the price of zero. It is not easy to fight for the rights of these people." She simultaneously blamed farmers, under the guise of capital, and Zimbabweans.

Coloured and Afrikaans residents described immigrants and migrants as threats to the imagined tranquility of the *rustig* (restful) countryside. Their discourse was different from many scholarly discussions about fear of immigrants' primitivity. Francis Nyamnjoh (2006: 43) describes South African beliefs that "if only these invaders could be contained, all would be well for authentic citizens of the new South Africa to fulfill their expectations of modernity." In the rooibos-growing area, however, discussions were not always about aspiring to modernity; they were also about maintaining the past. Residents depicted alien people, or black people, in much the same language as plants: They were threatening to the supposedly natural, delicate equilibrium of the social "ecosystem." The naturalizing of place-based belonging and literal partitions between racial groups showed the continuity of apartheid's control over people and its colonization of subjectivities, even though the layout of separate black settlements in the region actually occurred after the end of apartheid-era pass laws.

A couple of coloured policemen offered to drive me to the settlement. Like everything in town, the settlement was just a short walk from my home, but I thought it would be interesting to experience the area from a police car. We crossed the informal border between the "coloured area" and the "black area." Most people went into hiding when they saw the police, and suddenly the settlement seemed empty. No one remained on the streets except for a few young children kicking soccer balls. The policemen reminded me never to go there alone. "Do white people ever come here?" I asked. "No," they laughed. "Only farmers go sometimes to pick up workers." I spoke with a Xhosa man whom the police knew. They said that he was a leader of some kind. Under the watchful gaze of the police, I asked how long he had lived in the area. "I've been here for twenty years. I work seasonally on all the different crops, going from farm to farm. Farmers come to pick me up." I asked why he moved here, and he said that it was for the money. "There are no jobs in the Eastern Cape. I have sheep there, and my mother and father are there. I might return when I am a pensioner. . . . I work here, but my heart is there." He said that he sent his kid to school in the Eastern Cape. Despite the long duration of his stay, he had not put down roots in the rooibos-growing area.

Coloured community advocates spoke to the role of labor brokers in employing people like the Xhosa man and in maintaining the separation between coloured and black. Pieter, one such advocate, said that labor brokers used black workers to undermine attempts by coloured workers to demand better conditions. "Seasonal workers," he added. "Farmers make use of cheap labor. They use labor brokers to get workers from other areas, such as the Eastern and Northern Cape provinces. The labor brokers are a huge headache because farmers can pass the non-payment on to the labor broker and blame them. Seasonal workers are exploited. The community blames them for crime—and crime rates do increase." Another resident put the blame for discord between the coloured and black communities directly on labor brokers. "When the chaos [of the xenophobic conflict] broke out," he stated, "the farm brokers, they are not paying them what the Labor Relations Act says, so after the season is over, [black migrants] are squatting here." He described how labor brokers hurt both the coloured community and black migrants, but he also linked his comments to belonging in the region: "It's exploiting our people. It is human trafficking. This thing with the migrant workers, who does the Western Cape belong to?" While he spoke in support of improving black migrants' conditions, he still felt they had no right to be in the region.

When I spoke to a labor broker, however, she had a different take on race and labor conflicts, returning, as many farmers did, to sociological explanations rooted in ethnic inadequacies. She defended using migrant workers despite the high levels of unemployment in the region. An Afrikaner, she spoke slowly in English: "Local people . . . hmmm. . . . for people not from South Africa, it's hard to explain." She began by discussing race relations instead of focusing on economic conditions. "For [coloureds], the blacks are also foreigners. Whites and coloureds have always had the same tradition, the same language, the same church. When they get more money in hand, they are like children. They drink more, so the labor force has weakened. They also qualify for [social welfare payments], so they live off that. The attitude is very day-to-day." I looked to see whether the domestic worker preparing tea nearby heard these comments, but if she did, she gave no indication; her head down, she was seemingly focused on drying dishes. The labor broker continued: "The blacks have a different culture. They are very proud. They like to dress well, have nice cell phones. The other day when they went to a job, I was quite proud of them—they looked so nice. They work well with money."

Like Pieter, she moved back to ideas of belonging in the land. "This is not [black migrants'] proper home. . . . But when it gets to crunch time, the coloured man doesn't show up. . . . And I get a lot of work from farmers because labor is such a problem, the commitment." She differentiated the rooibos industry from other agricultural businesses in ways that reinforced a paternal, familial idea of labor relations. "Citrus and apple are company farmers. They need all the audits, so they won't use informal brokers." She described tea farms not as "company" farms but as "family" farms. Because of this distinction, she said, they were informal about obtaining labor. "They drive into the squatter camp, and someone comes up and says, 'Do you need workers?' And they fill their truck." She considered herself a formal broker, certified by the government, following all the rules. I asked whether it was the informal brokers who used undocumented workers, and she hesitated before responding. "Proper documentation is not," she paused again. "Most of the people in [the area] have been here for many years and still don't have documents. South Africa makes it so hard for them. . . . The rules change all the time. . . . It's all corruption. So the men keep on going [to the refugee office] and don't get helped. Traditionally, those are the people that do the work: Give *them* documents and know who is here. But I also understand the point of view of the farmer, if the farmer needs to harvest, especially with grapes and citrus, he needs it done, so he takes the risk."

We switched to another topic, but before I left, she returned to the issue of why brokers use black migrants instead of local coloured people for farm work. "Even though we [white and coloured] grew up together and played together, when they grow up there is not the same level of labor as with blacks. Coloured women sleep around like rabbits if they are not very religious. But if you are not raised to have a vision and a dream . . ." she said, trailing off. "I have one coloured female team, and I have to lecture them, 'Don't sleep around.'" I looked again to see whether the coloured domestic worker was listening, but she had moved to another room.

"You Can't Find Good Workers Anymore"

"You can't find good workers anymore," white farmers said again and again, re-inforcing the labor broker's tale. The discussion usually started with the words, "I'm not racist, but . . ." Then farmers would describe how local people did not want to work on farms, how they were lazy or drunk. "The day after 'All Pay,' people are too weak to work," one white farmer said, mentioning the day that the government pays out social grants.[5] "On Mondays, they have a hangover. Everyone needs to go to the doctor, but they just have hangovers. Even the best workers have 'Friday Syndrome.' They want the day to end so they can go home to drink." I discussed the *dop* system with some farmers. One farmer responded, "Let me tell you about the unfortunate dop system, or the seemingly unfortunate dop system." He went on to say that the dop system was not bad because it gave only a limited amount of alcohol for the whole weekend. White people had *control* over consumption. "Now you give them money and they buy as much alcohol as they want. It is not in them to stop drinking." Drawing on ideas of stewardship for land and for people, white farm owners described coloured farmworkers as like children who needed to be looked after—and not by the government, but by the farmers, who did a much better job.

Many farmers blamed government All Pay for alcoholism and the perceived lack of available workers. As one farmer said, "Government All Pay is a dop system that the government uses to keep people loyal." While "I'm not racist, but . . . " and phrases like it describe how previously paternalistic attitudes had been redefined since the end of apartheid, relations between white farmers and workers remained largely unchanged. Forms of both intimacy and tension characterized these relationships. When referring to workers, farmers used the words "my workers" or "my people." Workers also came attached to the land—literally. When a farmer bought a new farm, he sometimes "got" the people who lived on the farm, so transactions became about both people and land. And while the tension that comes with these relationships was clear, the intimacy often revealed complex understandings about the role of farmer and farmworker. Like farmers, many farmworkers' families had lived on the land for generations. Their fathers worked on the farm with the farmer's father, and rooibos knowledge passed down from one generation of workers and farmers to the next. As children, they grew up playing together. There was a strong sense that the postapartheid government disrupted these paternal relations, violating an unwritten social contract.

As a result of the perceived lack of local labor, because local people did not "want" to work on farms, the story continues, many farmers *had to* bring in black people from the Eastern Cape, Lesotho, and Zimbabwe. (Never mind that these workers were easily exploited because they were often desperate for work, far from their communities, non-Afrikaans-speaking, and lacking documentation.) So how did farmers explain the increasing informalization of work in the rooibos sector? The take-home message was: We did not decide to stop using permanent workers; we were forced to by the government and by the workers themselves.

Statistics for the percentage of permanent workers versus casual workers and for coloured workers versus black migrant workers did not exist for the rooibos industry in 2010 or 2011. Most evidence instead is anecdotal. In the South African agricultural sector more generally, full-time employment has decreased "significantly" since 1980, with half of all jobs falling in the seasonal or casual category (Munakamwe and Jinnah 2015). This trend was more prevalent in labor-intensive industries such as table grapes and citrus than in crops such as rooibos (Visser and Ferrer 2015). My observations, as well as comments from workers and farm owners in the region, suggest that seasonal workers made up less than half of the workforce, but the percentage was growing, in part because of their lower non-wage costs: Seasonal workers were less likely than permanent workers to receive pension funds, on-farm accommodation, or child care (Visser and Ferrer 2015).

The spatial layout of the community resulted in rumors and silences, in which some issues were made visible and others were hidden from view, creating an affective and sensorial landscape of denial that facilitated farm owners' explanations for their increasing turn toward migrant workers. According to many white people in the region, occasional acts of xenophobic violence had nothing to do with the white community or farms. This belief helped to make invisible the anxiety some white people felt about the growing non-white presence, as black and coloured people far outnumbered whites. Jonas, an Afrikaans farmer, gave his assessment. "Around or just after the time of the [postapartheid] transition we started to have problems with xenophobia in the coloured community. We are watching the situation closely," he said, taking on the role of policemen. "But I worry." A woman added, "There has never been a problem between white and coloured. It's between coloured and black." This distancing allowed white people to displace their anxieties and justify their role in local racial politics by framing themselves as innocent bystanders or even as mediators. A white farmer said that coloured people "are actually despised by black people, but . . . I have a good relationship with the coloured community."

At first glance, the presumed benign relationship between white and coloured seemed to render black migrants as nonpeople, reminiscent of Giorgio Agamben's *homo sacer*, or bare life (Agamben 1998; Hickel 2014). Black people may have been used by the community for labor, but they were forced to live in informal settlements, "zones of exception," from which they could be expelled or even killed if they proved dangerous. At a *braai* (barbeque) one night, a white farmer started telling a story about how his dog had "killed a black." I kept waiting for him to finish the story—a black cat, a black jackal—but no, I realized, he meant a black person. The fact that this death was so casually mentioned and the violence so normalized, without any sense of horror or complicity, exhibited just how nonhuman some residents perceived black migrants to be. "You see, Sarah," people would say, "the thing you need to know about black people is . . ." Or, "The thing you need to understand about the Xhosa . . ." They were the ethnographers, analyzing different "cultures," drinking their beer, wiping the sweat from their brows, and seemingly undaunted by the heat that overwhelmed me. In these narratives, black people appeared voiceless, confined to the kitchens or the fields, sitting in the backs of trucks, standing behind the grocery store drinking beer. To local farmers, black migrants, whether legally or illegally in the area, were mute, unable to cry out against labor violations or low wages.

Yet one of the many fantasies of apartheid control was the idea that whites might see individual black people as nonchalantly killable. When *individual* black people were in white South Africa, they were akin to homo sacer; they were available to exterminate, and "killing a black" became a way to exercise white sovereign command over property. The idea of homo sacer, however, was situational and intimately linked to territory. Behind assertions of power lay a deep fear that blacks, who made up about 80 percent of the country's population, might overcome the last vestiges of white territorial belonging. Taken as a group, black migrants did not represent homo sacer to white (and coloured) residents. Rather, it was the idea of the "stranger" that figured more prominently. Two concepts of the stranger emerge in this discourse: the stranger as irrelevant, a Derridian supplement, like the "black" killed by the dog; and the stranger as more dangerous than the enemy because he sits outside the social order of friend/enemy. As the supplement, the black migrant was neither a plus nor a minus, neither an accident nor an essence. The stranger may have been irreconcilably different, but this difference did not create hostility because it was irrelevant to local concerns of Afrikaans versus English or white versus coloured. How else could the brutal death of a person killed by a dog be spoken of so nonchalantly?

Alternatively, the perceived need for a dog to protect white families, and white women in particular, emerged from the black migrant (typically male) as the ultimate threat—unknown, virile, and strong. Strangers, as Zygmunt Bauman (1990: 294) describes, are not the "as-yet-undecided" but the "undecidable." A number of people mentioned that they owned large dogs to protect their sheep from leopards or other predators and to protect their women from rape at the hands of black men, a theme common on white-owned farms throughout South Africa. In such a context, Bauman argues, the stranger becomes a monster, terrifying because the stranger unmasks the fragility of the social order. Behind the stranger was something menacing: a commanding presence. Out of this fear, then, the black migrant became an easy and unquestioned target for certain forms of violence. In a world in which there are no clear lines, the presence of the stranger is more unnerving than in a world in which the boundaries are fixed.

The naturalization of differentiated racial characteristics informed this structural violence. White commercial farmers who critiqued the use of migrants used language that was strikingly similar to that of those talking about invasive species. To these farmers, strength was not an asset but a danger. Black people outcompeted coloured people. "I prefer coloured workers," one white farmer said. "Black workers are a problem. They are stronger and more aggressive, so they stay and kick out the coloured people." Like the dwindling native cedar tree, the locals were too weak to overpower the unceasing advance of black people. Dubow (1995) describes how coloured people were regarded as in a state of "terminal decline." Black people, by contrast, were conventionally portrayed as strong, and their fertility and "rate of increase" posed a threat to white civilization.

By extension, this masculine strength and fecundity could threaten the coloured population, which is often gendered as effeminate. To protect the coloured population from black workers, the South African Rooibos Council put in place mechanisms designed to give coloured residents labor preferences. Officially, the South African Rooibos Council stipulated that farmers "as far as possible hire only local people" (Pretorius et al. 2011: 18). At the same time, "When filling positions, we do not discriminate against anyone based on race, gender, religion or sexual preference." While espousing nondiscrimination (as outlined by the South African Constitution), the council still advocated for geographical discrimination, emphasizing a kind of undefined localness. What did it mean to be local? Did it mean that the worker was born in the area? That their parents were born in the area? That the worker was coloured and not black?

Despite these unresolved questions, the supposed need for protection seemed to go hand in hand with changing the "culture" of local coloured people so they would tolerate low-paying, unskilled work. The council recognized that rooibos uses "unskilled labour"; therefore, "It is necessary to develop an environment in the business where skills can be transferred and kept within the business. This means generating a culture among seasonal employees that would encourage them to return to the same farm every year." The idea that the local (meaning coloured) culture must be changed bore striking resemblance to some Afrikaans farmers' descriptions of coloured people as nomadic and lazy. It was the culture of the workers that needed to be changed, not the culture of the farmers or the conditions of employment. In a "stakeholder meeting" (which did not include workers) about these standards, everyone who spoke agreed that farmers already followed labor laws and therefore conditions on rooibos farms were acceptable.

Reacting to this discourse, coloured workers, unemployed coloured people, and coloured activists in the region expressed entirely different views. Because of the region's different harvest seasons (rooibos in the summer; citrus in the winter), black migrants could be "seasonal" workers all year long, a fact that hindered financial stability and labor organizing and often infuriated coloured residents. "They don't want to employ local people," one unemployed coloured resident and former farmworker said. "The black people work for lower wages, and they can't complain because they are far from home. They give the workers food but at expensive rates. Housing is in bad condition. There is no electricity or windows." I asked a coloured community worker about the contradiction between the claims of labor scarcity and the simultaneous unemployment in the area. He responded, "Look, if I was a business person, I would also employ people from Lesotho. South Africans know you can go to court; they know the labor laws, the minimum wage, overtime." Another coloured resident said that migrants placed a social burden on the community: "Migrants are in and out. Or they come to the area during the season and stay here, and that causes problems, too, because there are periods when there is no employment. Children are born, and then people are [leaving] the area. Children are left with no families."

What becomes of these children? Are they indigenous? How will their claims to belonging be negotiated in the future? These were questions I could not answer. Yet they highlighted how concerns about migrants both magnified and muted the noise around other kinds of threats in the area, such as decreasing employment opportunities that resulted from new, more mechanized farming practices and increasingly neoliberal economic policies, as well as structural and physical violence against the coloured community, uncertainty about the place of white and coloured people in a postapartheid future, and fear that climate change might alter the fynbos ecosystem. Concern over what would become of the children could have been reframed around questions of what would become of the region in the postapartheid political and economic climate. Or, perhaps more concretely for the coloured community, would they ever overcome the ingrained racism that denied them land, belonging, and economic power?

Good Seeds, Bad Seeds: Contextual Value and Weedy Outbreaks

The assumption of territorial and cultural congruence that has underpinned
the modern nation-state has as its corollary the need to sort those who belong from
those who don't: a process [similar] to gardening. . . . But the problem with maintaining
gardens . . . is the inevitable outbreak of weeds: "the uninvited, unplanned, self-controlled
plants" that are ever ready to subvert the established order. —NIGEL CLARK,
"The Demon Seed," quoting Zygmunt Bauman, "Modernity and Ambivalence"

During the dry months of summer, the rooibos-growing area's landscape was a
vision of contrasts. Having not received rain for weeks—or even months—the
mountains and rooibos fields turned a muted green-brown, interrupted by the
occasional blooming protea flower, whose ability to create color in the desert-
like dryness startled the eye. Yet interspersed in this vast brown landscape were
lush green groves of citrus trees that stretched along the Olifants River and up
into the hills. The citrus fields were a critical part of the regional economy,
so central that a town even bore the name, Citrusdal (Citrus Valley in English). Many farmers grew both rooibos and other crops, and they discussed
the dangers of invasive species, just as their irrigated citrus trees, grapevines,
and potato fields thrived under the care of pesticides, fertilizers, and water that
drained the region's water table and disrupted the indigenous fynbos ecosystem. The "thirsty species," then, were not just the Australian Port Jacksons, but
also the crops. One of the main reasons that water was so important to farmers
was that they needed it to grow these foreign crops, which would quickly die
in the dry climate.

What made a plant invasive? The answer for local farmers was clearly not
just being foreign. Rather, defining invasive species seemed inextricably tied to
notions of economic and cultural value and affective feelings of desire, danger,
and fear. The idea of alienness took on additional importance and nuance in
relation to rooibos's celebrated nativity. Pooley's investigation of nineteenth-
and twentieth-century botany in South Africa, and in the Western Cape in
particular, describes the significance of definitions. He focuses on early botanical uses of the words "indigenous," "aliens," and "natural."[6] "Aliens," according to Pooley, were introduced purposefully or accidentally by people.
Aliens become naturalized when they survive more than one life cycle without
human intervention. "Alien invasive" plants are introduced plants that reproduce quickly. "Weeds," by contrast, are undesirable but can be either foreign or
indigenous. According to Pooley, when "invasives" were first studied in South
Africa in the late nineteenth century, researchers actually focused on plants
that had invaded productive agricultural land and not "wild" lands. Whether
or not invasives were introduced or indigenous was of less importance than

their presence on farms—non-native species were considered alien only if they threatened agriculture. The idea of the alien, then, is contextual and unstable. Crops may have many of the qualities of invasives because farmers breed them for strength, adaptability, and reproducibility. Yet cultural perceptions and economic interests play a role in determining whether these crops are "useful" or "weeds." In these definitions, alien invasives emerge more as matter that is "out of control" than as matter that is "out of place."

While conservationists, farmers, and residents in the rooibos region talked incessantly about problems with Australian Port Jackson trees and other invasive plants, the industry itself had battled a poor environmental reputation, inspiring a biodiversity initiative that was later named "Right Rooibos." Conservationists and botanists cited uncontrolled expansion of cultivated rooibos into the "natural," "wild" environment. "I want to make rooibos thrive in harmony with nature and people of the area like it once did, not a monoculture. [We have to] make sure it does not destroy our heritage," one environmental worker said. His use of the word "heritage" was telling: If rooibos is the country's heritage, how could its growth simultaneously destroy that heritage? In a paper on rooibos biodiversity, Gerhard Pretorius (n.d.) describes indigenous plants threatened by rooibos. *Cullumia floccose*, for example, grows only near a small town in the sandy parts of the rooibos-growing area. The flower is listed as "critically endangered" because it is known to exist in only two sites. As a result of rooibos tea and potato cultivation, the flower has lost more than 80 percent of its habitat over the past twenty-five years. Despite farmers' and industry affirmations of rooibos's harmony with the ecosystem, its fecundity as a cultivated crop could turn the indigenous into the dangerous.

Conservationists typically blamed the tea's increasing popularity as a global commodity for the industry's rapid growth and its subsequent increasing pressure on the region's "critical biodiversity." In 2010, the total footprint of the rooibos crop was about 79,000 hectares (Conservation South Africa 2011). About half of this footprint lay in the Sandveld region, an area that, according to Conservation South Africa, was the second most highly threatened ecosystem in the country. The organization argued that farmers cleared an average of 2.7 hectares of northern Sandveld natural vegetation a day.

Through an environmental lens, rooibos became invasive. In a context in which ideas of pristine nature served as the moral arbiter of indigeneity, Conservation South Africa did not always consider rooibos "natural vegetation." Some scientists and environmental groups deemed the farming of cultivated rooibos harmful to wild rooibos, as rooibos made the transition from weed to commodity. One conservationist explained that land clearing was being investigated. She said that more than 70 percent of rooibos farmers regularly plowed illegally, even as rooibos was "put out there as indigenous and low-input farming." Plowing fynbos for rooibos, then, was akin to plowing a national treasure, only to replace it with another national treasure. What if the indigenous plant itself was a commodity that blurred the line between "good" and "bad," "in control" and "out of control"?

Conservationists envisioned removing or controlling invasives—including cultivated rooibos—to save an imagined, pristine nature. They employed discourses of morality different from those of farmers and private enterprises. This morality became even more complicated by the fact that rooibos is part of a global commodity market. Perhaps surprisingly, even rooibos farmers occasionally blurred the moral certainty of planting indigenous species. Albie, an Afrikaans farmer, said, "Many farmers keep the land too clean. They have huge monocrops of rooibos, and they leave no space for the endemic species." In Albie's language, rooibos can be both endemic and harmful to endemicism. Rooibos, then, was every category at once.

"Culture Makes a Difference"

White and coloured residents ascribed a volatile, contextual danger to migrants similar to the risks they associated with plants: Migrants could also be every category at once. Despite worries that foreign people would threaten safety and undermine long-standing paternalistic labor relations, farmers did not rely solely on the migrants who made their way to the area by hitching rides along the N7 roadway. White commercial farmers said that they would drive great distances for workers, and some even searched as far as the Lesotho border. Like the labor broker, farm owners sometimes pronounced black migrant workers the saviors of the region's perceived labor shortage and, more specifically, of its "coloured problem." "We *have* to import labor," an Afrikaans farmer stated. "It's like your Mexico problem. I bus my workers in from the Transvaal because they are willing to work." Yet like the discourse that follows the "Mexico problem," the farmer described the presence of migrants as both a need and a problem.

Some white farmers preferred black migrants' supposedly innate strength. "You get a much better quality of worker from other places," one farmer said. Farmers discussed in detail the essentialized qualities of each "tribe." "On the farm, we have forty permanent workers, all coloured, and sixty to eighty extra laborers, all black," he said. The black migrants were "extra" or excess—superfluous in their individuality, easily replaced and interchangeable. "The Xhosa are particularly strong, but lazy," he continued. "The Sothos and the Tswana are nice, but the Xhosas give them trouble." This evaluation shifted slightly from farmer to farmer. Another white farmer stated, "Black people are much better workers. The Sotho are good workers. Guys from Zimbabwe are harder workers. They have education and are willing to work for half the price. The Sotho are not drinking. They are always on time. The Xhosas are not reliable." Every farmer seemed to have his own preference, choosing workers based on their perceived cultural attributes. "Culture makes a difference," yet another white farmer said. He explained how black people were easier to manage and had a cheaper standard of living than coloured people. Using the same discourse that informed apartheid-era policies, he recoded capitalism and competitive advantage through a discourse of culture (Wolpe 1972). "The seasonal workers are black people," he said. "They will go and buy milk, maize. They don't buy like the local people. They eat different things, like *pap*. Their food is cheaper because of their culture. . . . Just look at what different cultures buy at Spar [the local grocery store]."

Conversations about cultural difference infused discussions of "legality." Many foreign workers were in the area "illegally" (although people remarked that the Department of Home Affairs rarely came to remote farms due to understaffing and lack of political will). An official described how to work legally in the region: "You must have a valid passport from your country, and then you must have a letter of appointment that says you can work. The farmers have to advertise in national advertisement so that South Africans can apply first." He discussed the idea of geographical preference, an emphasis on localness. "They have to apply to the department that they need X number of seasonal workers and X amount from X country. They must give information and the reason why they are not hiring South Africans and how many South Africans are employed on the farm. For example, if you want a tractor driver, you must prove that you cannot find anyone to do it," the official continued. "But the argument of the farmer is that the coloured people are lazy. They say it's not their fault. 'It's the coloured people. Coloured people are lazy.'"

White farmer after white farmer expressed similar feelings about the quality of black workers. "Previously," one farmer said, "it was said to be because [black people] would work for less. But it is not so much anymore because they are strict on minimums and there are inspectors. I think now it is because [blacks] are prepared to work very hard, unlike local people, who are not as eager to work very hard. It's very difficult to find people to work. It's a cultural thing. They have less respect for work. They don't want to work because of government money. They are not brought up with an energetic vibe to succeed." Another resident said that the rooibos-growing area has "illegal workers coming from Lesotho. During raids, they are hard to tell apart from black South Africans because they share the same Xhosa language. But generally, if they are good workers, they are from Lesotho." This statement only reinforced the view of black migrants as an undifferentiated horde: Sesotho and isiXhosa are entirely different languages.

Discussions of black workers echo what Peter Geschiere (2009) has described as colonial preference for migrants. Because migrants do not belong to the soil, they cannot challenge colonists' claims to it. In this manner, black people could both threaten *and* protect naturalized ideas of white belonging. One coloured resident echoed many of the white farmers' descriptions. But he added his own critique that reflected racially tinged discussions of migration and labor struggles around the globe, including what the farmers described as my "Mexico problem." He insisted that black migrants provided a means for white farmers to undermine labor laws. "South Africans have education. In Lesotho they have no standards. The Zimbabweans are very educated, but they are desperate," he said. "South Africans have family, so they won't work on the weekends. The Zimbabweans have nothing else to do. When you are a foreigner in South Africa, [the farmer] provides a house. And three hundred rands is enough for them." Three hundred rands amounted to approximately $25 at the current exchange rate. He continued by explaining why he thought local people might be hesitant to take farm jobs: "The wages are terrible. That's why some people don't see the value in being a worker. Nothing will encourage you to go be a worker." Another coloured resident explained that there were loopholes in the issue of legality that further undermined coloured workers. "The farmer will get twenty blank permits," he said. "Then he will go to the border and get people. It costs money, so the farmers don't want to bring them back. You are responsible for those people. But when the season is about to end, they chase people away or tell the police they have illegal people." According to this description, some migrants were not necessarily "escaping the control" of farmers but also being abandoned, too poor to make the trip back to where they came from and stranded in a land where they had no claim. This description differs drastically from what farmers said; they insisted that even when they returned the workers, the workers simply came back year after year, like the Australian Port Jackson trees.

Emile, an Afrikaans farmer, spoke at length about the region's changing demographics. We sat in his office, a hot dusty room with a hard cement floor and broken-paned windows next to a large concrete barn. He offered me tea prepared by his coloured domestic worker, and we sipped from our cups together as he described the many changes he had seen in the past thirty years.

EMILE: When I grew up there were two black people in the area, two Malawians. They are still here actually, in their nineties. Black people came in the mid-1980s as migrant labor, mostly from the Eastern Cape. The thing with migrant labor is they stay. Even up until five years ago it was different. But it's all changing, for better and worse.

ME: Why for better?

EMILE: There is a bigger pool of labor. I don't think people realize how much things have changed in the last twenty years. Agriculture wouldn't be where it is today without the labor. Migrant labor is black.

ME: Then what is worse?

EMILE: They brought crime, uncontrolled development which wasn't there before. It brought suppression of [coloured] people because they are a small minority with no economic might. They were the underdog under apartheid and now they are the underdog again. They have no bargaining power.

ME: Why don't they have bargaining power?

EMILE: The coloureds and the blacks don't like each other. As a culture, the coloured people are not in a good place.

ME: What do you mean they are not in a good place?

EMILE (ignoring or not hearing my question and pointing to people doing work outside): See, the workers are all black. The man in charge—let me wait for him to turn around, yes—the man leading them is coloured.

Our discussion touched on how migration patterns had changed since the end of apartheid laws. People were now "allowed to move from place to place." Emile described the racialization of labor in the region, as most farmers used black people for seasonal labor, but he also described the danger that these "aliens" brought with them. He expressed sympathy with the plight of coloured workers yet hired mostly black labor himself. This racialization—whites as farm owners, coloureds as permanent or domestic workers, and blacks as seasonal workers was common in many parts of rooibos country.

During harvest season, the presence of black people was obvious and increasingly part of conversations with white and coloured residents. There were more black people in town, at stores, and at the outdoor market. But the difference was especially acute on farms. During the harvest, I spoke with Koos, an Afrikaans farmer. I met him at his house, and we went to the farmyard. It was toward the end of the day, and the light was beginning to fade, leaving behind only the heat. As we chatted, large trucks came in from the fields. They stopped, kicking up dust around us, and people began jumping out. All of a sudden there were more than a hundred people in the formerly empty yard, coloured permanent workers on one side and black seasonal workers on the other. They quickly hushed when they saw the farm owner and stood looking at us, tea-cutting sickles dangling from their arms. "It's Friday," the farmer said. "You will see them all in town tomorrow. . . . We take them to town once a week on Saturdays to take money out of the bank to spend it all on alcohol." I wondered how my facial expression looked to the farmer. "You don't want to see them in town tomorrow," he added.

The farmer exchanged a few words about the day with his manager and then took me inside to talk. He explained that he paid his workers by the kilogram of tea harvested instead of through regular wages. Black seasonal workers made two or three times the minimum wage, he said, which at the time was about seven rands per hour, or less than $1 (Department of Labour 2016). He described a typical day for a migrant worker: "They don't have working hours, so they usually start really early in the morning until it gets hot, and then work again at night." He felt that local people would not agree to that schedule. "Our local people won't make normal pay. They have an easier way of life. They have medical, they have homes, but migrant workers don't have much food to get through the spare time of year," he said. "And the migrant workers, the blacks, they will work Saturdays. They are desperate for money. The farmer next to me has eighty people from Zimbabwe, a lot of them have degrees. They speak better English than I do." (Emile was a native Afrikaans speaker and wanted to speak to me in English to practice his language skills.) "Local people, if they can work on Saturday, will like to be paid more," he continued. "Our people got too much comfortable." Another farmer lamented that he now hired black people instead of local coloured residents, but "they work harder. In the end, the coloureds are the people who suffer. We aren't family ourselves, but close to family." Denying any genetic relationship, the farmer nevertheless felt that he was violating an unspoken social and moral contract, hundreds of years of paternalist master-servant connections solidified in the rooibos land.

Rooibos farmers often described this kind of morality in their discussions about the size of their farms, which many characterized as a "choice" to protect the community—defined by its ecosystem and its demographics—from change. Franz, an Afrikaans farmer, spoke about his hopes for the future of his farm: "Small is beautiful. It is a business, too, but with a heart. We have a small, conservative community to keep you in line. We have open space. We all work together. We help each other. We share tractors and workers." He said that he did not want to increase his rooibos production; instead, he wanted to maintain a way of life that, for him, extended indefinitely back in time. "It's how my forefathers would have liked," he explained. "I don't want a big commercial farm. We haven't strange people here. We are lucky. But we don't want to get too big. It's a good life we've got. I don't think there is a chance for big farming enterprises." But, he added, "I am happy and want to live like this away from outsiders."

"I Believed in White People"

This "guilt" over hiring "outsider" black workers, however, also appeared to be linked to fear. According to many in the white community, "escaped" black migrants could be politically and criminally dangerous. Rumors ran rampant that the ANC had bused black people to the area to gather votes for the first democratic election in 1994 and then again for the municipal election in March 2011. Supposedly, white people bused in black people for work, while black people bused in more black people for political power. The tensions and contradictions in these alliances and conflicts destabilized ideas of distance and difference among the white, coloured, and black communities.

In fact, in 2011 the rooibos region did experience increased politicization compared with surrounding municipalities in the Western Cape. On the day of the municipal election, hotly contested between the locally dominant Democratic Alliance (considered by many the "white party") and the ANC, I sat at a rural polling station on a farm. The polling station was quiet, a change from the rollicking party at the "coloured high school" in town, where music played, *rooster brood* grilled on *braais*, and people gathered to vote and socialize. At the farm station, I spoke with ANC representatives who sat on folding chairs under the shade of a tree. All of a sudden, a truckload of farmworkers came down the road, dust billowing up behind them, as it had been months since the last rain. *"Amandla!* Viva ANC!" they chanted, fists raised, calling out the Zulu/Xhosa word for power. *"Awethu!"* (Ours!), the representatives called back. Combined, the chant implies "Power to the People."

The use of this language, the language of the "black struggle," is significant because the workers and the representatives were Afrikaans-speaking co-loured people. Coloured political organizers and unions were using migrants to change the area's political power. While coloured-black political alliances were common in much of South Africa, that had not been the case in the rooibos region. During apartheid, the area was decidedly apolitical, with few people actively involved in the struggle, and the end of apartheid was met with an ambiguous response from many coloured residents. Some worried about losing their relative privilege vis-à-vis black South Africans. Or they feared black South Africans who were rumored to espouse revolutionary political views. In the first democratic election in 1994, the National Party, the primarily Afrikaans party of apartheid, maintained its majority in the Cederberg municipality despite overwhelming victories by the ANC in most of the country. Hermann, a coloured resident, spoke of his experience protesting apartheid. "We would have to go underground to visit the farms in the vineyards and fields of the farmers," he said. "We would do little things like stealing grapes." I asked Hermann what motivated him. "Well," he said, "because we were on the farm, I believed in white people. My father said, 'Those white people will never lie,' and I proved him wrong. They brainwashed our people and our parents. My relative was even a political leader of the New National Party." Another coloured resident said bluntly, "Clanwilliam was not active during the apartheid struggle.... The community was in love with, the whole community was in love with apartheid. I am speaking about the coloured community."

Denied land and denied a political identity, a preponderance of coloured people in the rooibos region voted to keep in place the very government that had codified their inferior status.[7] More than fifteen years after apartheid, some coloured rooibos workers still maintained this position. When I spoke with one coloured worker on that election day in 2011, he said, "There are immigrants from the African continent. It's actually quite scary. If you travel and leave the Western Cape, you feel everywhere you look, you see black. I don't feel that here. It's a feeling I'd like to maintain.... The black influence, the politics of this country are not good."

Yet the political climate was changing. Despite the continued xenophobia, the "aliens" (those, at least, who had citizenship) and the locals appeared to be voting together. While coloured residents remained separate and often hostile to black migrants socially, the two groups aligned politically in the 2011 elections. That alliance made the black migrants "dangerous" to white political power. While the Democratic Alliance, supported by nearly every white resident with whom I spoke, had held the majority of seats in the Cederberg municipality, the 2011 results left the ANC with five seats and the Democratic

Alliance with only four, despite the fact that the Western Cape was the only province not controlled by the ruling ANC. Often unable to communicate linguistically, coloured and black workers chanted "Amandla!" together.

Despite political unity between some black and coloured residents, many white farmers asserted that "their" coloured workers supported the Democratic Alliance and that the coloured people who voted for the ANC were being manipulated by outsiders. As a result of these perceived political betrayals, white farmers felt conflicted about migrants. Although farmers saw additional laborers as necessary to compete in a changing, uncertain global agrarian market, they also felt that "outsiders" contributed to a different kind of uncertainty, as the increased movement offered by the end of apartheid-era pass laws helped foster a rapid increase in the black population. Many coloured community organizers argued that farm owners said coloured workers were too expensive because of the government's new labor laws and thus preferred the more easily exploitable migrants.

Aliens among Aliens

The threat of migrants—of alien invasives—to both Afrikaans and coloured residents in the rooibos region was doubly problematic because of their own uncertain connections to the land. While no one disputed rooibos's indigeneity, the indigeneity of local residents was seemingly always precarious and relational. Allaine Cerwonka (2004) describes how even people who do not cross borders can become deterritorialized by increasing ethnic, racial, and cultural diversity that undermines understandings of local social relations. Coloured farmers' concerns over the presence of black people epitomized the potential for this form of deterritorialization, but they also challenged it. How do you "deterritorialize" a people—coloured people—who have never been allotted a territory in the first place, who are supposedly always alien to everywhere and whose very identities are denied cultural or place-based authenticity?

Jason Hickel (2014) argues that interpretations of xenophobia as strictly involving the anomie of neoliberal globalization and its attendant flows of goods and people misunderstand how communities comprehend and incorporate social disruptions. By examining the 2008 xenophobic violence in Durban, South Africa, he maintains that when migrants become connected to local communities, they can cease to be dangerous. Yet the rooibos region reflected still more complex notions of incorporation because of residents' own uncertain belonging. In *Purity and Exile*, Malkki (1995: 4) explores how refugees in Tanzania are imbricated in issues of classification and liminality. They are, she describes, out of category in "anthropology and in the national order of things." She shows how refugees become abominations to our understanding of human taxonomy, citing Victor Turner's work on liminality. "Transitional beings," Turner writes, "are particularly polluting, since they are neither one thing nor another; or maybe both; or neither here nor there; or maybe even nowhere (in terms of any recognized cultural topography), and are at the very least 'betwixt and between' all the recognized fixed points in the space-time of cultural classifications" (1996: 7). How do we understand these cultural topographies in a place where everyone seemingly is considered taxonomically problematic, where everyone could be a transitional being? In such a context, violence against perceived others could be easily legitimized and "blurry lines" rendered intolerable.

Who and what, in this context, are the weeds? Certainly, Afrikaans and coloured residents described black people and Australian plants as foreign. Black migrants came recently. They did not own land; their blood had not mingled with the soil. Or perhaps more accurate, the fact that local farmers rendered black migrants' labor invisible made their connections to the soil invisible. They could be easily argued away in claims to cultural rootedness. Like alien invasive plants, they arrived from elsewhere, bringing good, bad, and at times unforeseen consequences. Black people provided cheap and supposedly strong labor, but they also brought the potential for politicization. It was when they stayed and were no longer transitional beings—when they became involved (or were perceived to be involved) with politics; when they "mingled with local women," as one coloured resident said—that they became dangerous. At the same time, Australian Port Jackson trees sucked dry the few water sources with their insatiable demand for water, while citrus and grapes brought relative wealth to the region.

Conclusion

"The local species can't compete," Willem, a white conservationist working in the rooibos region, explained. "The alien invasives are too strong for them. They beat them out of their habitat." Willem described the Port Jackson trees that had taken over precious water and land from the fragile local ecosystem, disrupting the delicate balance of endemic plants, soil, and insects. This fear of alien plants' comparative strength directly mirrored the language used to describe black people. "The town isn't the same as it used to be," Japie, a coloured resident, told me shortly after my conversation with Willem. "There are so many black people. It's scary." Japie's assertion drew both from a concrete concern over job competition and from centuries of discourse about the character of black South Africans.

This chapter described how coloured and white residents articulated an alien invasion of foreign plants and people that threatened indigeneity and local belonging. Yet in the rooibos region, the alien people and plants were potentially both pariahs and saviors. Farm owners saw migrant workers as solving a perceived labor shortage and providing a less expensive labor force to help them maintain profitability in a shifting agrarian landscape in which family farms were losing ground to corporatized agribusinesses. However, an uneasy alliance was forming among coloured workers and black migrants, as many attempted to challenge the local political dominance of the Democratic Alliance and the economic power of the white farmers.

Tensions remained, however, around exactly what constituted foreignness and when this foreignness was and was not acceptable. Some conservationists pardoned invasive plants that helped the agricultural industry. To help stop erosion on rooibos land, for example, the *Right Rooibos Handbook* (Pretorius et al. 2011) actually mentioned planting grasses native to India. Farmers, industry leaders, and conservationist justified this slippage by invoking economic and environmental reasons. Yet central to these discussions remained the concepts of indigeneity and belonging, who and what had a rightful claim to the soil. Foreignness was not necessarily mapped to the boundaries of the modern nation-state. Rather, the concept of the alien was regional, even ecological, in scale. Drawing on discourses of fear, morality, and economic necessity, discussions of alien invasives were highly emotive, even as they used the supposedly neutral language of science and economics.

How were the ever-shifting concepts of good and bad aliens resolved? Among the rooibos-growing community, the tensions were never resolved, with people often contradicting themselves multiple times within the same conversation. While residents articulated concerns over the foreign in highly localized terms, Nyamnjoh (2006) describes the "growing preoccupation with belonging" in Africa and in the world as part of neoliberal globalization. The attendant "paradoxes of flows and closures, empowerment and enslavement, hope and disappointment," he argues, contain new inclusions and exclusions (Nyamnjoh 2006: 4). Comaroff and Comaroff (1999: 17) ask why "immigrants—those wanderers in pursuit of work whose proper place is always elsewhere—become pariah citizens of a global order in which, paradoxically, old borders are said everywhere to be dissolving?" They describe this seeming incongruity as one of the tensions inherent in contemporary capitalism. The only things that remain "pure" are endemic plants such as rooibos.

Thus, the stakes for claiming a cultural connection to rooibos are economically and symbolically high.

Yet rooibos farmers simultaneously relied on a "scaling-up" of rooibos's commodity chain beyond the region to finance their insular way of life. This "scaling-up" had its own consequences, as the unique fynbos ecosystem became increasingly visible to the national and international environmental community. International environmental groups often emphasize that "we are all one world" and that the environment should be protected for the greater good of humanity. The area that includes the fynbos ecosystem is a World Heritage Site; it is in the *world's* interest to protect it because is one of the *world's* biodiversity hot spots. It is important, one conservationist involved with the rooibos industry said, to appeal to the "consumer perception internationally." As rooibos "spreads to the world," he continued, it must follow international standards about environmental sustainability. A World Heritage Site and a globalized commodity, rooibos became the world's possession and not just the local people's or the local ecosystem's.

Nigel Clark (2002) critiques what he sees as a new international environmentalism, which he believes is premised on the idea that, undisturbed by people, nature is harmless, maintaining its proper, natural place. Clark points to a contradiction in responses to alien people and alien plants: "We are being called on to act as cosmopolitans as we explore the potentialities of culture, but to revert to an older construction of environmentalism when we consider the fate of nature" (Clark 2002: 5). Culture is "allowed" to be dynamic, "both self-transforming and responsible for the mobilization and transmutation of the material world."

In the rooibos region, moral valuations of indigeneity and foreignness had vastly different meanings and consequences for plants than for people. Some residents were "resigned" to the fact that the arrival of black people was inevitable. "We have to work with it," a white resident said. Other residents were finding possibilities in the changing demographics, while still others claimed that they would fight off foreigners at all costs. Notions of local, national, and international belonging informed some social and environmental initiatives in the region at the same as other initiatives attempted to delineate and harden local borders. As Douglas (2002 [1966]) describes, disorder can symbolize both danger and power: We recognize that disorder is unlimited, and its potential for patterning is indefinite. What this potential holds for the rooibos region's future was uncertain and linked to narrations of rooibos's past and rumors about its present.

{ 4 }

RUMOR, CONSPIRACY, AND
THE POLITICS OF NARRATION

There are bigger political things happening, and people get
sidetracked [by] conspiracies of who benefited and this and that.
—LOCAL COMMUNITY ORGANIZER

There are animosities and sympathies
in rooibos on a personal level. —LOCAL RESIDENT

While I had been in uncomfortable situations during my time in South Africa, this time felt different. I received a call while I was in the library. My phone signaled "Unknown Number," and I thought it might have been a farmer whom I had been trying to reach. "I don't like people going behind my back," the voice said. "You can't talk to anyone without me present, and I am too busy. I can talk to you next year." He hung up abruptly. I had somehow wandered into a politically charged situation about which—at that moment—I had no clue. I walked home from the library going through a million reasons I might have received this call, and they all led back to the same thing: the government-subsidized rooibos factory just across the border in the Northern Cape.

Of all the rumors that dominated conversations in the rooibos-growing area, none was more controversial than this factory. Rumors spanned the entire spectrum of cronyism and corruption, job creation and job destruction, racism toward coloured people and racism toward white people, and positive hopes or dismal prognoses for the future. I never heard the same story twice. The confusion the factory generated and people's inability to situate it as "right" or "left," white, black, or coloured forced it into a liminal space. This liminality seemed to transform the factory into an abstract painting: It could be interpreted to confirm either hopes or fears about the postapartheid future. One farmer even asserted that the government used "rumor mongering" to cover up its lack of transparency and public participation.

In a small farming community, rumors such as the ones that surrounded the rooibos factory were an everyday part of social and business interactions. Narratives of Shakespearean-style betrayals, public fights, political graft, and corporate greed informed gossip exchanged among farmers, farmworkers, and other residents. Battles over rooibos became so heated in one religious community that congregants refused to share a communion cup. People repeatedly warned that "rooibos is a minefield" and "rooibos is run by a mafia." These discussions were typically not about the crop itself but, rather, about the personal, racial, and religious feuds that surrounded it. "What's the story about the tea?" one farmer asked. "There is always stories . . . always gossiping and wondering."

The gossip and feuds drew on the seemingly infinite number of rooibos cosmologies expressed by farmers, workers, and industry players. As I described in previous chapters, for many the heritage of the tea was synonymous with their own heritage. Emotionally charged discussions of cultural ownership— whether the tea belonged to coloured farmers or to Afrikaans farmers or to workers or even to South Africa as a whole—were tied to the region's historical structures of inequality, to dispossessions of land, to the tight controls of apartheid, and later to the uncertainties of a postapartheid future. Against this backdrop, rooibos farmers had much more at stake in the plant's history and speculation about its future than a recounting of facts or the creation of a story palatable for consumers. Numerous people asked me which "version" of rooibos's history I had heard so that they could set me straight.

This chapter uses "versions" to explore how the rumors surrounding rooibos were entangled with political and economic struggles over labor, livelihoods, and social belonging. Beginning with rooibos's founding parables, the chapter pays particular attention to how these narrativized histories both affected and were constitutive of people's understandings of current political, economic, and environmental trends. I want to emphasize that the truth or falsity of these narratives is not my main concern. Rather, I take seriously how rumors, gossip, and cosmologies influenced local residents' worldviews and had concrete effects on the people and the plant. As other scholars of rumor have argued, regardless of verfication, stories and their ideological contexts—whether historical transition, social dislocation, or power hierarchies—can create intimacy or disunity, cause violence or foster hope (Haviland 1977; Stewart and Strathern 2004; White 2000). Rooibos rumors were not necessarily a result of farmers' ignorance about the workings of political economy (although some residents did make that argument). Rather, they were tied to a lack of communication and to the energy involved in shaping the region's place in a postapartheid and "globalizing" world. Rumor forged residents' dynamic understandings of and contestations over their lived experiences.

While previous chapters underscored the ecologies of belonging and exclusion in the rooibos region, this chapter addresses the issues about which residents spoke most often and most passionately. Through a discussion of their narratives, I show how written histories can go only so far in describing the area. Instead, I articulate the history that was *at work* in the region. Some of the histories, rumors, and gossip that I describe may run counter to official narratives, but these were the stories that people repeated. They were the daily, lived histories that became sedimented in the landscape. Through their retelling, the stories gained lives of their own.

Rooibos narratives provide a regionally specific lens through which to address how the macroeconomic, globalizing processes of neoliberalism interweave with fights over a distinctly ecological notion of cultural belonging and indigeneity. The term "neoliberalism" has taken on a scholarly life of its own with multiple definitions, making it a "slippery, hazy and contentious category" (Wacquant 2012: 68). Following James Ferguson, this chapter will refer to neoliberalism as a macroeconomic doctrine that includes a valorization of privatization at the expense of the state, a fetishism of the free market, a desire to eliminate tariffs, and an enterprise model of the state that would allow it to "run like a business" (Ferguson 2010: 179). At first glance, the rooibos industry appears to follow the classic narrative of neoliberal economic transition: After decades of state subsidies and pricing controls, the industry privatized in the early 1990s. Privatization led in part to the consolidation of land and wealth in the hands of a few and to rising economic inequality. Concurrently, the region saw an increase in the presence of global agribusiness as the end of apartheid marked the opening of barriers to international trade. Changing economic and political policies also resulted in the rise of public-private partnerships within the industry, and nongovernmental organizations (NGOs) began taking over roles previously controlled by the government, including many social services. As the rooibos industry turned to cultural marketing, the area also experienced a rise in the commodification of an "indigenous" ethnicity.

Yet this rendering of the rooibos industry's history would miss how neoliberal policies interacted with the local social, political, and agrarian landscape (Bernstein 1996; Hart 2002). Rooibos's "tea stories" show what happens when the idea of neoliberalism comes into contact with a government whose implementation of and desire for neoliberal reforms is haphazard and with an agricultural product that farmers refuse to call a "commodity" because it acted as an everyday, inalienable part of their existence. Hardly a case of pure market fundamentalism, discourses of postapartheid hope and excitement about new farming practices and about the potential for economic expansion ran alongside heated discussions of blame for changes to the landscape and the community: blame the farmers, blame the outsiders, blame the government, blame the workers, blame the rooibos companies, blame nature, blame international certifiers, and so on. While the privatization of the rooibos industry was reflective of an increasingly neoliberal global economic climate, it also interrupted grand narratives of neoliberalism: Privatization marked a continuation of economic policies that often focused on racial politics first and the market second. Rooibos's "family farms" represented not relics of a bygone form of agriculture but, rather, sites where the tensions in neoliberalism were contested through the interconnected lives of people and the crops on which they depended.

Rooibos rumors moved among the individual, the political, the personal, the local, the national, and the global while simultaneously blurring the distinction among these scales. Through a selection of rumors, I consider how residents negotiated, made sense of, and attempted to control a shifting agrarian landscape. The stories provide insight into the constitution of the object—rooibos—rather than just casting the object as a thing of truth. Emphasizing the power of narration, I show how rooibos's commodity history interweaves the language of globalization, nostalgia, and class with highly emotive ideas of ecological belonging and changing but persistent structures of inequality in the region. As I outlined in the first three chapters, claims to rooibos were critically important for the coloured population, whose pathologized heritage made a place-based identity uncertain and who owned just a small percentage of rooibos land. Rooibos ownership was also crucial to the Afrikaans farming population who linked their personal and cultural identities with the tea and the farming lifestyle that it imparted. What, people asked, is "a boer without boerdery" (a farmer without a farm)?

In addressing the industry's history and the stakes of this history for coloured and white residents, I lay the groundwork for the final chapter in which I discuss the sense of anxiety and foreboding in the region regarding its political, economic, and environmental future. Rooibos *was* becoming a globalized commodity, and its rising economic value led to the increased value of the previously marginal land. Yet the increased value resulted in a variety of consequences that did not always signal an improvement in livelihoods or access to land. The final chapter tackles issues of land and politics directly by showing how the bravado expressed by many white farmers hinted at fears about the security of their tenure on the land—and in the country as a whole—just as coloured and black residents negotiated the seemingly unmovable force of failed postapartheid hope.

Rumor, Gossip, and Cosmologies

People do not speak with truth, with a concept of the accurate description of what they saw, to say what they mean, but they construct and repeat stories that carry the values and meanings that most forcibly get their points across. People do not always speak from experience—even when that is considered the most accurate kind of information—but speak with stories that circulate to explain what happened.
—LUISE WHITE, *Speaking with Vampires*

In the mid-century, the South African anthropologist Max Gluckman (1963: 307) declared gossip and scandal to be two of the most important "societal and cultural phenomena we are called upon to analyze." While it may seem trivial, gossip was central to social dynamics in the rooibos region. More than any other topic, making sure that I understood *their* perspectives on local rumors became the driving force of my conversations. During some interviews, residents would ask to check my notebook to make sure that I had gotten the details of their narratives correct. In other interviews, people would ask first to hear which account of a rumor I had heard so that they could provide the counterargument—or the "true story."

Gluckman argues that gossip is central because it creates social ties of intimacy, maintains unity, and enforces morality. He asserts that the actual subject of the gossip is secondary to the act of gossiping. Instead, he offers a functionalist interpretation: Gossip and rumor reinforce social norms. Like Gluckman, Mary Douglas (1970) sees narratives as explanations for how ambiguities and discrepancies in meaning can be tolerated and resolved. Other scholars describe gossip and rumor as means to increase social standing (Paine 1967), entertain (Rosnow and Fine 1976), explain cultural change (Turner 1996 [1957]), and police deviance (White 2000). As the psychologists Sarah Wert and Peter Salovey (2004: 77) note, "Almost as many functions of gossip have been argued as writers to write about gossip."

Gluckman points to the significance of exploring people's narratives about their social worlds, but his comments also signal a common terminological slippage between "gossip" and "scandal," as well as rumor, legend, myth, historical memory, allegory, satirical commentary, and accusation. According to Pamela Stewart and Andrew Strathern (2004), gossip takes place primarily among people within a group, while rumor travels to wider networks. In her work on spirit possession in northern Sudan, Janice Boddy (1989) argues that through gossip, women come to possess and manage politically and economically valuable information that in turn gives them social power over matters such as marriage and kinship. In a similar way, rooibos residents alluded to gossip's gendered qualities, invoking the word "gossip" when they trivialized others' versions of stories. "Gossip" was mere "women's talk," not to be given import.

Psychological and gendered discussions of gossip are not the focus of this chapter, however. Instead, I follow Luise White (2000), who asserts that concentrating on labels and deciphering differences among rumor, gossip, and accusation can foreclose a space for credibility. White sees rumor as a matter of degree: Rumors are significant not for their accuracy but for the intensity with which they spread. Like White, I take seriously the content of the "tea stories" told by farmers, workers, and other residents of the rooibos region. Rather than trying to distinguish between scandal and gossip, I explore how rooibos narratives were dialogic. Each version continuously evolved in response to other narratives, and the debate revealed larger cultural processes at work in the region and the world. In a sense, rumors did not reflect but, rather, constituted "reality" for residents.

In her work on vampires in Central Africa, White asserts that scholars should not reduce the idea of rumor to anxiety, fear, or superstition. Rumor is not a mechanistic response or misunderstanding that merely deforms actual events. Instead, White argues that language and event are not opposites; they are in constant dialogue. In their work on witchcraft, Stewart and Strathern (2004) describe rumor as part of a broader discussion of conflict creation and resolution. In rumors, they see a "logic of explanation." To Stewart and Strathern, rumors are processual: They flourish in certain circumstances and give further impetus to those circumstances. Rumors can even act as a kind of witchcraft. Like witchcraft, they have both explanatory power and seemingly supernatural force; stories can create harm (Austin 1962). Rooibos farming was not supernatural in the sense of witchcraft or vampires, although farmers did infuse the plant with charismatic qualities. However, research on the supernatural can illuminate the qualities that make rumor more than mere words. Rooibos rumors not only had explanatory power, but also had concrete impacts on the landscape.

The concrete effects broadened the idea of rumor in the region to speak to local cosmologies. Stanley Tambiah (1985: 3) describes cosmologies as "frameworks of concepts and relations which treat the universe . . . as an ordered system, describing it in terms of space, time, matter, motion, and peopling it with gods, humans, animals, spirits, demons, and the like." Tambiah emphasizes the significance of relations in cosmologies, relations that incorporate perceptions of space, time, and God, in addition to humans and animals, much like those in the rooibos region. Yet research on cosmologies often retains an essentialist quality in that scholars envision cosmologies as having their own, coherent logics. They are, as Tambiah describes, "frameworks," or, as Jean Comaroff (1980) defines, symbolic repertoires of causal principles that are predicated on a deeper structural order. The cosmologies in the rooibos region, however, were distinctly unstructured. They emerged from constant, dynamic, and at times contradictory struggles over the plant's histories, meanings, and relations. In her research on Hutus and Tutsis, Liisa Malkki (1995) connects cosmologies with what she calls "mythico-histories." She shows how descriptions of different "versions" become struggles over both events *and* categories, such as "self" versus "other" and "good" versus "evil." If solidified through the telling and retelling of histories and rumors, these categories could lead to extreme and even genocidal violence.

While Malkki focuses predominately on the nation-state, I bring a discussion of "versions" to rooibos's social and ecological world. In the rooibos landscape, cosmologies shifted from person to person depending on his or her social location, but they also differed even for the *same* person at different moments. Struggles over cosmologies can begin to account for contemporaneous ways of viewing the world. As such, multiple and contradictory rumors could simultaneously exist as narrative fact. Cosmologies can inform strategic and flexible ways of inhabiting the landscape, just as they can provide frameworks and structures. They were part of the articulation between people's thoughts and larger sociopolitical, economic, and ecological events. Nevertheless, the ability to articulate these cosmologies in the form of a forceful rumor was linked to power. Dispossession could constrain and silence narrations that fell outside the dominant framework.

I, too, became a part of the flow of rumors. I gave voice to some narratives while potentially silencing others. The rumors, gossip, and cosmologies conveyed by residents may have expressed not only their "versions" of events, but also the "version" that they wanted me to hear. In these instances, it may not be the particular *interpretations of* rooibos stories told by residents that matter so much as the *reasons behind* the stories they told. Rumors can act as a kind of meta-commentary in which they become ethnographies in and of themselves (Boddy 1989). White (2000) asserts that even rumors' inaccuracies allow scholars to view the world the way the storytellers view it. I argue that the role of rumor is still more complex: Through rumors, we not only see the world the way storytellers do; we also see the world the way they *want* us to see it. Through the act of retelling rooibos rumors, I am transforming them from oral histories or circulating gossip to concrete, academic histories—solidifying them, giving the tales the apparent permanence and authority of the written word. I believe that this tranformation was one of the reasons people in the region urgently sought me out. They wanted their "versions" recorded.

When Did Rooibos "History" Begin?

"There is not an idyllic story in [rooibos]," Jon, a prominent Afrikaans farmer, said. "The Khoisan used to live here. They are responsible for the rock art.... At the end of the day both the Khoi and the San dissolved in Cape Town. The language is nonexistent. . . . Apparently they started with rooibos." Jon reiterated the now familiar tale of Khoisan extinction and wove this extinction into the history of rooibos. Cosmologies can serve as explanatory accounts of already existing phenomena. In the case of rooibos and its indigenous heritage, the consequences of these explanations were substantial: The people who "proved" that they owned rooibos's heritage could argue that they rightfully owned the land, as well. Underscoring the emotional, moral, and practical premises for controlling the rooibos narrative, I begin with a brief description of rooibos's commodity history, followed by a discussion of local people's various rooibos origin stories.

Rooibos's history as a crop differs from that of many colonial commodities. These commodities, such as sugar, coffee, and black tea, helped to consolidate colonial power and connect the colony to the metropole through dependencies on export-oriented trade networks. With a focus on extraction, colonial development projects created infrastructure aimed at bringing raw materials out of Africa for processing and distribution. However, in the early colonial era, rooibos figured little in a regional settler economy that was already rebellious against the metropole. Afrikaners in the region did not focus on producing cash crops for export; instead, they attempted to realize an Edenic dream separate from the perceived sins of Europe. Rooibos did not become a globalized commodity and achieve its current economic value until the late twentieth century. Instead of contributing to colonial dependencies, rooibos producers became reliant on global trade in a postcolonial, postapartheid, and increasingly neoliberal economic context. The timing of the industry's expansion affected both the structure of the industry and the rumors that surrounded it.

Most people in the rooibos-growing area began their industry histories around the turn of the twentieth century. They described an immigrant Jewish trader, Benjamin Ginsberg, who journeyed through the Cederberg Mountains to buy wild plants from white and coloured residents. Perhaps a Jewish trader supplied an aura of neutrality. He was neither Afrikaans nor Khoisan, British nor coloured. He was foreign and "alien," not part of the conservative and mostly Christian population. Yet he was still white, so his role could negate coloured claims to rooibos's cultural ownership. The figure of the "Jewish guy" held an ambiguous place in rooibos cosmologies that do not fit easily into narratives of anti-Semitism in South Africa. Historically, Afrikaners often conflated Jewish and British South Africans as greedy figures of capital—the ultimate foils for Afrikaner identity in a context in which nonwhites figured little because they were considered invisible or less than human. While anti-Semitism was certainly present in the rooibos region, most white farmers' and industry narratives describe Ginsberg as one of the founders of the modern rooibos industry. They could operationalize his whiteness. He became part of justifications for rooibos's white ownership: A white man, even if he was Jewish, began the industry. Since few Jewish people resided in the area, he did not serve as an antagonist in contemporary struggles in the way that British farmers did.

Aside from the founding figure of Ginsberg, people debated the origins and cultural ownership of the tea. Some in the white farming community pointed to a lack of "proof" for any definitive historical origin. A scientist working with the industry said that "descendants of the Khoisan, 'or whatever,' are coming after the fact to make claims. It's political. Please bring me the evidence." Another Cape Town–based scientist reiterated that coloured people did not discover rooibos. "It is difficult to say who in South Africa owned rooibos. It is definitely not the coloured. The Khoisan? Bushmen? Whites? There is no literature, it is all just anecdotal," he added. In discussing the history, "We have to make links to Khoisan, but can't make that claim, simply no proof. We had to stick to generic, 'early people.' Or even 'early settlers.'" For the scientist, a lack of specific "scientific" evidence of ownership left the cultural heritage of rooibos open for question. Nevertheless, he was certain that coloured people did not own it.

During conversations with coloured and white farmers, the first question I asked usually centered on the history of their farms. With white commercial farmers, this question often led to people pulling out family trees and photographs of great-grandparents. Most of the commercial farms in the area had been in the same family for at least three generations, and some from as early as the eighteenth century. When I asked who lived on the farm before their family, many people did not know or simply said, "No one." One farmer asserted, "If we stole [the land] from anyone, it was the Bushman. . . . And they died more from smallpox than anything else." Farmers excluded natives from the rooibos landscape in ways that allowed them to include themselves.

While most—although not all—white farmers said that the original inhabitants of the area—whether they called them Khoisan, Bushmen, or San—consumed rooibos before Europeans arrived, there was still a strong sense that rooibos was an Afrikaans drink. One woman involved with industry described a tourist from Great Britain. According to her, the tourist demanded to see an "Indigenous rooibos tea ceremony." "I've been to Japan," the tourist had said, "I know how Indigenous people drink tea." We laughed at the idea of a rooibos ceremony, and she continued: "And besides, rooibos was started by commercial farmers anyway." A number of white farmers in the area used "biological" rationales to deny the tea a Khoisan heritage. As one farmer stated, "Khoisan people didn't drink the tea because it made them hungry."[1] However, most coloured rooibos farmers firmly asserted that the history of rooibos was theirs and that the knowledge of the tea was stolen from their forefathers. A man in his late seventies who still worked on a rooibos farm explained, "My elders drank the tea. We drank the wild tea. The tea is ours."

Narratives of history, Malkki (1995) asserts, can be politically and symbolically powerful, cumbersome, threatening, or irrelevant to the formation of a local and national consciousness. Citing Claude Lévi-Strauss, Malkki reminds scholars that history is never merely the recounting of historical facts; rather, it is "history-for." Collective histories, Malkki argues, thrive in places where they have a meaningful use in the present. The many rooibos histories certainly had a meaningful use in the present; they informed and were constitutive of contestations over rooibos's economic, symbolic, political, and affective role in the Cederberg region and in South Africa's larger attempts at a postapartheid national identity amid persistent poverty, inequality, and violence.

Cederberg Histories

Rooibos was like gold and diamonds that they found here.
—COLOURED ROOIBOS FARMER

Ten years after the arrival of the Settlers in Africa (1652), the first
visitors arrived in Clanwilliam, but it was not until 1725 that people settled
here permanently. The town was first known as Jan Disselsvalleij but was changed to
Clanwilliam in 1814 by Sir John Cradock who named the town after his father-in-law,
the Earl of Clanwilliam. Clanwilliam is one of the ten oldest towns in South Africa.
—FACEBOOK PAGE, Clanwilliam Museum and Family Heritage Centre (2013)

Debates over rooibos's heritage were influenced by the structures of inequality present in the region since the arrival of Europeans in the seventeenth and early eighteenth centuries. Rumors were a part of the Cederberg's history from its founding. "The first white colonist—oh what's the politically correct term?—was sent north by Van Riebeeck to investigate the area in 1660," an Afrikaans farmer said. "There were rumors of great wealth up here." Few historical records exist about the expansion of the Dutch into the rooibos region. Many of the early settlers who pushed north were barely literate, and no official newspapers existed prior to British occupation. The Khoisan did not keep written records, though they did leave significant archives through the rock art that covers boulders across the region. Drawing on various sources, the historian Nigel Penn (2005) attempts to piece together what he calls South Africa's "forgotten frontier," providing the most comprehensive written history of the area. In this section, I briefly describe Penn's Cederberg history and place it in dialogue with coloured and white rooibos farmers' versions of events. For Penn, the history focuses on the creation of private property and the solidification of the idea of landownership. For coloured residents, however, the idea of historical landownership as synonymous with rightful belonging in the region was contentious and, for many, seemingly irrelevant to contemporary claims.

Penn describes the first colonists, or *trekboers*, as entering the Olifants River area in 1712. The term *trekboers* (lit., migrant farmers) refers to farmers who moved north from Cape Town, then the center of Dutch colonial society in the region. As they moved from Cape Town, colonists destroyed Khoisan culture through violence, the spread of disease, and the use of Khoisan as slaves or laborers. Penn emphasizes that trekboers created their own myths—most prominently a firm dichotomy between civility and savagery—despite the fact that miscegenation was common. Trekboers typically represented the Khoisan as naked to demonstrate that they were as "far removed from civilized humanity as the Cape was from Europe," at the outer margins of humanity or not human at all (Penn 2005: 6). These depictions helped justify the commando raids against nonwhite people that marked much of the early stages of colonial expansion. Penn describes how colonists envisioned hunter-gatherer societies as the ultimate "other," therefore justifying a style of fighting that "approached the genocidal" (Penn 2005: 9). Khoisan and fugitive slave groups in the area responded with significant resistance to the trekboers, causing white settlers to retreat south several times.

By the beginning of the nineteenth century, however, the "Caledon Code" served as the first attempt by the (now) British government to regulate relationships between colonists and the Khoisan. The code, ostensibly driven by the goal of "civilizing" the natives, mandated that Khoisan have fixed residences and that they carry a valid pass if they wanted to move from one locality to another (Adhikari 2010a). This pass, a precursor to apartheid-era pass laws, attempted to emplace "natives" to oversee them and secure land tenure for white colonists. Added to the code was the decision that Khoisan who were not in colonial service or living in mission stations would not be given passes and would be considered vagrant and punished accordingly. By mandating service, the state transformed the Khoisan into wage earners dependent on employment on white farms. The code, then, effectively entrenched state power over laborers, thereby "closing" the frontier. While authorities in the Netherlands insisted that the Khoisan should not be enslaved, the colonial government had little enforcement over their labor status, and most Khoisan laborers remained, if not enslaved, then "unfree." Khoikhoi laborers "were often treated worse than slaves. . . . The non-slave status of the Khoikhoi counted against them: a slave, being property, had more value than the Khoikhoi labourer" (Penn 2006: 147).

Cultural encounters occurred not just between Dutch farmers and the Khoisan, however. According to Penn, Dutch fugitives, escaped slaves, and other groups fought for a place in the region. These groups—including the trekboers—practiced a kind of transhumance, or seasonal movement, in which property boundaries were less important than features in the landscape such as waterholes. They followed seasonal rains to eke a subsistence livelihood out of the dry climate, a climate that dissuaded later colonists from settling in the area and augmented the belief of many Afrikaners that they were a hardier group, more suited to the land than the outsiders who purchased farms in the last decade. Through long descriptions of their ancestors' hardships, Afrikaans farmers who descended from early settlers painted a "history-for" continued landownership that transcended the invocation of private property rights. They believed that their struggle with the ecosystem had endowed them with a natural and inherent right to the land. Settler colonists received loan farms from the Dutch East India Company and, later, from the British government. These loan farms eventually transitioned to secure private property.

Despite claims to natural and pure Afrikaans belonging in the land, coloured people living in the rooibos-growing area described histories of fluidity between the white and nonwhite populations in the eighteenth, nineteenth, and even twentieth centuries. A number of white and coloured families shared surnames. Some white farmers ascribed name sharing to the fact coloured people had no last names of their own, so they took on those of their white slave owners or employers. Many in the coloured community, however, told different stories. People described their white ancestry, pointing to specific farming families with whom they were related. Lizette discussed her family's history on the land: "My parents were born here in 1919. The area started with the de Villiers Boer from Holland. There are lots of people here named de Villiers. There was a man that married a Bushman woman. But there were many other people who married Boers, too. . . . What happened to the other people? I think they were forced into work on other farms maybe."

Significantly, for Lizette and for many others, conversations about Cederberg histories focused more on farm laboring than on indigenous ownership. While these conversations could seemingly reinforce Afrikaners' ideas of rightful ownership, the conclusions drawn by Lizette and by other coloured residents were more complex. They never used the discourse of landownership as implying or justifying cultural ownership. Rather, people—whether coloured or Afrikaans—belonged because they worked and loved the rooibos ecosystem.

The Rooibos Marketing Board and the Postwar Period

While rooibos's indigeneity informed ideas about belonging in the ecosystem, its transformation into a national and then international commodity mirrored the history of more mundane and less "charismatic" agricultural products in South Africa during and after World War II. Local narratives about the industry's expansion in the postwar period reflected political and economic concerns among rooibos farmers, many of whom straddled a fine line between desiring government protections and criticizing the government's restrictions on private enterprise. Should the apartheid government act as a paternalistic welfare state helping Afrikaans farmers to maintain their economic and social distance from coloured workers? Or did government interference undermine the notion of the hardy, independent Afrikaans farmer living in his own personal Eden?

Before World War II, many whites from other parts of South Africa viewed rooibos as a "poor man's drink," associated with lower-class Afrikaners. Unlike the higher-status "English" (or black) tea, rooibos could be found in large quantities in hospitals, schools, jails, and the military because of its low cost. When World War II halted imports of black tea from the region then called Ceylon, however, South Africans turned to rooibos, and the tea soon commanded the same price as "English" tea. The increase in rooibos consumption around the country was marked by linguistic slippages in local tea terminology. Whenever I walked into a South African's home (across class and racial boundaries) in the Western Cape, I was often greeted with the offer, "Would you like some tea?" and more specifically, "English or rooibos?" or "Normal or rooibos?" Rooibos was an everyday commodity, a part of the hospitality of the region, both culturally fraught and offered without a second thought. Yet rooibos was not "normal." The language signifies it as a deviation from norm. Even though "English" tea (while obviously not English but tied to colonial networks of trade) was typically imported, it was rooibos, indigenous to the area, that people described as unique. In other parts of the country, people frequently referred to English tea as black or Ceylon, signaling different ideas of exoticism. In the rooibos region, the distinction between the niche and the everyday commodity fell apart. Just as Afrikaners saw themselves as God's chosen people, rooibos was both special and natural.

Rooibos's transition from something imagined as wild to something described as Afrikaans and local to a beverage on par with English tea reflected social dynamics at the time, as the country slowly distanced itself politically (if not economically) from Britain. Responding to the industry's growth, the apartheid government created a centralized marketing board, a model common to South African agricultural industries at the time. The marketing board imposed production quotas on farmers and attempted to control price fluctuations. Although apartheid-era sanctions somewhat limited possibilities for international growth, rooibos became a staple in the South African diet. Children drank rooibos in schools; parents gave their babies rooibos alongside breast milk; and middle-aged white men reminisced about the huge sugary vats of rooibos they drank during their mandatory military service.

The marketing board and other apartheid-era social safety nets such as farm subsidies allowed white farmers to survive, if modestly, on a combination of rooibos and other crops able to grow in the low-nutrient, low-rainfall area. Louw, an Afrikaans farmer, described his view of the marketing board's history. He was a relatively young farmer and considered himself a modern trailblazer, more creative and enterprising than older Afrikaans farmers who had dominated the industry in the past. Instead of delivering his tea to one of the larger processing plants, he was attempting to do his own processing. "There was the Rooibos Board," he began. "All rooibos had to be sold through them. There were quotas on the farms and for the buyers." He said that the board officially began in 1954 under the revised Marketing Act of 1937. "When Afrikaners got to power, there was bitterness because of the history with the British," he added, neglecting to incorporate coloured actors in his history of the industry or in any history of bitterness in the region. "They gave bursaries to the smartest Afrikaner kids to go to university. They got degrees in agriculture, because Afrikaners are farmers.... The deal was that they had to then work for the government for some years, so they often got jobs at places like the Rooibos Board."

Louw felt that marketing boards stifled growth by prioritizing redistributed wealth across the white population. Indeed, powerful marketing boards helped to stabilize industries and shield Afrikaans farmers from poverty, thus protecting the white race from "falling." Under apartheid, the Rooibos Board dictated prices in a fashion that rejected economically liberal values of market competition. Sovereignty was founded not on liberal understandings of freedom or a universal juridical subject but on race. The government controlled the market with the aim of maintaining the separation of races through institutionalized support of white farmers (Nattrass 1991; Wolpe 1972).

Apartheid-supported capitalism's communal—but distinctly non-Marxian —values emerged in local tales of apartheid-era industry setbacks, rumors, and nostalgia for the paternalist apartheid state. One of the primary setbacks to the rooibos industry occurred in 1984 when traces of salmonella were found in the tea. This incident fundamentally changed the industry by further centralizing production as new regulations required expensive and technologically challenging pasteurization processes. One industry member describes it in this way: "It was right at the height of the tea's growth curve. The whole thing originated in Australia. Someone in Australia had a grudge against us, against rooibos. It was because of our connection with the Japanese." He blamed an unknown saboteur. "There was a little news item in Australia about rooibos having salmonella. And within a month, we had almost no sales." This story is indicative of many people's reactions to the salmonella—blame resided outside the farming community. "We all thought the salmonella was an orchestrated move to discredit the industry," a farmer fumed.

Many farmers described years of hardship following the "salmonella incident," as they often labelled it in hushed tones. "We had eleven million kilos in our stores," one commercial farmer said. "It took us back nine years to get rid of the stock." In addition to conspiracies about Australian "lies," the burgeoning international presence of rooibos as a commodity affected farmers' and the industry's response. Tea processors had to figure out a way to sterilize the tea. "We tried irradiating. I mean, in South Africa nobody worried about it, they just kept on buying, but for overseas. And Germany and Japan freaked out because they were still in 1945." Some farmers felt that the marketing board saved them. "There was a huge effort from the government to subsidize the industry," a farmer explained, before describing how the Rooibos Board helped him with loans and interest. However, another, very different narrative about salmonella also circulated. "The salmonella scandal was politically motivated," one white farmer stated. "There was a man in the area, a coloured man, who was high up in the church. It was apartheid politics." These competing rumors—was it foreigners or coloured people who upended the industry?—reflected the uncertainties, fears, and hopeful possibilities provided by two major changes in the agrarian landscape: the end of political apartheid and the increasingly international agricultural market.

Postapartheid Rooibos Rumors

FIELD NOTES, JUNE 2011: *I sat at Jan's dining room table. We drank the rooibos that his coloured domestic worker had poured for us, and I shivered under my jacket and scarf. Winter winds blew through his rickety, single-paned windows. Jan seemed unfazed by the cold, just as he had seemed unfazed by the searing heat of the summer. He took a loud sip of tea and began speaking:*

JAN: My great-grandfather . . . bought all this land in 1878. It was a horse farm with seven hundred to one thousand horses for plowing. He also had mules. But during the English [South African] War, the English took the horses for the war. That is why we are not that fond of the English. We love playing them in rugby *[laugh]*. Losing the horses put him in financial trouble. . . . So he sold [the land] to my great-grandfather on my mother's side. Then my father put up fences in the 1940s and 1950s. "You've never tasted blood in your mouth," he used to tell me. "When you have nothing." My grandfather had to pay a price. In 1954, the farm was transferred to my father, and in 1998 the farm was transferred to me. . . . We started farming with rooibos in 1960. At first, we sold to Ginsberg, the Jewish guy. At first, since [my father] had a lorry, he bought up the rooibos from the other farms, and he made quite a bit of money, but then he started planting his own. I joined the farm in 1980. We started doing red bush on a bigger scale. I have green hands.

ME: Why did you join the farm?

JAN: I joined my father because it was just the natural thing to do, to take the farm from Dad. There was a time when the farm was too small for the two of us [so I worked as a programmer]. My father was eighty-six when he stopped farming because he died. There was a land claim against our farm in the 1990s. Our neighbors is coloured guys. The guy who owned the farm before my family was named Baard—that's the same name as the coloured guys. He had seven sons. One son married a Khoisan woman. They got their farm then. They had their land from 1870, but they thought the fences weren't in the right places.

ME: How much land was it?

JAN: It was almost ten thousand acres. It went to the Supreme Court and cost a lot of money. But I won the case. But the courts said because of their level of education they didn't have to pay because they didn't know any better. In this country, if you are black or brown [trails off].

Afrikaans farmers' historical narratives of the rooibos industry often moved seamlessly into their descriptions of the industry today. Much of Jan's tale was typical of other Afrikaans farmers in the region. They began farming with rooibos because the nutrient-poor land could not sustain other crops. They struggled for years with and against nature in ways that were central to their identities as Afrikaners. Even though English farmers—and a "Jewish guy"—also lived in the region and played central roles in the development of the industry, they were positioned as the greedy figures of capitalism. In contrast, Afrikaans farmers argued that *they* loved the land; *they* "tasted blood on the land"; *they* worked the land until they died; *their* sons took over the land because it was "the natural thing to do." And, according to Jan, "those coloured guys" were being coddled by the postapartheid government, even as the government denied land claims—claims that brought out intense emotions and anger from the coloured farmers who made them.

As Jan's story indicates, the postapartheid rooibos narrative is hardly a straightforward tale of political and economic liberation. In the first democratic election, the majority of coloured voters chose the National Party, the very apartheid party that had cemented their oppression, and farmers such as Jan were able to fight off attempts by coloured farmers to redress the inequalities of the rooibos landscape. Themes of changing political and economic governance dominated industry rumors circulating between 2010 and 2011, a time that municipal elections led to an increased politicization of the region and the African National Congress (ANC) challenged the formerly Democratic Alliance–dominated local government. During this period, sides were drawn not necessarily along racial lines (although any cross-racial socialization was rare) but between those who felt the area had lost its core values and those who celebrated or took advantage of the political and economic upheaval that often appeared to bring more change than it actually did. Yet the government's involvement in the rooibos region was hardly a unified project. For that reason, the industry provides a lens through which to address how the macroeconomic processes of neoliberalism merged with the government's postapartheid rhetoric and with local fights over ecological notions of cultural belonging.

When discussing the rooibos industry today, white and coloured farmers alike more often than not used two words: greed and corruption. "People got greedy when they started making money with rooibos," an Afrikaans farmer said. "They started acting funny—wearing certain clothes and driving certain cars." The gradual transition from the apartheid government to a democratically elected postapartheid government brought with it the loosening of apartheid-era economic sanctions. In the mid-1990s, opening markets combined with the burgeoning popularity of "alternative" or "exotic" foods and beverages, a healthy rooibos crop resulting from ideal climate conditions, and the recovery from the salmonella scandal. These positive growth factors led to an increase in rooibos farmers' personal wealth. At the same time, life for farmworkers became dominated by shakiness and unpredictability (du Toit and Neves 2014; Neves and du Toit 2013). In the 1990s and 2000s, farmwork moved toward seasonal and temporary employment. It appeared to many in the rooibos region that a surfeit of people would never find permanent jobs in agriculture again.

In the years leading up to 1994, privatization consolidated power for one company, Rooibos Ltd., which took over the assets of the marketing board under the guise of free-market capitalism. By the early 1990s, it had become clear to industry insiders that the current government and its policies of protecting the Afrikaans farming community through subsidies and other economic policies would not last much longer. Simultaneously, the expanded rooibos market and the increased wealth experienced by some farmers made a deregulated industry seem both appealing and inevitable. One farmer described this transition: "With the marketing board, all farmers had to deliver there, and all buyers had to buy there. It was a time when quality and standards were developed, centralized, standardized. With the end of apartheid, the [marketing board] became just another buyer. That opened doors. You had Freshpak, Laager [two large South African brands]. The board had to do generic marketing. It got the tea out there in the South African market—and it kept most other herbal teas out—that's why it's just English or rooibos."

While the government-controlled marketing board may have helped the industry to grow, the farmer continued, it ultimately reached the end of its economic efficacy. "They could only handle bulk. No value-add for the farmer. In 1993, they voluntarily privatized. It was political. They didn't know what would happen with the new government. Unlike other marketing boards like wheat, they had all this infrastructure, and they didn't know what the new state would do. So, they thought, let's take a more cautious route. The production facility that exists now was built by the levies from the producers."

This narrative provides an example of how farmers moved in and out of supporting and challenging apartheid-era agricultural policies, of both wanting government protections and feeling that government regulations stymied economic growth through restrictive buying patterns. The apartheid-era rooibos industry could handle only "bulk" and could not bring "value-add" to the area. In other words, farmers said, the apartheid industry paid little attention to quality or to improving regional profitability. By dealing in bulk tea, it simply shipped massive amounts of medium-grade tea to other parts of the country for distribution.

White and coloured farmers' use of the term "value-add" was common in the region, but only in certain contexts. It was woven into policy documents and industry materials and spoken of in commercial and small-scale farmer meetings. Many farmers proposed doing their own processing and packaging to "add value" to local farms instead of large corporations. Even those who claimed they just wanted to farm and disregard the business side of commodity production expressed a desire for more value to accrue through regional packagers and processors. This desire often led to rumors about how rooibos's economic value was being stolen—by someone, often undefined—and hoarded in Cape Town or Germany or other "greedy" places that did not have the same pure intentions that a life on the farm supposedly fostered. Fuming, one farmer said, "I want to understand where the value adding is happening, because farmers are struggling. They see figures like 'rooibos contributes five hundred million rands to Western Cape GDP,' but [we] don't see the money.... The value should be here, but all the processors are in Durban [in the eastern part of the country]." One thirty-one-page "development plan" for rooibos mentions "value add" no fewer than thirty-seven times. Typically, industry meetings took place almost entirely in Afrikaans, but farmers would shift to English when referring to terms such as "value add," "sustainable development," and "stakeholders." Adopting the language of foreign NGOs and international development agencies, Afrikaans and coloured farmers alike learned to (or attempted to) operationalize these words toward their own ends.

Many industry narratives described the move to break apart the marketing board as motivated entirely by a desire to protect farmers from the uncertainty of a new government—and to create "value add"; this account, however, masked how privatization consolidated power for one company under the auspices of the free market. Anticipating that the end of apartheid was nearing, key white players in the industry attempted to safeguard their financial interests and power. Yet the tale of privatization was not just about protecting capital from the uncertainty of a postapartheid state. Some farmers' use of seemingly neutral economic language rendered invisible the race-based implications of rooibos's privatization. So while privatization in the industry might appear to mirror the turn toward privatization in an increasingly neoliberal global economic climate, it also marked a continuation of economic policies that addressed the needs of the white population first and the idea of a free market second.

The discourse also masked political upheaval within the white farming community. The decision to deregulate spawned many rumors. As one farmer explained, "In 1993 when we were deregulating, there was a chap that presented the whole scenario. . . . The last words he uttered were, 'Guys, just remember that if you become deregulated, on the statute side there will be nothing to control anyone. You should come to a gentleman's agreement to remain under this roof.'" But the farmer felt quickly betrayed. "He hadn't walked out of the door before people were breaking away. The pirates started undercutting the prices to get into the markets. As soon as the buyers realized this they started negotiating, and the prices are still way down."

According to this "version," when the Rooibos Board privatized, the first people who split away (the "pirates") were "conservative" Afrikaners, most of whom were members of the Afrikaans Protestant Church, or AP Kerk. The AP Kerk had about 125 congregants in Clanwilliam, and perhaps more from the surrounding area. One member of the Dutch Reformed Church stated the AP Kerk broke away because of the "political situation." He said, "They were afraid about sharing a building and their faith with coloured people. It is 90 percent Afrikaans-speaking farmers. But the theology is the same." While the majority of Afrikaans farmers who attended church went to the Dutch Reformed Church, the AP Kerk had the reputation of being a "farmers' church," and church membership played a role in the dynamics of the rooibos industry during its privatization. This discourse focused almost entirely on white-white relations, despite the fact that the impetus for privatization was allegedly fear about a new black government.

Nearly everyone involved on all sides of the privatization debate described the marketing board's split as "quite political." According to one of the self-proclaimed "rebel farmers," a director of Rooibos Ltd. came up to him and a group of like-minded farmers during the deregulation talks and said, "Let's talk about it. We are not in the business of spades and forks." But, the farmer said, one man disrupted these discussions: "*He* is trying to steal from us. This was a fight in Clanwilliam amongst [the] farmers. . . . *He* manipulated then, and *he* is still manipulating the prices. He manipulates every step of the process." The "he" in this story was Michael, the managing director of Rooibos Ltd., whose British ancestry already made him and his family members suspect in the eyes of the Afrikaans community, despite the fact that the family had lived in the area for generations.

A number of times, farmers who heard about the American doing research reached out to me because they wanted to tell me their version of Michael's or Rooibos Ltd.'s supposed evildoings. Other rumors included the claim that Rooibos Ltd. planted media stories; that it controlled information about planting and how to prepare seeds; and that it hid research results from the rest of the industry, despite the fact that each farmer had to contribute to an industry-wide research fund. I was even the target of rumors. Some people wondered if I was an agent of Rooibos Ltd.

Rumor as Resistance

The shock and feelings of vulnerability vis-à-vis the huge but strangely anonymous forces of global finance capital are palpable in countries like India and South Africa that until the early 1990s had sheltered their economies behind high tariffs and heavily interventionist economic regimes. — THOMAS BLOM HANSEN and FINN STEPPUTAT, "Introduction"

The farmer is coming into a threatful situation to survive. Where is that coming from? It is [Michael]. — ROOIBOS FARMER

"The rooibos industry, what worries me the most is the tendency at one moment to be up and then the next down," a farmer said. "One moment you are a beggar and the next a king. . . . No one seems to have an answer for it." During the postapartheid transition, discussions in the rooibos industry did not directly engage changing trends in global and South African agriculture, such as deregulation, mechanization, and increasing consolidation into larger and larger agribusinesses. Rather, conversations focused on personal and religious feuds and betrayals of gentlemen's agreements. Farmers described the disunity after deregulation as violating both economic and social contracts—social contracts that they saw as crucial to maintaining the cohesiveness and stability of the (white) farming community in the face of postapartheid uncertainty. Compounding what Margareet Visser and Stuart Ferrer (2015: vii) have called producers' "perceptions of their own vulnerability" were trade liberalization, deregulation, and shifts of structural power downstream to markets and retailers that are woven into the global value chain. Fears relating to broken social contracts were ever present and explained in a variety of ways, one of which was the persistent allegation that Rooibos Ltd. was trying to steal farms by keeping prices unnaturally low. A number of farmers said they believed Michael, as Rooibos Ltd.'s director, wanted to put farmers out of business so he could buy their farms and control the market. Global agricultural trends were described *personally* in the rooibos industry, giving a specific target to blame for the changing agricultural landscape.

Rooibos Ltd. controlled the majority of the domestic and export rooibos market. Each year, the company set the price that it paid farmers per kilogram of tea, and, with the exception of fair trade– and organic-certified farms, other processors generally followed suit. If prices were low, as they were in 2010, Rooibos Ltd. and Michael became the symbols of all that was evil in the community. Low prices led to many theories. "It's a corrupt system," farmers said. "Price fixing." As for the director of Rooibos Ltd., farmers alleged, "*He* controls the hands of the market."

To explain this belief, Henk, an Afrikaans farmer, described his under-standing of free-market capitalism. Bread prices, he asserted, are determined by the cost of grain; by local, national, and international demand; and by the amount of money a baker needs to make a profit. But with rooibos, he con-tinued, "Prices are not determined by the market. . . . Everyone waits for [Mi-chael]. To me that is not a market-related price. They wait for [Michael]. It's a corrupt system. . . . [Michael] is ruling this industry. Why wait for competi-tion?" Through stories like Henk's, farmers expressed resentment that seemed to come from contradictory sources: nostalgia for the controlled market of the apartheid era and anger over the *perceived* controlled market of the post-apartheid era. Tinged with anti-British sentiments, the narrative featured the figure of a physically strong Afrikaans farmer who loved and worked the land for pure ends battling a greedy English-speaking capitalist who manipulated that farmer. As Henk's neighbor described, "We Afrikaners, we are farmers, not businesspeople. . . . The previous generation would believe anything, and Rooibos Ltd. identified that weakness." Many coloured farmers agreed. Rooi-bos Ltd. took advantage of farmers' lack of business acumen, a coloured farmer insisted. "[Michael] says 'trust me,' but he is rolling in money."

"It is a monopoly—no more, no less," Jonas, an Afrikaans farmer said, de-scribing Rooibos Ltd. "That is the beginning and the end of it." "They are afraid of competition," Jonas's son said, jumping into the conversation. "So they rather let the price drop and buy all the tea from farmers, even if they make farmers bankrupt. Buy as cheap as possible and sell for a bigger profit. That's why they drop prices now and then, and they smile all the way." He leaned closer and closer and pounded his fist on the table. "The Rooibos Council, it should fix the price. . . . [It] should find out what it costs to produce and then say this is what we should pay, 'but that's not democratic.'" Jonas and his son seemed to want the Rooibos Council to take over the job of the old marketing board. Jonas wanted a monopoly, but one controlled by the nonprofit industry group and not by privatized capital. He believed that he was in an intractable position, and his strong emotions reflected his feeling that he was politically impotent.

Diedrik, another Afrikaans farmer, was older and did not have any sons, so he was especially concerned about the future of his farm. He felt it was "very important" that I have the "correct" version of rooibos's history, and the his-tory of the privatization in particular. Because he was so insistent that I record each part of his narrative—and repeatedly interrupted himself to check my notebook for accuracy—I include many of his own words: "In 1993 it became a public company on the thirtieth of September. It is important that you write down that it is a public company. With private companies the shareholders are not more than fifty people (PTY Ltd.) [He paused and scribbled the letters down in my notebook]. A public company had to be more than fifty people. It was made up of people who produced tea in the last three years, so [Michael] is by far the biggest shareholder."

Diedrik started describing "personnel schemes." I got confused. He rattled off numbers that I didn't understand but that he made sure I wrote down. "It's very important that you record this," he said:

> Two million approved shares one million, one hundred of which were A shares, which in the beginning were only producers and nine hundred B shares which can be anyone but preferably people who worked there. But they were not all allocated, and they bought back shares from people who got lots. There were very few B shares issued, some as a bonus. There was a share bank, so people would sell their shares to the bank and then the bank would sell them to others. The important thing for you to know is that the reserves of the old control board were not paid out to the government or to producers, but in shares that stayed in the company, so we didn't pay them any money. That's why Rooibos Ltd. was solvent right from the start.

I was uncertain what his narrative meant—he presented me with a jumble of numbers and letters. I tried to get him to clarify, and he responded that Rooibos Ltd. had reacted to the "threat" of the postapartheid transition by maintaining control of the company rather than letting farmers or the government gain a share. My recording of this information was crucial to Diedrik. He wanted to make sure that I passed his narrative along.

In what follows, I attempt to remain true to many residents' fervent pleas to "get the facts right," even as I became increasingly confused about the details of these "facts." The opacity was productive in maintaining the uneasily alliance between the power of capital and the power of government. At the same time, the opacity revealed a central component of the rooibos story that few white farmers discussed: coloured farmers and workers. So removed were they from the narrative of the postapartheid transition that some people in the region joked that workers on remote farms had not heard that apartheid was over, the horror and violence of such a statement hidden under smiles and hearty laughs. The seeming banality of dates, labels, and numbers juxtaposed the idea that dispossession was so total on some farms that people might not even realize their liberation had come.

People Are Worshipping a New God, and That New God Is Rooibos

I am freed from the market of sin. I am free.

—AFRIKAANS ROOIBOS FARMER

"Who among the rooibos tea farmers are really benefiting?" Ruan asked. "It is not the poor. Today no one has an equal opportunity to land." Ruan, a coloured community organizer from Cape Town, used the rhetoric he had learned as a comrade in the struggle against apartheid. He had been involved in a number of legal and political actions that tried to benefit the coloured rooibos farming community living on Moravian Church land. He leaned farther across the table. "There are elites, and not in the Marxist sense, but their status, their role in the community . . . it dates back one hundred years with capitalism and a market-driven approach. . . . There is no more petty production, but everything is at a capitalist scale. There is further differentiation. All are resource poor, and the rooibos price determines so much." He shifted back in his chair and paused for a moment. "It is becoming Moravian PTY, Ltd." Instead of focusing on Rooibos Ltd., Ruan believed that both Rooibos Ltd. and the Moravian Church epitomized postapartheid capitalism and that both represented a betrayal of the comrades who had fought for a socialist state. The Moravian Church, in his narrative, had become its own corporation.

Before and during apartheid, one of the only areas where coloured farmers maintained some degree of independence was mission land. On church-owned land, coloured farmers labored not for Afrikaans farmers but, rather, for the church, for the community, and for God. Wupperthal, a town of about three thousand people with a series of remote mountain "out-stations," was founded in the 1800s by German missionaries who incorporated local Khoisan families.[2] When the colonial government officially abolished slavery in the region in 1838, the population of the mission station grew as many freed slaves moved from nearby white-owned farms and converted to Christianity. In Wupperthal, missionaries came to "uplift" and "civilize" the population. By 2010, the missionaries had long since left or become integrated into the local population, but the church's role in the area continued to be complex and contradictory, a fact that takes on critical importance in the rooibos story because of the church's central place in coloured farming.

According to Penn (2005), missionaries contributed to the social and economic transformation of the Khoisan by making them more dependent on colonial commodities and by increasing state control over the tumultuous region. The Khoisan were open to conversion, he continues, because the social fabric of their societies had been torn apart by years of commando raids, enslavement, and disease. This "cultural and psychic trauma" was fertile ground for Christianity, "especially when its spiritual securities were coupled with prospects of a more stable political order" (Penn 2005: 251). Early missionaries in the region focused on creating an agricultural community with small trade in *veldskoene* (Bush shoes). Mission stations also came to serve as labor reserves for the surrounding farms, providing cheap, seasonal labor. One activist described Wupperthal as a buffer against apartheid: "As much as you can romanticize it . . . you can see how agriculture has been systematically destroyed in mission stations to provide a labor pool for surrounding areas." Yet the Moravian Church also had a radical history during the apartheid struggle, taking part in the Council of Churches with Desmond Tutu. The South African Council of Churches was founded in its current form in 1968. Active during the apartheid resistance, the council's goal is "to express the never-changing Gospel in the changing scene of South Africa through the years of apartheid, transition and democracy."[3] Mission stations, then, had conflicting relationships with white farmers and with the rooibos industry. On the one hand, the church provided land and livelihoods for coloured people that left them some independence from the labor regime of the apartheid-era farming system. On the other hand, the church and its elders retained control over the land and eventually over the rooibos. In this context, rumors about and among the Moravian community could take on operatic proportions, with tales of family betrayals, fights in the streets, lawsuits, and people refusing to share communion cups with those whom they believed had wronged them.[4] When referring to a small-scale cooperative operating on church land, one Moravian said, "People are worshipping the new God, and the new God is rooibos."

The presence of both the church and rooibos physically dominated the small town. The processing plant was located just behind the church, and the sweet fragrance of drying rooibos reached the pews. Small rooibos fields grew in front of houses and up into the mountains, and a tiny shop sold rooibos beauty products. Needing a place to talk, Jacob, a Wupperthal resident, and I sat in the church. He believed that the increased value of rooibos was destroying the community. "There were personal problems and money," he began. "Money because there is no economy here, no industry, and everyone needs money. They say, 'I don't care how I get it.'" He shook his head and looked around the church. "Will there be peace? This is what we hope for. . . . It is sometimes heartbreaking. We are supposed to be brothers and sisters. They all come together in the church. But they walk away from the church without taking communion because there are people that don't want to greet each other."

These rooibos stories were augmented by the belief that some people were ruining the region's heritage with their greed. Francois, a coloured farmer who lived on Moravian land, narrated a history of avarice that he felt coincided with a distortion of religious faith and a changing political and economic situation. "In 1991 [the town] was still a complete, complete backwater. It was still donkey carts," he said, describing the mode of transportation that many farmers used to negotiate the poorly maintained dirt roads on Moravian land. "Within the space of 1991 to 1995, suddenly there were pick-up trucks. It coincided with South African political and economic changes and money and rooibos. . . . It definitely changed, the economy, and it's not just deregulation but also the lack of sanctions." Deregulation opened up a space for new rooibos cooperatives, but Francois saw this opening in a distinctly negative light. "With the deregulation, the first people to break away were pariahs," he added. Money and rooibos: Instead of emerging as a tea of salvation, rooibos was a tea of temptation.

The idea that rooibos's growing economic value led to a fall from Eden crossed racial boundaries. As I described previously, the biophysical aspects of the tea influenced its history because the land where rooibos thrives is sandy and receives little rainfall. Before rooibos's increased commodity value, many farmers struggled with wheat, sheep, and other crops. Lucas, an Afrikaans farmer, described what he saw as the transformation many of these "humble" farmers underwent. When tea prices rose in 2000, "a lot of farmers made a lot of money. Poor farmers got rich very quickly. When the price went down, they had to maintain that standard of living, the Mercedes and John Deer."

Tales of a previously austere and authentic farming community undone by the corruption that accompanies sudden wealth were common. Abe, an Afrikaans farmer who lived deep in the mountains, had a reputation in the rooibos industry for being an "overly aggressive" evangelist. One of his neighbors gave me his phone number, but only after his wife had told him not to. "You really think she should talk to Abe?" his wife had asked. They exchanged looks. "Well, I suppose she should." I was curious and a little apprehensive when I pulled my car in front of his modest farmhouse surrounded by acres of rooibos land. His wife opened the door, and I sat in the living room waiting for him to return from the fields. All around the room were copies of Bibles, prayer books, and religious pamphlets.

When he finally greeted me, Abe began our conversation by asking if I were a Christian. "I was raised in the church," I explained. Not wanting to go into my own uncertain thoughts about religion, I changed the subject to his rooibos farming. He narrated his tale as though it were a morality play: "I was a greedy man. I invested in townhouses in Cape Town, Jo'burg, and all over. My father told me, 'You must stay in farming.' I said, 'No, you must diversify.' My goal was to get rich." He paused and stared at me briefly. "On my way there, my life was transformed by God. . . . You need discipline. You are sinners." He looked at me again, and I felt myself shrink under his gaze, uncertain whether he was saying that *I* was a sinner or rich farmers were sinners, or whether the distinction even mattered. He said that the Dutch Reformed Church was satanic and talked on and on about sodomites and lust. I stopped taking notes, tried to avoid his piercing eyes, and frantically thought about how I could turn the conversation back to rooibos. "Where do you sell your tea?" I asked. He said that he refused to sell his tea to the new processor that had opened in his town. "I don't sell there. I don't want to arrive in Hell. Satan is the ruler of the earth. . . . I tell my [workers], 'Eventually God will give up.' I won't sell my tea to that plant. My life must be an example to the world."

An hour passed, and I was unable to interrupt again with a rooibos-related question. I decided to leave, and Abe continued proselytizing as he walked me to my car, as I shut my car door, and even as I closed my car window and drove away. Certainly, his narrative was largely due to his eccentric character—Abe was notorious for preaching about Satan. It was also partly indicative of the increased presence of evangelical and apostolic churches in the region. Some white and coloured residents were leaving the area's more traditional churches, saying that they wanted a closer connection to God, to encounter God personally and individually through their bodies and their emotions. Scholars such as Daromir Rudnyckyj (2010) have explored connections among religion, neoliberalism, and new "spiritual economies." In the rooibos region, however, Abe's proselytizing also marked a continuation of the relations among God, rooibos, and ideas of a pure, moral connection with the plant. In Abe's mind, the corruption in rooibos stemmed from farmers' losing sight of what matters: an ecological, affective, and spiritual belonging with the ecosystem.

"The Politicians Are a Bunch of Capitalists"

Feelings that capitalism was corrupting the region permeated race and class. "I can't see any benefits in politics. Here in Clanwilliam, when someone is elected, he doesn't worry about the community anymore," Bern, a coloured resident, said in the days leading up to the municipal elections of 2011. I asked him whether he planned to vote, and he shrugged: "I don't know." Scholars have written about the disillusionment following the hope of the postapartheid "miracle of transition" (Chari 2008; Hart 2007; Kagwanja 2008). Economic inequality and unemployment have remained high since 1994. While the political arena arguably has become more representative of the country's population (racially, if not economically), many South Africans became disenchanted with the government's potential for enacting or enforcing substantive transformative policies. Bern was left frustrated. "The politicians say they are democratic, but they are really just a bunch of capitalists." To Bern, the idea of capitalism and democracy were held up in diametric opposition. One could not be democratic and capitalist at the same time. This belief likely stemmed in part from the antiapartheid struggle's socialist underpinnings. Yet the rumors that linked politicians, corruption, and capitalism spoke more immediately to government's inability (or unwillingness) to enact change in the region.

Perhaps in response to this inaction, in 2011 the Cederberg municipality became the rare municipality in the history of South Africa to have a mayor representing the Pan Africanist Party of Azania (PAC). For many people, the result was shocking. The PAC, largely black, operated on the platform of African nationalism, socialism, and continental unity, a platform that seems incongruous with local white and coloured declarations of Western Cape exceptionalism and concerns over increasing black migration to the region. While a closer examination of the results reveals a more complicated alignment of events—the PAC did not win a majority but gained the position as a condition for allying with the African National Congress (ANC)—the election was nevertheless politically significant: It marked a reversal of recent political results, in which the Democratic Alliance (DA) had won the majority of council seats.[5] As I described in chapter 3, the DA (which many in South Africa considered a "white" party because its president was white) won the majority of votes in the Western Cape, including in the areas surrounding the rooibos region.

Local people interpreted the election results in different ways depending on their social locations. One conclusion white farmers drew was that the ANC must have bused black people to the area because coloured workers' voting for the ANC would be a betrayal: "Not our people!" This rumor brought together concerns about political change, economic uncertainty, and shifting national and global agricultural trends. One moment a rooibos farmer said that he bused in his workers from the Eastern Cape, and the next moment he complained that the ANC bused people in from the Eastern Cape to win votes. The increasing informalization of agricultural labor combined with a loss of political control and with a change in the town's social relationships.

Another white farmer asserted that the ANC threatened workers into voting for the party. "One of my workers told us that," he said. "They tell us a lot of things. And we don't understand why they go and kill farmers. And of course they spread the news that all farmers are bad." I wondered if he was questioning what I had learned during interviews with workers. "There was a BBC reporter here, and he said to a farmer 'How racist you are.' But the reporters should live on a farm and see. They kill you. People from Europe or the outside don't understand." But he then added a more positive spin: "But the Western Cape is like a different country. We are family. We help each other. We have some blacks on the farm, and they are fine. Most are coloured and speak Afrikaans.... The whole world is against you. They don't see that farmers really help people on farms." He returned to expressing betrayal, again blaming outsiders—and the state broadcaster in particular—for any unease in the region. "The SABC [television crew] comes here and stirs people up, and says the farmers should give you a better house, but you give them a nice house, and they destroy it. There are animals in the house, a pig in the bathtub. They drink and break windows," he said.

> There are new laws that if people don't work for you, you can't make them leave. What other employer gives a house? You have to give water, electricity, and you can't get them out. The black people, seasonal workers, smuggle drugs.... The sad thing is the permanent workers, the coloureds, buy alcohol for twice as much from black people as they would in town. They give their clothes to the black people to get drugs and alcohol. We give them nice work clothes and Sunday clothes, and they give them away. It's sad because it's very nice people and they are family.

The farmer refused to believe that "his" workers might want to change the "natural" hierarchical relationship between white and coloured. Black people, the ANC, and even the media came under fire for destroying his social world.

"His" workers had very different views on what farmers provided them. One Friday, I walked the aisles of Spar, selecting groceries for the weekend. Since Spar was the main store in town and located prominently on Main Street, I often ran into people I knew: white farm owners stocking up for the week or coloured residents I had met at the nearby Anglican Church. But I was surprised to see Anneke, a coloured farmworker whom I knew did not have easy access to transportation. She was heading to the checkout counter with a man I had not seen before. She smiled, recognizing the "American *meisie*," and stopped to talk. She was in town only for the day to shop, having caught a ride with a group of people who lived near her. "This is Dirk," she said. "He works on another farm." She wanted me to know how much he was struggling with wages. Dirk said that he earned below minimum wage and was trying to get a new contract. Anneke pointed to her small shopping cart: "This is a week's worth of pay." It was enough food to last me maybe two or three days, but I did not have a chance to ask how many people she planned to feed with it. I looked down at my own cart, filled with the expensive brands of pasta sauce and cheese. Dirk talked about trying to switch farms, but he did not know who was hiring. "See," Anneke said. "I want you to see this, to understand." Her words echoed those of the coloured man in the hospital who insisted that my American friend look as a dead body was wheeled past us. "It isn't hard. It is life," he had said. "That's why I wanted your friend to look." With these haunting testimonials about "life," farmworkers seemed to be asking me to bear witness, to pass along their stories. Yet farmworkers did not necessarily long to leave behind the rooibos world. Rather, they dreamed, as one farmworker said, "to maybe someday leave the [commercial] farm and do my own rooibos and sheep." Or, as another put simply, "I love farming." Despite this love, I was told, workers "still experience apartheid physically and emotionally." Ostensibly, the government was working to change that.

The Government-Subsidized Factory

In principle the new factory is great. It started off really well. One or two guys got greedy. I think it will recover. If you get the right driver it will succeed. I am still positive about it. —WHITE ROOIBOS FARMER

The new factory is not about Black Economic Empowerment. That was the concept but not the reality. Reality is that government is running it. . . . It's a lie. They are using small farmers to get funding. It is 90 percent commercial farmers and 10 percent emerging. —COLOURED ROOIBOS FARMER

The factory opening was a smoke screen for a political rally. —WHITE RESIDENT

In February 2015, South Africa's *Mail and Guardian* newspaper ran the story "Rooibos Farmers: 'Empowerment Isn't Our Cup of Tea'" (King 2015). The provocative title seemed aimed to entice readers: What formerly disadvantaged community would not want to be empowered? The article described the debates surrounding the new government-subsidized factory in Nieuwoudtville, the northernmost part of the rooibos-growing region. Built in 2008 by the provincial Department of Agriculture as an "empowerment scheme," the factory's goal was to serve as a production and packaging plant for local rooibos farmers. But the factory was shrouded in mystery and controversy, as the phone call I received about it in the library indicated. The *Mail and Guardian* article discussed the relationship between the factory and members of the Heiveld, a rooibos cooperative consisting primarily of coloured farmers. According to the article, the factory (ostensibly designed to help these farmers) is forcing the Heiveld to sell it 70 percent of its harvest. Otherwise, factory overseers would confiscate the tractors and other farming equipment donated by the provincial department. Because the factory is not certified organic, factory prices would be lower than selling to their cooperative. "Many of the farmers are illiterate, so [they] did not know what they were agreeing to. And then you threaten them with losing their tractors and diesel. That's not right," the article quoted the Heiveld's general manager Alida Afrika as saying. One farmer linked the government's actions directly to life under apartheid rule: "During apartheid [we] could only sell to the large-scale white farmers, who controlled the price. After that it was companies controlling the price." He felt that working for their own cooperative was the first time coloured farmers had control over their destinies. "We worked so hard to get this and just as we are growing they want to destroy it."

Farmers were confused about the role of government, neoliberal economic policies, and postapartheid politics. In his examination of postapartheid social assistance, James Ferguson (2007) describes how the government incorporated the rhetoric of neoliberalism *and* social welfare to bring the formal and informal into a new relation. This relation, he argues, could be made appealing to both the left and the right under the guise of revolution or neoliberal technocracy. By examining the rumors surrounding the government-subsidized rooibos factory, I explore how this "new relation" of government and capital manifested itself in the rooibos region in ways that were not necessarily "new."

Unlike the social grants that Ferguson shows could be made palatable for the right and the left, the government factory seemed to occupy a different space. The official narrative described by people involved with the factory and in government press releases was that it would provide job opportunities and support both white and coloured farmers in an idealized vision of the Rainbow Nation. White and coloured farmers would work together to create opportunities and "value add" in the area. The plant supposedly cost about 120 million rand ($18 million). The ostensible model was that commercial farmers (meaning white farmers) would own 34 percent of shares in the company, "formerly disadvantaged farmers" (meaning coloured farmers) would own 26 percent, local and international investors would own 10 percent each, and the Northern Cape Department of Agriculture would own 20 percent (Genis 2011).

Discourse about the purpose of the factory shifted between the goal of establishing globalized agricultural markets and statist calls for government protection *from* globalized agribusiness. Local people's reactions were decidedly mixed. A number of white and coloured farmers were excited about the possibility of having a factory in their region and avoiding the hassle and cost of transporting tea to the main processing area about an hour and a half's drive to the south. Many people in the area felt strongly that they produced better quality tea and should be recognized for it. They wanted freedom from what they saw as the tight control of Rooibos Ltd. With the new factory, the post-apartheid government appeared to be intervening to help nonwhite farmers in the same way that the apartheid government had supported white farmers during the years of subsidized marketing boards. Yet both white and coloured residents expressed concerns about corruption. Many white farmers criticized the government's intentions and feared that the people running the factory did not know what they were doing—or, worse, that they were intentionally trying to destabilize the industry. On the other side, many coloured farmers, like the farmer quoted in the *Mail and Guardian* article, felt that the government factory was undermining their efforts to create a sustainable livelihood from rooibos.

"The factory don't speak about BEE anymore," a coloured rooibos farmer said, referring to the government's Black Economic Empowerment program designed to help redress inequality through programs such as hiring preferences, skills development, and preferential procurement for black, coloured, and Asian people. Conversely, another coloured farmer stated that the factory was *too* BEE. "Someone from the ANC said that you need to replace coloured workers with black workers," she said, perhaps expressing a concern that black migration might find its way to this remote part of the rooibos region. "Only ANC people get a job," a third coloured farmer asserted. The rumors continued:

> JOHAN (coloured farmer): The rooibos factory was never necessary. They cannot justify it commercially. It provides few jobs.

> JON (white farmer): The opening was a bit of an election campaign for the ANC. There were chants about who to vote for. The committee was there, buses from all over, premiers, a VIP buffet. Everyone got food. It cost around four million rands. It was basically government funds for an election campaign.

> MARIE (coloured farmer): The factory is using water to water the decorative plants when there is no water in town.

> PIETIE (white farmer): The government was impetuous.

There were even rumors that Julius Malema, the controversial, banned ANC Youth League leader and founder of the opposition Economic Freedom Fighters, was involved in some way. People talked of court cases, of farmers being sued, of neighbors fighting, and so on.

Of all the myriad rumors, two dominated: The factory was re-marginalizing coloured farmers in favor of white commercial farmers, and—in direct contrast—the government was undermining white farmers by disrupting the natural workings of the market. Many residents believed that the idea for a factory in the area had actually stemmed from a group of coloured farmers. "It's strange because they put out a proposal to the government for just such a factory, and people from the government came out a few times. [The government] hijacked the process." It is "for the whities," a white farmer stated, "and the emerging [coloured] farmers are just pawns." Someone even said that the government sent a woman to speak to white and coloured rooibos farmers in the community, but the woman spoke in English, despite the fact that most coloured farmers understood only Afrikaans. Supposedly, the woman said that the factory needed white farmers' help to succeed. "Thankfully," said a white farmer who had attended the meeting, "the emerging farmers couldn't understand." In this instance, Malkki's (1995) struggles over "versions" became struggles not only over the ownership of rooibos but also over the role that white and coloured, government and private-sector, and local and global civic organizations would play in forging the postapartheid social, political, and economic landscape.

The government representative's statement about "needing white farmers to succeed" would have resonated with the many coloured farmers who argued that, despite the end of apartheid, the government remained in cahoots with Afrikaans farmers. Yet just as many white farmers expressed anger over the factory as coloured farmers did. Some white farmers cited government greed and antiwhite racism. "Corruption," George said, "is a very big thing. It is part of this whole system . . . , because [under the black government], there is a new thing in South Africa: You don't 'steal'; you only 'mismanage.' That's why you don't go to jail." George argued that the sterilized language of mismanagement replaced ideas of immorality and illegality. Most farmers, however, worried that the factory would upset the "natural" workings of the tea market. They feared that the factory was paying farmers too much money and that they would—in some unforeseen time in the future—dump the tea cheaply on the market and undermine the rest of the industry. The government, a farmer said, "ignored market signals."

The racial aspects of the factory controversy were less straightforward than many antigovernment tirades I heard in other parts of the rooibos-growing region. In these areas, people talked about how black people were only out for themselves, how they were greedy and corrupt, and how much better the apartheid government was. However, the government factory complicated this narrative. "A lot of the coloured people are mistrusting. They like to talk about the new factory because it was the white people," Bert, a white farmer, said and laughed. His assessment moved back and forth between white privilege and black privilege, in which, once again, coloured people were left behind. "The black guys from government come with their laptops and leather cases and ask us questions about rooibos. If you do business, you must look at your partners," he said. "We asked them, 'Where do you want to sterilize?' 'We don't know.' 'Where do you want to market?' 'Africa.' It is supposed to be for the coloured guys, but that doesn't make sense. It is going to a chief in Limpopo province." Limpopo is located in the far north of the country, bordering Botswana, Zimbabwe, and Mozambique. The province is nearly 98 percent black, a fact that was not lost on Bert, though he could not remember where he had heard about the Limpopo connection. His voice grew louder. "But the plant is taxpayer money. If they put it up for the coloured guys, it would make some sense. They say you were left behind in apartheid. I tell my workers, in eternity you weren't left behind," he continued. "Left behind is the wrong principle. If you have something to blame, you are on the wrong path. The people at the new plant didn't want to work with Rooibos Ltd. because they are white guys. That's Africa."

While Bert was decidedly against the new factory, some people who supported it gave a historically informed retort: "Rooibos Ltd. was also a government project just like us. They forget." In this narrative, history, free-market capitalism, and government assistance were racialized, just as they had been under apartheid. Only now, with the future uncertain, no one was sure which racial group was the beneficiary. Perhaps more urgently, some people speculated that the factory was making coloured farmers unwittingly lose their fair trade or organic certifications and thus their ability to make a living off small parcels of land.[6] According to one resident, "emerging farmers" were tempted by the factory's promise of free but nonorganic rooibos seeds. In a column for the South African Civil Society Information Service, Glenn Ashton (2010) describes "Lessons from Rooibos" as warnings for other small-scale farmers:

> Rooibos is as uniquely South African as Champagne is French and Parmesan Italian. It should be one of our roaring success stories while providing a platform for the upliftment of its traditional owners, the indigenous people.... Despite these challenges some emerging indigenous farmers made remarkable headway in establishing niche markets through

the support and assistance of non-government organisations, funded mainly by Northern donors during the post democracy heyday. . . . What has specifically happened in this case is a microcosm of what has befallen our agricultural markets more generally. Political interference, whether building or dismantling systems, has inevitable unintended consequences. Neo-liberal and free market influences imposed on South Africa's agricultural system since our democratic transition have undermined true transformation of the sector by throwing our farmers to the wolves of international trade.

Ashton's comments (with the exception of referring to the emerging farmers as "indigenous") reflected many of the stories told by farmers and activists in the area. Ashton critiques government involvement *and* market forces, praising benevolent northern donors *and* condemning northern "wolves." The fact that the government seemed to undermine rooibos—the quintessential South African product—made the neoliberalization and corruption (two words often invoked together) of government practices all the more objectionable to Ashton.

"It's Different Up Here"

If you don't know someone, there is always stories. The poor producer is always in the dark, always gossiping and wondering. That's why they are so easily manipulated. —AFRIKAANS ROOIBOS FARMER

You don't know this but producers, they are a funny group. They wouldn't invest their money in Rooibos Ltd. or in anything; they would just spend it. —ROOIBOS INDUSTRY INSIDER

Citrusdal [a town on the southern end of the rooibos-growing region] competes more with the global citrus industry. The other countries don't grow rooibos. We are a community of rooibos producers. The perception around here is that it is big. But it is a small industry. It's big here, but not in the world. Citrus is big, but it is in the world. We are very small area, but for this area it is huge. —ROOIBOS FARMER

In competing rumors about the rooibos industry, another common refrain emerged: Rural farmers were too ignorant to take advantage of the globalizing possibilities of a postapartheid world. "It is different farming up here," a white farmer said. "If you are isolated you start believing what you think. It is a fairly close-knit community and fights among people, but everyone knows everyone." Many people in the industry asserted that farmers did not understand the economy or the rooibos market. This potentially willful ignorance, some insisted, was the reason for the rumors and feuds; there were no deeper, structural reasons.

Notably, many farmers who delivered to Rooibos Ltd. told stories that were quite different from those voiced by farmers who believed Michael or the company "controlled the hands of the market." To the people who stood by it, Rooibos Ltd. was attempting to counteract farmers' and other processors' greed—a greed that led to overplanting and an oversupply of tea. "If prices are too low, farmers will neglect their farms. If they are too high, farmers over-plant," one industry insider said, remaking the farmer as an automaton, a *Homo economicus* driven entirely by market forces. "We just want to work with the soil," another farmer said, differentiating himself from the "automatons." "We aren't concerned with economy unless it becomes too bad." In this view, the farmer was above the market, desiring only to belong with nature.

Through these farming narratives, a picture of romantic nationalism emerged in which the soul is bound up with the soil. One of the biggest farm owners in the region, however, scoffed at these sentiments. "Most of the people on rooibos tea farms spent 90 percent of their life on the farm and they can't do anything else. . . . They are afraid of losing the farm and going to work for someone else or trying to do something they can't do. Most don't have much education." Many people said that rooibos farmers were lower class than citrus farmers and thus less able to cope with changing agricultural circumstances. A farmer who cultivated both rooibos and citrus explained this position: "Clanwilliam, they are more 'Karoo' people. . . . Clanwilliam is older people with older attitudes." I asked what him what he meant by "Karoo people." He replied, "The Karoo people are mean, rural, plain, common."

Class dynamics combined with persistent English-Afrikaans tensions to inform rumors that erased the coloured presence. Some Afrikaans farmers felt that the English took advantage of their forefathers because of their cultural attributes. One Afrikaans farmer spoke about his frustration with the Rooibos Council and the fact that more farmers were not actively involved: "For Afrikaners, this is a big problem in life. They want to do it on their own. It's an independence thing." Dawie, another Afrikaans farmer, explained the "problem" with the Afrikaner: "It is interesting to know the politics. Among Afrikaners, there's a self-destruct button. . . . They will buy [someone's] farm for one-third the price and then say 'Hi' to him in church. There may be politics in the industry, but it's the Afrikaners." Even community leaders expressed frustration at the Afrikaans population's lack of cohesiveness. "Individuals are doing a lot, but as a team they are not doing anything. I am supposed to be their shepherd. But they are not pulling in the same direction."

Others dismissed both coloured and Afrikaans farmers. "They don't understand supply and demand economics. At the farms, and even in town, their world is so small," a farmer said, distancing himself from other rooibos farmers. "They don't want to know about climate change and global finances. They just want a roof over their heads. They don't care about the outside world." A stereotype of a backwoods farmer trying desperately to hold on to a bygone life emerged, but there was something more at play. Certainly, the changes brought on by a political transition coupled with a more globalized, commoditized agricultural landscape were unsettling to people's views of life. Despite the stereotype, most residents seemed to have a thorough understanding of changing ecological and economic circumstances. They preferred to label *neighboring* farmers ignorant. Perhaps by doing so, they were able to gain a sense of control.

Conclusion

How does one tell the history of an industry? In exploring this question, I return to the comment from a community organizer that began the chapter: "There are bigger political things happening, and people get sidetracked [by] conspiracies of who benefited and this and that." The organizer labeled himself an ardent comrade in the fight against global capitalism. He felt that rumors distracted people from the real struggle: Stopping neoliberal policies from undermining efforts to combat centuries of white hegemony. Through descriptions of competing rooibos cosmologies, however, I argue that residents' conspiracies represented more than just a distraction from larger political and economic issues. Rooibos rumors had force.

Fighting in the streets, lawsuits, eternal damnation—to farmers, narratives were not just about economics or politics or land rights, but also about rooibos's cosmology and how that cosmology would be represented to the world. More than rehashing a tale about the neoliberalization of the rooibos industry— and South Africa as a whole—I take seriously how rumors, gossip, and cosmologies affected residents' worldviews and had concrete effects on the people and the plant. It was crucial to people that I got the "correct" version of rooibos's history according to their particular worldview. In the context of a fused human-plant social and ecological world, the force of these sentiments and the stakes involved were high. The battle over history was not only about looking to the past, but also about determining the course of rooibos's future and attempting to protect that future from the seemingly unstoppable effects of globalization and climate change. To some in the area, projects such as the new government rooibos factory marked a continuation of apartheid attitudes. Attempts at neoliberal economic policies were intersected by a force more potent: race.

At the same time, the lifting of international sanctions after apartheid allowed agribusinesses to gain a foothold in the rooibos-growing area. The post-sanction milieu solidified large companies' control over the industry, but it also opened spaces for other industry actors, such as foreign donors, NGOs, and small-scale coloured farming cooperatives. The region was pursued by international and national development agencies and community organizers, all too happy to attach themselves to the photogenic landscape and the redemptive qualities of a healthy African beverage. Gillian Hart (2002) highlights how the powerful discourses of neoliberal globalization can delimit action and political identities, becoming "disabling" in light of seemingly inexorable market forces. Yet some rooibos farmers used the discourse and economic benefits of globalization to *enable* different possibilities. Some took advantage of the government-subsidized factory to gain new markets for their tea. Others joined with international certifying bodies to create fair trade farms that sold their tea at higher prices to wealthy consumers in the Global North. However, for the majority of the coloured population, eking out a livelihood, let alone owning a rooibos farm, remained frustratingly out of reach. The rumors and uncertainties coalesced in the ideas I discuss in the final chapter: anxieties about the future, anxieties that centered on struggles over land tenure, fears over the alienability of rooibos, and concerns about the role of climate change.

{ 5 }

PRECARIOUS

LANDSCAPES

After the thrill of liberation has gone and our cosmopolitan
romance with South Africa has waned, the specter of history repeating itself casts
a pall as the iniquities of apartheid continue to resurface and linger.
—LYNN MESKELL, *The Nature of Heritage*

[The 2013] annual Clanwilliam Wildflower Show . . .
will pay tribute to the unsung heroes of the floral spectacular: the millions
of tiny creatures that pollinate these plants. Birds, bugs, insects, rodents—
you name it, every living creature found within the floral kingdom plays its
own unique role in the pollination of the flowers, ensuring their survival
for generations to come. But it is a fine balance, an ecosystem so sensitive
to change that it literally is balanced on a knife's edge.
—FACEBOOK PAGE, Clanwilliam Wildflower Festival (2013)

"Rising Tensions Explode in Grisly Violence at South African Mine," a CNN
headline read in August 2012. While strikes and labor unrest had been a nearly
constant part of South African economic life for years, the violence at Lonmin
mine in the country's North West province attracted international headlines.
In a scene eerily reminiscent of apartheid-era violence, the police opened fire
on striking miners, killing dozens. The violence at the mines—and the waves
of strikes that followed across different sectors—pointed to the fragility of
postapartheid labor relations. In the Western Cape, including the rooibos region, many agricultural workers began striking in an attempt to raise their daily
wages from sixty-nine rands (about $7.50) to 150 rands (about $16.50).

"The situation outside Clanwilliam remains tense as police are trying to stop a group of striking farmworkers from marching to the town centre," reported the South African Broadcasting Corporation.[1] By February 2013, farmers and workers across the Western Cape had reached an agreement to raise the minimum wage. I visited the region a month after the strikes ended. Knowing that most rooibos farmworkers were not unionized, I was surprised to learn that the strikes had unsettled Clanwilliam. "The farmworker strikes were really scary," an Afrikaans resident said. He described his fears about his girlfriend's safety when strikers came between her and their home. For coloured residents, the end of the strikes brought out distinctly different concerns. A government employee predicted that the increased minimum wage would lead to more evictions of farmworkers: "Farmers are saying they can't afford the wage. . . . Illegal migrants will get the jobs because they will take anything. Local people will get fired." Petrus, a white resident, agreed: "The farmers are now turning to more mechanization so they don't have to have farmworkers." Foreign bodies and machines seemed primed to take over the roles that coloured farmworkers had formerly held, despite what appeared to be a victory for labor. "Will the local government help?" I asked Petrus. "There is drama in the municipality," was his only response.

Behind the strikes, a constellation of fears manifested itself in ways that seemed to touch on nearly every aspect of the region's social relations. Wages were too low to support farmworkers' livelihoods; migrants and neoliberal economic policies were unsettling coloured and Afrikaans labor relations; technology was making farmworkers expendable; residents did not trust politicians; and white farmers worried that coloured workers were becoming radicalized. Expressions of generalized anxiety lurked behind nearly every interview, every meeting, and every social event. "Maybe," Willie, an Afrikaans farmer, said, "there are so many rumors due to that everyone is a bit nervous. They are trying to make money as quickly as possible because they don't know how long it will last. It is emotional." When I probed further about farmers' apprehensions, conversations took a number of directions. We discussed people's concerns about the African National Congress (ANC) government and "corrupt fat cats." Farmers worried that global agribusinesses would buy rooibos land or that land redistribution would unsettle the sanctity of private property. People described dramatic conspiracies regarding local and international competitors, regarding a unified nonwhite community, and even regarding the influence that rooibos's "cultural marketing" might have on Afrikaans and coloured residents' precarious claims to belonging in the region. Others worried about the impact of HIV/AIDS, drugs, and violence.

Today, life for many South Africans is defined by social, political, economic, and ecological precarity. In the rooibos region, anxieties came together through the feeling that something—whether it was the climate, the government, the market, or changing demographics—would betray them in the future. The anxiety took different forms depending on residents' social locations, but commonalities also existed across social boundaries. Residents feared that rooibos would become a commodity and lose its "miracle-like" qualities. The certainty of rooibos as a stable object, anchoring uncertain lives and precarious indigeneities, seemed to be unraveling through the destabilizing economic, political, and climatic changes apparent to many farmers. In other words, fears about rooibos's commodification connected to the ultimate anxiety: The possibility that rooibos's very identity as an indigenous crop might become uprooted from its territory if climate change shifted the rooibos ecosystem southward.

Drawing on these highly emotive issues, I show how anxieties were related to issues of entanglement and alienation. Karl Marx (1988 [1927]) describes alienation as estrangement, or the separation of things that "naturally" belong together. In the rooibos region, these symbiotic connections included rooibos, farmers, and the indigenous ecosystem. Yet the symbiosis expressed by farmers also erased the very people whose lives remained the most precarious: farmworkers, the poor, and the unemployed. According to Marx, alienation can take on multiple forms. In *The Economic and Philosophic Manuscripts of 1884* (1988 [1927]), he describes four types of alienation within capitalist modes of production: alienation of the worker from the product of his labor; alienation of the worker from the act of producing; alienation of the worker from himself as a producer; and alienation of the worker from other workers. In all of these forms of alienation, Marx specifically focuses on the worker. He argues that the worker loses the ability to determine his life when he loses the right to conceive of himself as the director of his actions. In the rooibos region, it was not just the worker who feared alienation; it was nearly everyone whose livelihood and sense of belonging depended on the plant.

In this context of entanglement and estrangement, farmers and workers repeatedly told me, "We don't want rooibos to become a commodity." The statement appeared to have two different, yet overlapping meanings. Because they believed in rooibos's unique value and because their livelihoods depended on this value, they did not want to lose the rooibos "brand." Just as designers try to distinguish their luxury brands from generic knockoffs, farmers wanted to ensure that "the market" recognized the high value of the indigenous plant and thus priced it accordingly—not as an ordinary commodity, but as a unique and charismatic substance.

But branding was not their only concern. Political economy theories define a commodity as a good or service produced by human labor and sold on the market. Many farmers insisted that rooibos was not a commodity because it was not necessarily produced by human labor at all. Rather, it represented an interdependent relationship that blurred the boundaries between man and nature. If rooibos became a "commodity," it risked being estranged from the fynbos ecosystem, from residents' livelihoods, and from their senses of belonging. Commodification in this context implied a rupture in residents' concept of an indigeneity forged with the rooibos plant. Their feelings about the market, however, were complex. While they did not want to call rooibos a commodity, they also did not block it from commodity exchange. The sale of rooibos was necessary for farmers' livelihoods, *and its commodification gave the plant and the land the very economic value that allowed the triadic relationship among plant, person, and place to sustain itself.*

This chapter examines how farmers resolved this ambivalence by allowing rooibos to be a commodity in one sense but not in another. They used a strategy of localization, or geographical indications (GIs), labels used on products to indicate a geographical area of origin, so that, like champagne, tea could be called "rooibos" only if it grew in its "proper" territory. By codifying rooibos's regional specificity—its indigeneity to *this* landscape with *these* people—farmers could protect its charisma from a placeless idea of global commodity production and exchange. Yet a strategy of localization led to its own, profound anxieties. If rooibos farmers claimed their belonging through the plant, what would happen if the plant acted in a way that undermined the relationship between specific people and specific ecosystem? What if rooibos was indifferent to farmers' love?

In addressing these questions, I divide the chapter into two parts. The first part explores the landscapes of precarity, disillusionment, and anxiety that were seemingly central to being South African more than fifteen years after apartheid. By 2011, the country had experienced a retreat from the hopeful and redemptive language of the Rainbow Nation to something more uncertain and potentially threatening. The second part addresses the commodification of rooibos and farmers' strategy of localization as they attempted to codify rooibos's indigenous belonging in a specific landscape. Concerns about rooibos's commodification spoke to a deeper anxiety. Residents' uncertain claims to belonging *in place* merged with uncertainty of the *rootedness of place itself.* I conclude by addressing industry efforts to delineate and control these ambiguities and potential forms of alienation through the use of supposedly neutral scientific methods such as mapping, classifying, and measuring with satellite technology.

Landscapes of Anxiety and Disillusionment in the New South Africa
In the post-colonial, post-apartheid, neo-liberal new South Africa poor
and marginalized citizens continue to struggle for land, housing and health care.
They must respond to uncertainty and radical contingencies on a daily basis.
—STEVEN L. ROBINS, *From Revolution to Rights in South Africa*

FIELD NOTES, JANUARY 2011: *"There is fear at the moment in South Africa,"*
Barend, an Afrikaans farmer, said as he opened his beer and sat down on a dirty
folding chair near a fire. He stirred the coals, rearranged the grill, and tried to
get the flame to catch. "Are you afraid?" I asked. He shook his head, "I don't have
fears." Placing the meat on the grill, he continued. "But there is fear about [the
evictions that occurred on white-owned farms in Zimbabwe beginning in 2000].
Most farmers just have agricultural degrees, so it's hard to start over in another
country. Some people are coming back who moved to America and Australia be-
cause it doesn't have the same quality of living." He turned the meat, and the smell
of dripping, burning fat reached my nose. I coughed. "We don't have subsidies,"
Barend explained. I was unsure if he was comparing his situation to that of Amer-
ican farmers—I often heard that complaint—or if he was describing a nostalgia
for apartheid-era subsidies. "There is fear if you have young children; you want to
give him a new future." I noticed that he said "him" and smiled to myself. As usual,
male farmers left women out of discussions of landownership.

Poking at the fire, Barend changed gears. "In the end, the people who will
hurt the most is workers because everything will fall apart. These are the fears of
the average white farmer, even if you are a black or coloured farmer. You should
go overseas while young or wait." But some people don't want to leave, he con-
tinued. "I lived here, my father lived here. People will not give up. There will
be armed resistance." I was uncertain what he meant by "even if you are a black
or coloured farmer," but I was unable to press further because he got up from his
chair and yelled to his friends, who were drinking beer at a nearby table. "The
meat is ready!" Armed resistance? I thought to myself. This wasn't the first time
a farmer had mentioned that to me. These farmers were not part of a far-right
Afrikaans resistance movement (although "everyone knew" which families had
belonged to the Afrikaans Broederband, a "secret" organization dedicated to Af-
rikaner nationalism). Yet the idea that nothing would disrupt their primordial
attachments to the land appeared central to their attempts to find some kind of
peace as racial minorities who no longer controlled the government. In moments
of candor, white farmers sometimes expressed concerns about their own poten-
tial estrangement from rooibos land by "global capitalists" or by the nonwhite
government.

Following the end of apartheid, the late 1990s marked a period of economic stagnation and changing relations of production in South Africa's agricultural sector. These combined forces led to a surfeit of unemployed people who wondered whether they would ever find jobs in agriculture again. Postapartheid euphoria met with people's confusion about the role of the new government, neoliberal economic policies, postapartheid politics, and the realization *or* abandonment of the apartheid resistance movement's revolutionary, leftist rhetoric (Peet 2002). Anxiety became part of a "structure of feeling" that was seemingly central to being South African.

In using the term "structure of feeling," I draw on Raymond Williams (1961). Addressing the idea of cultural change, Williams (1979) uses the word "structure" to describe how feelings can become patterns of impulses, restraints, and tones. In this sense, feelings are not random or merely sentimental; rather, they become social experiences that are actively lived and felt. Through "structures of feeling," Williams (1977) describes how social change is not directionless flux; it leads to new "starting points" and new "conclusions." Building on this idea, I focus on the structures of anxiety that accompanied the uncertainty of what new "starting points" and "conclusions" might imply in a postapartheid landscape threatened by climate change. In South Africa, generalized fears magnified daily concerns about the impact of globalization on the country (du Toit and Neves 2014). Yet the anxiety in the rooibos-growing area crossed class and racial borders in complicated ways, with different stakes and different potential consequences. These concerns merged fears of lost cultural homogeneity with declining biological diversity, as plants, commodities, and people traveled across space and seemed to upend the region's social and ecological relations.

Anxiety has a particular history in South Africa. During apartheid, literature and research on South Africa highlighted the idea of uncertainty and nervous expectation. J. M. Coetzee's novel *Waiting for the Barbarians* (1999 [1980]) describes the state of anxiety that residents of the Empire (understood to be South Africa) experienced in their daily lives, as they feared attack—seemingly always on the horizon—by barbarians whom they could never fully control. Vincent Crapanzano's ethnographic piece *Waiting: The Whites of South Africa* explores similar lurking fears. "South Africa today is caught up in a deadened time of waiting," he wrote in 1985. "For most whites, waiting is compounded by fear; for most blacks, however great their poverty or despair, waiting is illuminated by hope, by a belief that time is on their side. For the Coloureds and Asians, there is both fear *and* hope in waiting" (Crapanzano 1985: xxii). The racialized idea of waiting described by Crapanzano implied a lack of movement. Crapanzano articulates the stasis before the change.

With the end of apartheid, the "wait" was presumably over, but the anxiety remained and took on new and perhaps even more uncertain qualities in the rooibos region. Apprehensions acquired two opposing qualities. For some, anxiety was about constant, uncontrollable change; for others, it was about the fact that, after years of "waiting," little had actually changed. Unanswered questions seemed to float in the air, invoked by different people at different times. Is the "barbarian" the black immigrant or the invasive species that I described in chapter 3? Or is it the "radicalized youth," fed up with continuing inequality? Or is the barbarian not black at all but, rather, the "global capitalist" waiting to descend and steal rooibos land and profits?

Despite the particularities of the rooibos region, the narratives of anxiety reflected similar themes throughout the country: continuing—and even exacerbating—poverty among the rural poor, enduring white economic hegemony and the emergence of postapartheid opportunism. For the white and coloured populations of the rooibos-growing area, these postapartheid uncertainties also built on historical fears about being minorities in a majority black country. They worried about losing their racial privilege and distinction. The apartheid government used fear as a kind of social control, and this form of control hardly ended with the first democratic elections. In the rooibos region, some commercial farmers were able to capitalize on the uncertainty by taking over land abandoned by white farmers frightened at the prospect of a majority-black government. Other white farmers attempted to use the uncertainty to keep their coloured workers dependent on them. And outsiders—white, black, and coloured—leveraged the uncertainty to gain access to the industry's economic resources. The anxieties, however, worked alongside continued expressions of hope for new, nonracial possibilities. In this context, the symbolic value of rooibos as South Africa's *national* beverage and rooibos's role in notions of *local* belonging made ownership of rooibos land all the more fraught.

"Farmers' Concerns Are Pure Racism"

The "land issue" dominated newspaper headlines as much between 2010 and 2012 as it had during the postapartheid transition of 1994. Politicians and the media debated reforms to government land acts, and Julius Malema, former leader of the ANC Youth League, called for immediate land redistribution. "The settlers committed a black genocide and made the black landowners into slaves. . . . If the leaders of this revolution are not prepared to fight for this land, the economic freedom fighters will," Malema told a group of supporters in Soweto, adding that South African land must be returned to its "rightful owners" (Bauer 2012). White people, he emphasized, did not bring the land with them from Europe. Malema's speech about land redistribution consumed journalists, and people involved in local Cederberg politics often mentioned it.

Despite Malema's fiery rhetoric and Barend's discussion of the Zimbabwe farm evictions, few white farmers in the rooibos-growing area expressed worries about losing their land. When I asked farmers such as Barend about land redistribution, they were resolute in insisting that their ancestors were the first to live on and cultivate the land. Yet white farmers often added a caveat, an expression of anxiety that made its way past the bravado. Pierre, one of the biggest farmers in the area, replied that land redistribution "doesn't really affect us. We're more concerned with how efficiently our taxes are used." I asked him what he thought about Malema. "As a business and from a supply base it doesn't worry me," he said. "And anyway, black people don't want land. They don't want land—they just want space for a few cows and to have cell phones and nice things. It's all political." He focused his attention instead on the attitudes of other white farmers: "The concern you have here amongst farmers is pure racism. They haven't lost anything. They are not threatened. If anything, they are economically better off." Pierre viewed his rooibos land as a business and believed that he held an economically rational view of the political system.

Corporate-style rooibos farmers such as Pierre often assumed that global capital would function seamlessly no matter what the political situation, despite the fact that the charisma of rooibos's indigeneity trapped them firmly in place. According to Pierre, the ANC, once the leading force in a Marxist-influenced liberation movement, would never let Malema interfere with the workings of capital. Some white farmers were emotional, he argued, moved by an irrational fear resulting from their loss of political power, even as they made substantial economic gains. His comments about black people also revealed his own essentialized views of race. He was not concerned about losing his rooibos land because he believed that economics transcended politics, but he was also not concerned because he believed that black people were childlike, attracted only to "nice things" and uninterested in land or development.

Other white farmers expressed emotions that vacillated among hopelessness, faith, and anger. "People don't take Malema seriously, but that's a problem," Bert, an Afrikaans farmer said. "You should worry about things that you can do things about. See, I am also a religious man. I have faith in myself, my wife, the people that work for me. We can make a success anywhere in the world. At this stage, I love this country, and I love what I am doing. If I listened to everything, I wouldn't be in South Africa anymore. But if it happens,

I'd burn my farm and then go, so they can start with nothing like we did." He paused, "I'm worried, but I can do nothing about it. But it does make me angry." Bert trusted that he could move to a different country and still manage to succeed. Unlike some farmers, he asserted that his livelihood was not completely tied to the rooibos land, despite his love of it. Yet his final comment was telling: "I'd burn my farm and then go." He explained that he did not want black people to get anything for "free." They would have to "earn" their right to the land like his ancestors supposedly did through their blood and sweat. For Bert, rooibos land was not an inalienable part of his existence; he could move on. But he could not allow the farm that he built to pass on to someone else. He would destroy it first. In this sense, while the land was alienable, his toil on the land—his relationship with the land—was not, *even if coloured and black workers did most of the actual labor.*

A slight distinction existed, however, between larger-scale commercial farmers such as Pierre and Bert and smaller-scale white commercial farmers with respect to whether Malema and people like him posed a threat. While corporate farmers presumed that no one would disrupt the mechanisms of agricultural capital, Marius, an Afrikaans farmer who worked on a small farm with his father and a few workers, was bold for a different reason: He claimed that farmers would never surrender. "Farmers are definitely not fearful. Farmers won't let anyone stop them. They will fight," he declared. "They are farming because it is in their hearts. They are not concerned. There is no way farmers will let their rights go. It will be a civil war. Government acknowledges that."

Yet Marius's bravado went only so far—he expressed a fear, always there, always lurking. "With the 'Shoot the Boer' song, they are stirring people up. It's scary. They imprint it in people's minds. There is always, it's always in the back of our minds." He referred to a trial about Malema's singing an apartheid struggle song, "Shoot the Boer," or "Shoot the Afrikaner/Farmer." The trial was ongoing at the time, and it infuriated many residents. Discussing it, one white farmer said that some people were abandoning their land and moving to Australia. "If they stay here," he added, "the chances are good that they could lose everything." Another white farmer and his wife expressed outright concern. "We have fear of redistribution of land. You are not so sure that you will get your money that you have invested in a lifetime, no, over generations." He wife jumped in: "We have a very insecure future here. There is a lot of legislation. We have to wait and see. But our son doesn't want to go to the States or the U.K."

These uncertainties reflected a broader anxiety about how to negotiate a changing agricultural market in the context of South Africa's political transition. To white farmers, the stability of the rooibos market was predicted in part on the certainty of land tenure and private property. Despite worries that the nonwhite government might take land from white people, Afrikaans farmers rarely mentioned apprehensions about their own workers and their desires to own rooibos land. For most white farmers, coloured workers remained invisible, their erasure serving to naturalize white landownership. In white residents' descriptions, rooibos was spiritual, inalienable, and created not through labor but through the grace of God and nature. In treating rooibos as kin rather than a commodity, white farmers fetishized it. Making rooibos strictly "natural" rendered coloured labor invisible.

Rooibos Workers, Rights, and Species-Being

"The situation is that farmworkers have no rights," a man stood up and yelled in a worker-related meeting. His worn blue uniform had the name of the commercial farm where he lived and worked emblazoned across his chest. Applause erupted around the room. People began shouting, "*Amandla!*" the ANC chant that means "Power!" While he employed a rights-based discourse that evoked politicized ideas of power, the man sitting next to me expressed another desire. "I just want a life; that's all I want," he said, his wrinkled eyes evidence of years of labor under the hot Cederberg sun. Unable to respond to him among the chaos of the meeting, I wondered: What does it mean to "have a life" as a worker? A black government employee quieted the crowd; he stood in the front of the room and spoke about efforts to ensure greater workers' rights to housing on commercial farms. Coming from a distant province, he spoke in English rather than in Afrikaans. Since many workers did not understand English, they waited impatiently for the translation, grumbling audibly. The use of English made many people in attendance angry. "We don't understand English," the workers said repeatedly. One man yelled, "We are in an Afrikaans area. Speak Afrikaans." During the meeting, government employees handed out a report about workers' rights. The report was in English, so even though people took copies, I wondered how they would understand it. The significance of language use cannot be underestimated. The man who translated to workers was an ANC Party member and a candidate for reelection to the Municipal Council. By spreading the word of workers' rights, he endeared himself to workers in a way that had resonance for many in attendance. When the translation finally occurred, a woman sitting in the row in front of me repeated one word quietly to herself: *waardigheid* (dignity).

The harsh conditions of farmworkers in the Western Cape have been well documented: food insecurity, high levels of disease resulting from cramped housing, and often total dependence on farmers because of isolated locations. Marx argues that laboring to produce commodities turns the *worker* from a human being into a *commodity*, "the most wretched of commodities" (Marx 1988 [1927]). Speaking about South Africa, Franco Barchiesi (2011) describes how a neoliberal shift to work-based social citizenship rendered workers "commodities" in a country whose constitutional guarantees of inclusion no longer appeared sufficient to protect them from systematic socioeconomic violence.

In this political and economic context, workers faced an existential form of anxiety: They feared their conditions might never change. Yet many coloured workers who had lived with and farmed rooibos for generations expressed a connection to the plant and a belief that they could regain their dignity through their cultural ownership of it. Like the man sitting next to me at the meeting, they wanted a "life"—a desire, I realized, that went beyond a generic idea of rights. Indeed, when I spoke to workers about what they meant by "rights," they almost always mentioned having access to land so that they could farm their own rooibos. Only rarely did they mention wages.

Despite the focus on access to land, workers' conditions remained a central, if rarely addressed component of the rooibos industry. When the man yelled, "The problem is we have no rights," he spoke to this frustration. In rooibos-related meetings, workers were mentioned as an aside, included in documents such as the *Handbook for Implementing Rooibos Sustainability Standards*, but skipped over in every industry meeting I attended. "Oh, we already comply with the legislation. That is not an issue," an industry member said at one meeting, and people nodded in agreement. The use of the term "rights" often entered these discussions. A teacher who worked at a local farm school described some of her lessons. On Human Rights Day, she said, "We teach them about their rights, but also about their responsibilities." The teacher's instruction about responsibilities and rights could signal the training of a new generation of self-governing neoliberal subjects and the internalization of neoliberal discourse in the South African school system. The discourse was echoed in the worker-related meeting that I discussed earlier. "Workers have rights and duties," the government employee read from the pamphlet, "and farmers have rights and duties." Issues of race and power were seemingly erased in this moment. Everyone had obligations to everyone else.

While I have discussed relations between white farmers and coloured and black workers elsewhere in this book, in this section I explore workers' alienation as it specifically relates to Marx's concept of species-being. As he explains the concept: "The life of the species, both in man and in animals, consists physically in the fact that man (like the animal) lives on organic nature" (Marx (1988 [1927]: 75). Yet he draws a distinction between man and animal. Human nature, he continues, cannot allow a person to be separated from his activity as a worker. Thus, species-being implies a worker's innate potential as a person. Marx's use of the concept "species" is significant. He draws from Hegel's idea about the uniqueness of man as a result of man's consciousness, his ability to reflect on his condition (Hegel 1977 [1807]).[2] Marx (1988 [1927]: 76) explains: "The animal is immediately one with its life activity. It does not distinguish itself from it. It is *its life activity*. Man makes his life activity itself the object of his will and of his consciousness. He has conscious life activity."

Marx describes conscious life activity as distinguishing man from animal. But he extends the idea further: He believed that the distinctly human attribute was not merely consciousness but also free labor. Consequently, for Marx free labor determined man's "species-life": "Through this production, nature appears as *his* work and his reality. The object of labor is, therefore, the *objectification of man's species-life*: for he duplicates himself not only, as in consciousness, intellectually, but also actively, in reality, and therefore he sees himself in a world that he has created. In tearing away from man the object of his production, therefore, estranged labor tears from him his *species-life*, his real objectivity as a member of the species and transforms his advantage over animals into the disadvantage that his inorganic body, nature, is taken from him" (Marx 1988 [1927]: 76). Historically engrained racism may have rendered coloured and black workers less than human in the eyes of many white farmers, but if one follows Marx's concept of species-being, their alienation as workers also rendered them animal.

Through their sense of belonging with rooibos, however, coloured workers were not "torn" from the world that they created, and they often expressed a love of the land and the plants with which they spent their lives. Yet their expressions were largely unheard in the industry, rendering them invisible in the rooibos-farming process. In 2010–2011, most of the efforts by NGOs and government departments centered on small-scale farmers who already had access to land, as opposed to labor organizing or workers' rights, outside of housing security. Even a prominent *union* focused more on small-scale farmers than on workers.

While the erasure of workers by white farmers may have served to justify white belonging in the soil, the erasure by union organizers could have stemmed in part from a history in which black South Africans resisted wage labor and viewed independent agriculture as an alternative to capitalist production relations. "With rooibos, I need to organize a black voice," said George, a labor organizer from outside the region. He used the word "black" to describe a unified, nonwhite community that he envisioned he would foster in the rooibos-growing area. "We will have economic liberation only through organizing. . . . Then you can engage the captains of industry. I know their level of arrogance. They have a soup-kitchen mentality. We want economic change. What is happening here is 'fronting,' where they use our black people and co-opt them into something and give them a title that is impressive but useless, and they give them some money, but it is window dressing." We sat in his urban office surrounded by ANC posters and boxes of ANC T-shirts that he planned to hand out in anticipation of the upcoming municipal elections.

While George was not officially part of the ANC, people said that he was well connected and "more ANC than the ANC." Over the noise of traffic outside his building, we discussed the creation of a new farming cooperative for coloured rooibos farmers in an isolated, mountainous part of the region. The co-op, George explained, would be free of white interference and white capitalist relations of production and would allow rooibos farmers to change the industry in a profound way. He would help this community, whom he called "lost sheep." George would be the shepherd. Taking a messianic tone, George responded to the intense anxieties among coloured rooibos farmers. Part of the community decided to join George's proposed new co-op, but another part was suspicious of another outsider trying to mine the region's rooibos gold. Out of this division, the community became embroiled in lawsuits and feuds over the tea.

Paul, a farmer who sided with the new co-op, said that before George came "we were not getting any money for our tea. . . . The [old co-op] had lawyers, the [Democratic Alliance] regime, the Department of Agriculture. How can you side with these corrupt fat cats? They are driving around with their SUVs with girls. . . . If we make one solid voice, we cannot be manipulated." I admit that I had trouble imagining "fat cats" with fancy cars driving around the resource-poor community with pothole-filled dirt roads. "Ridiculous," a farmer who stayed with the old co-op told me later. Outsiders like George, she continued, "just want to steal from them." A coloured farmer from another town sighed when I brought up the new co-op. "Every time it's someone from the outside coming in . . . they want to talk to me, but . . . ," he said, trailing off. George's, Paul's, and other residents' passionate narratives conveyed the stakes involved in controlling rooibos's symbolic and economic power. Significantly, though, George did not reach out to workers on commercial rooibos farms, who in 2011 remained almost entirely nonunionized. In his work on plantations, Eric Wolf (1982: 355) describes how "even labor historians were more interested in efforts to transcend a condition than in delineating that condition itself." This statement had resonance with rooibos labor organization and its attention to creating small-scale farms rather than improving conditions on commercial farms. Even as George tried to "organize a black voice," he ignored the voices of the workers. In the rooibos context, the significance of land remained paramount even in the imaginary of a labor organizer, despite the fact that rooibos land seemed increasingly unattainable.

The Uncertainty of Coloured Land Tenure

The northern end of the rooibos-farming region is a dry, desolate place. After driving to a plateau at the top of a windy pass more than a thousand feet above sea level, you can feel the transition from one climate zone to the next. A tourism website for the area calls it "a place where the experience of silence, space and stars contribute to a tranquil way of life."[3] While life is not tranquil for coloured workers, farmers, or the unemployed, the vastness of the silence, space, and stars is haunting. I spent many nights watching the crisp, clear moon rise over the small rock formations that dotted the otherwise flat plateau, broken up only by the occasional farmhouse, sheep fence, dirt road, or rooibos field. Farms stretched for miles, as the nutrient-poor soil could not sustain most kinds of agriculture, and farmers often earned livelihoods from herds of sheep that rotated from one large grazing area to another. I once sat on a porch for hours, as day turned to dusk and then to night, watching hundreds of sheep file silently from one field to the next.

Here, miles from any city, a group of coloured rooibos farmers owned their own land—and had owned it since before the days of apartheid. Most residents said that they came to possess the land because a relative married a white man long ago. They maintained ownership throughout the apartheid era largely because of the land's isolation, nutrient-poor soil, low rainfall, and the fact that, as one farmer stated, "I think no one sort of wanted it before the tea." Rooibos's ecological requirements gave the previously marginal land economic value. Despite the fact that only a small number of coloured farmers owned land, few land claims or land transfers from white to coloured hands had occurred.[4]

Arend, a coloured farmer, worked in an office to earn extra money when he was not tending his rooibos. He had obtained rights to cultivate a parcel of farmland (though not live on it) but needed to supplement his farming income with another job. He described the effort he and his small group had put into accessing land. "We sent a proposal to the government in 1998," he began. By 2002, they had obtained some funding. "Initially, we used some of our money to rent the land . . . , but we negotiated with the government, and the Department of Land Reform bought the land for us [to use for farming]. . . . The land then cost 180,000 rands," he explained. "Now, it would be a lot more, like 1.5 million rands [about $150,000], especially with the new rooibos company built here." I asked him who had owned the land they purchased. "We got it from a white commercial farmer," he said. "He was one of the first commercial farmers to sell land to emerging farmers. We did not notice that it was a significant parcel until we saw the rooibos plants."[5] For Arend, finding rooibos plants was like finding gold. Instead of attempting to eke out a livelihood from sheepherding, his group could form a rooibos cooperative and sell their tea into the international market. "God blessed us," he said. His group, however, was having trouble earning enough to sustain every member. "I am not a small-scale farmer," he added, referring to one of the euphemisms used to describe coloured farmers. "A small farmer chooses to be small. I am only a small farmer because I have limited access to land. Access is the main problem."

His group consisted mostly of former farmworkers; they were trying to get more land so they could farm full time, but "the government says rooibos land costs too much money," at more than ten times that of sheep land. "But we say that rooibos is indigenous." He explained that rooibos land should cost more because of its indigenous value, but that its indigeneity should also make the government more invested in transferring it from white to coloured farmers. Rooibos became a blessing and a curse, and the government's relation to it was confusing to Arend. The plant offered the possibility of earning a livelihood. He asserted that the previous farmer did not do much with the land. "We've made it productive," he insisted. "The municipality sees this and now they want to give land to their friends."

Rooibos's economic productivity made obtaining rooibos land seemingly impossible for people such as Arend because it increased the land's market price. According to Arend, government corruption, combined with the government's "willing buyer, willing seller" model of land redistribution, exacerbated the difficulty of transferring land from white to coloured farmers. "Willing buyer, willing seller" was a market-led model of agrarian reform influenced by the World Bank and other international institutions. Under this pro-market model, previously dispossessed people, such as the landless coloured of the rooibos region, could ostensibly apply for grants to purchase land from "willing sellers" at "fair market prices" or to purchase shares in existing commercial enterprises. The model, however, had been largely unsuccessful in redistributing land. As one government worker said: Why would a farmer willingly sell productive land?

Despite the intense desire for land—and the feeling that owning rooibos land was central both to their livelihoods and their sense of self—few landless coloured people used the language, "The whites stole our land." Rather, they spoke in general terms about how everyone had land but them. In contrast to many definitions of indigeneity, most people whom I interviewed did not describe a primal attachment to specific land areas. As much as they were simultaneously entangled with and estranged from the rooibos landscape, they did not ask for the return of "their" land but, rather, for land in and of itself, for a place to live and to farm rooibos. A black community organizer in the area explained the situation in this way: "You should look at the Western Cape differently. There is a long history of dispossession. It is the missing link in restitution." He argued that, unlike residents in other parts of the country, the region's inhabitants had been estranged from land for so long that they had no legal claims or, often, concrete evidence to assert ownership of land. While some people wanted land in and of itself, many coloured residents desired rooibos land specifically for its affective and economic value and for the "dignity" of growing the indigenous plant. In such a context, the idea of land tenure was not about a one-to-one relationship between people and place. Instead, it was about regaining a relationship between coloured livelihoods and subjectivities, their means of production, and the objects of their labor.

Strategies of Localization in an Unstable World

South Africa is the monopoly producer of the tea, but unlike in many other industries it has been unable to extract a price advantage from this fact. Willem Engelbrecht, director for cultivation research and producer affairs at the South African Rooibos Council, told journalists on a media trip to the region that the tea, pegged against prices for black tea, was distinctly undervalued for a product that grew nowhere else in the country— or the world. —MARY DONNELLY, "A Treasure Traded as a Commodity"

Commodification in the Marxian sense implies turning a "thing" into cash. Rooibos farmers' lives, livelihoods, and identities depended on this transaction, and farmers have traded rooibos for more than a century. Farmers' fear of commodification was both different from the Marxian and twofold: First, it was not of rooibos turning into cash but, rather, of rooibos not turning into *enough* cash; and second, it was of how the alienating effects of commodification might interrupt the triadic sense of indigeneity among farmer, tea, and land. Rooibos was a commodity because they sold it, but it was not a commodity because it had an unalterable relation to a particular place and a particular group of people: white and coloured residents whose claims to belonging and whose very essences were inextricably tied to it. Rooibos, people stated again and again, was a "miracle." When I asked farmers to explain what they meant by such effusive statements, they would say that rooibos was exceptional and that, like the "rugged" farmers who cultivated it, the plant grew naturally in the arid, hostile biome.

In an attempt to reconcile their dual understandings of rooibos's commodification, farmers wished to create a space outside the market but still engage in it. Because they believed in rooibos's high value and because their livelihoods depended on this value, they wanted to ensure that "the market" recognized the value and thus priced the tea accordingly—not as an ordinary commodity, but as a unique substance that derived its charisma through the miracle-like properties it developed with its proper cultivators in its indigenous ecosystem. When they explained the tea's value, they typically spoke not of price, but of an intrinsic significance of the plant and the tea that existed outside "market economics." Being "undervalued," as Engelbrecht described to journalists, was not just about rooibos's being pegged to the price of black tea, but also about consumers, traders, and marketers failing to understand its "specialness."

For farmers, rooibos was not a possession or even necessarily an object external to themselves. Rather, they used the language of human-nonhuman kinship—or as Marshall Sahlins (2011) describes, a "mutuality of being"—underscored by an idea of indigeneity that implies an inseparable relationship among farmer, plant, and ecosystem. Kinsmen, Sahlins (2011: 11) explains, are "persons who belong to one another, who are co-present in each other, whose lives are joined and interdependent." While he focuses on human connections, he notes that this same mutuality of being can exist in trans-species relations. Kinship relations in the rooibos-farming region were not entirely between person and plant or self and other. Rather, the person was partly vested in the plant. The plant was in the soil; the person was in the plant; the plant was in the person.

Rooibos was a "thing" enlivened and animated not solely through *relations of exchange* between people but also through its *relations of dependence* between people and the ecosystem. Marilyn Strathern (1988) describes "things" as parts of chains of obligations and desires that circulate through exchange. Objects, she argues, are not "things-in-themselves" but, rather, social relations. Commodities in the strictly Marxian sense are social phenomena endowed with thing-like status and embedded in economic calculation. When farmers said, "We don't want rooibos to become a commodity," they implied their own—partial—resistance to classic politico-economic concepts. They insisted that rooibos was not an object at all. It was *more than a thing*. They described an aura to rooibos, an affective feeling not so much of awe, but of reverence: a connection among the plant, the ritual of daily consumption, and the "holy act" of cultivation. According to Walter Benjamin (1986), aura inheres not in the object itself but in its external attributes, such as its known line of ownership, its restricted exhibition, its publicized authenticity, or its cultural value. Rooibos farmers, however, found aura both in the tea itself (its chemical composition) and in its external attributes (its authentic indigeneity), an aura that persisted through the mechanical reproduction of the tea in its heavily processed form yet would be lost if consumers did not value its uniqueness. It was this "excess," this "aura," that farmers needed to protect.

Paul, a white farmer-processor, explained: "We need to play in the free market system, but protect and not prostitute the product." He seemed uncertain about how to strike this balance. Because of the firm belief in the "rooibos miracle," farmers could not understand why the price for the tea ever dropped. "If rooibos is that exclusive, why the extensive ups and downs? If the world is familiar with rooibos, why do prices have to fluctuate?" Paul asked. His concern over the "ups and downs" drew from the apartheid-era marketing board's regulation of the tea's price, a regulation that had afforded (white) rooibos farmers some stability by "protecting" the tea from the vagaries of the agrarian market. Perhaps more important, however, Paul's incredulity stemmed from a belief that rooibos should be immune to the world market (unlike local citrus and grapes—generic, placeless products in rooibos farmers' minds) because of its totem-like qualities and its inalienable connection to residents' belonging. Deeply Christian, rooibos farmers did not worship rooibos per se. Instead, they included God in their descriptions of interdependencies between themselves and nature. Farmers did not pray to rooibos, but many believed that rooibos formed part of their spirituality.

Nelson, a rooibos packer in Durban who was not tied to rooibos's history or its ecosystem, told a story that confirmed Paul's fears about the "prostitution" of rooibos. "I realized we should look at tea as a commodity. . . . We should buy it when the price is low and then sell it when it's high," he said, and then spoke to nearly every rooibos farmers' concern. "I think it would be good if they grow rooibos other places. Wherever we get our tea, if it's from Australia or Rooibos Ltd., if they sell it to us at a lower price." I probed further by discussing how most farmers and even most marketers in the country valorize the fact that rooibos grows only one place. "It's also a business," he responded. "We can't be selfish." Nelson brought his own morality to the equation, arguing that keeping rooibos from the regular functions of the market would be "greedy."

Instead, farmers wanted to *control* the market. In the unregulated postapartheid, globalized rooibos market, farmers feared the idea of uncontrollable economic forces. While rooibos farmers typically explained these global dislocations with localized sentiments about production and the plant itself, their livelihoods—and the growth of the industry—depended on the global flow of goods. Farmers expressed desires to protect rooibos from becoming a "commodity," but the global expansion of the tea market allowed for the creation of economic worth on previously "unproductive" land. They attempted to resolve this apparent disjuncture through a strategy of localization that helped them feel they had some power. Yet this disjuncture also created a new relationship to the land. By first examining the limits of cultural marketing, I explore this new relationship through farmers' strategies of localization, strategies that ultimately could fail if climate change shifted the growing region southward.

Cultural Marketing and Unpalatable Subjectivities

Americans think there are no people in Africa.
—COLOURED ROOIBOS FARMER

What does a taste of Africa mean to you?
—WHITE TEA MARKETER

"You need to give the tea a culture," a marketer at a major rooibos company said. We sat in the company's boardroom surrounded by posters from marketing campaigns: images of Bushmen, African animals, and the kinds of landscapes pictured in safari guides. "We looked at our competitors," he continued. "Our old box. . . . Foreigners loved the animals, but locally, the [animals alone] don't move us. We wanted to give the brand a stronger presence on the shelf. So we went with animals with a haiku. It's African and Asian. The Haikus are an Asian connotation. The box is white, simple and pure." He paused: "A brand is like a person." The marketer's use of the word "person" appeared to have two meanings: creating the character of the product, but also creating the characters of the rooibos producers themselves. If the rooibos "brand" is a person, who is it? Is it white, coloured, or racially neutral? What does it mean to be "African"? And what "person" is marketable to consumers in both South Africa and the sought-after international community? Certainly, marketers did not consider the racial ambiguity of Afrikaners and coloured people palatable.

In her research on coffee production, Paige West (2012) explores how marketing connects fantasy and desire to politics, native authenticity, nature, and Euro-American ideas of progress. How, she asks, do Euro-American desires "feed back to the material lives of coffee producers?" (West 2012: 23). The potential "feedbacks" worried some people in the rooibos region, such as Lindie, a coloured saleswoman who worked in a country store. While waiting for her to finish with a customer, I fidgeted with a rooibos tea box, spinning it around. Because it was a holiday weekend, Lindie thought the store would be quiet, so she asked me to interview her between transactions. Turning back to me, Lindie noticed the box in my hands. It had an image of a woman on it. I did not recognize the woman, even though I had gotten to know many of the people in the farming community. "Why do you think she was chosen?" Lindie asked me. Not waiting for me to respond, she answered: "It's because she is darker. And even though we are from here, it doesn't fit the image." By "it," she meant the lightness of their "coloured" skin. A white marketer, she explained, had designed the box to appeal to international consumers who wanted to see their fantasies of the Dark Continent associated with an African tea.

For consumers, part of the affective value of rooibos involved the idea of being transported to some imagined African space, a space that did not necessarily map onto a particular location. Drawing on Marx's commodity fetishism, Michael Taussig (1980) discusses how social relations between people can be disguised as social relations between things, as labor is hidden in commodities. Marketers often "hid" laborers by emphasizing the naturalness of a tea growing wild in the African Bush. But they also occasionally sold rooibos using connections to idealized images of small-scale producers laboring on rugged African farms. For some consumers, drinking rooibos for its health benefits was less important than "drinking a piece of Africa" or "helping African farmers." The rooibos commodity chain did not mask relations by focusing exclusively on things. Instead, it idealized a relation that disguised the poverty, violence, and hardship experienced by both small-scale farmers and workers.

For marketers, controlling and creating a rooibos narrative was crucial to the tea's sales. "We did market research," an industry member who focused specifically on the African tea market said. "We asked people, 'What does a taste of Africa mean to you?'" When he posed the question to employees in the boardroom of the Durban-based tea distribution company, they said, "Sipping gin and tonics in the Bush on a verandah." They evoked a colonial fantasy of a carefree life in nature. "But in our market research [that sampled South Africans across race and class boundaries], it was poverty, crime," he continued. "For them, the taste of Africa is not a very good taste. They aspire to be like Europeans." In the marketing narrative the company created for South African consumers, he removed the "Africa" from the packaging, instead showing muted colors and descriptions of the tea that focused on health. Rooibos became another placeless commodity.

This kind of marketing, however, was not well received in the growing region. In response to what they felt was a failure to celebrate rooibos's "specialness," many local producers tried to take action. "We need consumer education. Rooibos of origin. Estates like wine. Name by region, description, and so on," a farmer who had recently started his own small tea company said. He, like many farmers, wanted to emphasize the land and the people who created the plant. Much of South Africa (and the developing world more generally) has turned to cultural/ethnic marketing as a form of "sustainable development." Lynn Meskell (2012) describes how South Africans have leveraged their heritage to transform histories that once ensured racial subordination into capital. The rooibos region was no exception. The Chamber of Commerce, farmers, cooperatives, and processors tried to draw on rooibos's indigeneity to create a rooibos heritage route. Yet according to people involved in local tourism, these attempts had been largely unsuccessful. Perhaps, some posited, the problem was the people's precarious indigeneities.

Geographical Indications: Governing Plants and People

Marks indicating countries of origin, such as geographic indications, create
new borders around newly valued forms of cultural difference, producing places, and
constituting borders of identity, while potentially linking producers and consumers in
new relationships of identification. —ROSEMARY J. COOMBE and
NICOLE ALYWIN, "Bordering Diversity and Desire"

The globe is on our computers. No one lives there. It allows us to think that
we can aim to control it. —GAYATRI SPIVAK, Death of a Discipline

Awie was a hulking environmental worker whom I had gotten to know through several rooibos-related events. On a summer day, we sat in his office and stared at large computer monitors opened to images of different maps—climate maps, soil maps, cadastral maps, conservation maps, and other maps that I could not decipher. I found the property lines particularly confusing; they seemed to wiggle around with little regard for natural features such as streams or hills. "That's because [individual farms] usually started out as one big plot, but then the farmer had three sons and split it up and so on," Awie explained, showing how farmers' genealogies had become mapped onto the rooibos landscape. Property lines, however, were not the reason that he wanted to show me the maps. As an environmentally focused scientist, Awie cared little about who specifically owned rooibos land. Instead, he wanted to bound, through maps, where rooibos *should* grow. As far as he was concerned, anyone could grow rooibos as long as the farmer lived within the borders of the "natural" rooibos ecosystem, an area that he and a team of scientists determined from a variety of factors that included, but were not limited to, areas where wild rooibos grew.

Awie was working with the South African Rooibos Council to create a geographical indication so that tea could be called "rooibos" only if it grew in its natural, indigenous territory. "A border geographically has been defined," Awie explained. "The idea is that if you are illegal, you can't sell your tea as rooibos." By giving the tea a label based on a specific geographic area, Awie and others involved with the project asserted that the region could maintain exclusive ownership and classify people and plants outside the region "illegal." Rooibos officially secured its GI in 2014 in an economic partnership agreement between southern African nations and the European Union. (In the agreement, South Africa had to concede "feta" cheese, a protected designation-of-origin product in the European Union since 2002.) Rooibos Ltd.'s newsletter from September 2014 celebrated the victory, proclaiming, "Storm in teacup finally over for South Africa's Rooibos."

By legally cementing rooibos's regional specificity, farmers believed they could shelter it from a placeless idea of global commodity exchange (Coombe et al. 2015). Yet the desire to bound rooibos's proper place became more than an issue of classifying and mapping. Mapping initiatives centered on protecting the plant not only against theft by other people but also, significantly, against theft by other landscapes. Instead of stressing "intellectual property," the initiatives emphasized the "geographical" aspects of ownership by focusing on connections among plant, farmers, and place. They discussed the spiritual relational qualities of farming a plant where God originally intended it—and not the local, human knowledge of how to grow rooibos.

"It worries me to death that somewhere else in the world they would start growing rooibos," a fourth-generation rooibos farmer said. The rooted, place-based quality of GIs emphasized that products should not be estranged from their territory. In their discussion of GIs in Europe, Rosemary Coombe and Nicole Alywin (2011) describe how one of their purposes was to create "place-based foodscapes" to counter brand-based placelessness that led to the alienability and unaccountability typically associated with commodities (Besky 2014). Coombe and Alywin describe how GIs create new, hard borders and in the process construct new forms of cultural identity: You are either within the GI's boundaries or you are not.

Coombe and Alywin question whether GIs provide possibilities for de-fetishizing commodities by unveiling locations of production or if they actually imply new forms of fetishization. Edward Fischer and Peter Benson (2006) describe a "double-commodity fetish" of food. People want to be ignorant about some aspects of food production (a kind of deliberate fetishism), yet they are also captivated by the lore of food origins (Cook and Crang 1996; Guthman 2009). The campaign for a rooibos GI did both. In some respects, farmers attempted to de-fetishize rooibos to celebrate, maintain, and even strengthen the relationship among farmers, land, plant, and product. In other respects, the GI may have exacerbated the estrangement of workers—or those unable to access land. These issues came together around the question of traceability.

According to the *Handbook for Implementing Rooibos Sustainability Standards*, "Every Rooibos field must be mapped and marked physically with signs showing its name or number. You should be able to point out a field on a map where a specific batch of certified Rooibos was produced, and signage should be used to clearly mark the field" (Pretorius et al. 2011: 22). The idea of traceability combined with satellite surveillance to form a kind of panopticon. The panopticon, however, was not focused on labor. Rather, it emphasized space, place, and plants. Despite the constant, probing surveillance, little monitoring of workers' living conditions, job security, or wages occurred. Again, physical geography seemed to trump human conditions, and workers remained alienated, despite efforts to protect rooibos against estrangement from the landscape.

Awie shifted in his chair, turning to me with a renewed intensity. "The farmers don't realize that we can monitor them now," he continued. "The images are right here on Google Maps." Mapping and satellite images rendered visible whether or not rooibos had strayed from its indigenous home and whether or not farmers were taking proper care of the ecosystem. Awie added, "I can use Google Earth and GIS [Geographic Information Systems] to monitor farms. I can use satellite imagery. I can tell how the soil is doing because if there is no evaporation, no cooling, it means the soil is dead. It hasn't struck home to farmers that Big Brother is watching." Nikolas Rose (1999: 221) argues, "To govern a problem requires that it be counted." In strikingly similar language, the *Handbook for Implementing Rooibos Sustainability Standards*, referred to by the faintly Orwellian nickname *Right Rooibos Handbook*, claims, "If you can't measure it, you can't manage it" (Pretorius et al. 2011: 82). By labeling—and then monitoring—the tea based on a specific geographic area, Awie and others involved with the project asserted, the region could maintain exclusive ownership.

What is significant in the rooibos context, however, is that it was not so much other countries that rooibos farmers worried about—although farmers certainly expressed concerns that French, U.S., Australian, and Chinese producers were trying to "steal" the tea. Rather, the movement of the tea's ecosystem itself risked undermining the commodity's kinship relations—its "mutual belonging" with the landscape and its people. Awie had his eye trained specifically on the effects climate change might have on rooibos's *terroir*. *Terroir*, according to the study of artisanal cheeses by Heather Paxson (2010), refers to "taste of place," shared customs, and affective senses of belonging. In many ways, this description explains rooibos farming—the affective relations between people and plant and a shared (if unequal and structurally violent) history of growing and consuming tea among white farmers and coloured farmers and workers. Yet startling questions emerged in discussions with farmers, workers, and environmentalists: Would the terroir lose its significance and authenticity if rooibos's growing range moved? If rooibos's ecosystem "moved," would rooibos become indigenous to new landscapes? What if it was "nature," and not "man" that the farmer had to fear most? Awie might be able to create location-based protections from other growers through GIs, but how could he halt the effects of climate change?

Through attempts to combat these simultaneous threats, battles against people and nature were indissociable. Human virtue and the virtue of "true" rooibos that grows in its "proper" place were intertwined. The potential movement of rooibos and the climatic conditions that helped it thrive, that created its "taste of place," unsettled people's ideas of rootedness and permanence and their place-based concepts of indigeneity. Property lines may have defied natural features in Awie's maps, but rooibos appeared to have had just as little regard for property lines. If rooibos no longer possessed a regional specificity, it might surrender its charisma to a placeless idea of global commodity production and exchange.

Farmers said that losing this specificity could undermine marketing messages, the price of tea, and local livelihoods. Despite attempts to draw borders around it, *the plant still moved*, and it was highly unlikely that farmers would be able to move with it if its ecosystem shifted to other farmers' land. The apparent inalienability of private property disrupted the surprising mobility of rooibos's geography and potentially undermined the delicate webs among rooibos, people, and their senses of belonging. Private property seemingly foreclosed the possibility of a migratory indigeneity for residents, rendering the people immobile. In contrast, as it faced the effects of climate change, rooibos acted. Just as new farmers found that they could cultivate rooibos, rooibos also found new places that it could grow. Wild and cultivated rooibos plants showed that they could *do* things; they responded to climate change with mobility.

Rooibos's Southward Creep

In 2011, the United Nations Convention on Climate Change hosted its meeting in Durban, South Africa. The convention spawned a number of newspaper and Internet articles on the potentially "disastrous" effects of climate change on rooibos, all invoking an impending crisis to the industry and the country's iconic plant/beverage. Articles frequently described rooibos as a canary in the coal mine, its vulnerability to climate change a marker of South Africa's vulnerability in an uncertain postapartheid future. Because rooibos is almost entirely rain-fed, its cultivation is particularly susceptible to climate shifts that farmers have already observed. Some scientists predict that cultivated rooibos could lose up to 75.5 percent of its climatically suitable habitat range by 2070, and wild rooibos could lose up to 88.7 percent (Lötter and Maitre 2014). In interviews, scientists speculated that climate change might cause rooibos's unique ecosystem—its soil, rain, and insects—to creep slowly southward.

"The center of tea production has shifted south. It used to be Clanwilliam and north. Now, it's more Citrusdal," Jako, a producer from the southern end of the growing region, said, describing the success of his experiments with cultivating rooibos on land that he had previously reserved for wheat. While Jako's eyes gleamed with economic possibilities, rooibos farmers in the "traditional" growing area felt that their own autochthony was disrupted by the movement of the indigenous plant. The certainty of rooibos as a stable object now seemed to be unraveling in a human timescale, the deeply destabilizing change apparent to many farmers and researchers. When I spoke about rooibos's movement to a retired industry leader, he shook his head, responding, "The biggest challenges are climate change. To be able to supply markets in the future, we will have to find alternate places to grow quality rooibos." For many in the region, the industry leader's idea of looking for new places to grow the tea was tantamount to sacrilege. He seemed ready to betray his kin and the symbiotic relationship between *this* land and *these* farmers to create new producer relationships in different lands. What would this alienability mean to farmers' sense of belonging? Would rooibos become "indigenous" to the new landscapes?

Hansie was a young coloured farmer whose family had been growing or harvesting rooibos for as long as he could remember. I mentioned that a farming community had started cultivating rooibos in the Southern Cape, well beyond what most people considered the rooibos region. He looked to the ground and dug the toes of his shoes into the soil, thinking about what I said. Wiping his brow, he turned to me and said, "The Southern Cape. I am not too much into that. It's bad news to me. It shows there is no limit." Hansie introduced me to another farmer in his community named Diederik. Standing with Hansie, Diederik and I discussed this "bad news." "It is important to protect the rights of people of tea so it can be a unique South African product," he said, using a more nationalist discourse than Hansie. "We must protect the growers." He described his feelings about Nestlé, one of the multinational corporations involved with rooibos distribution. "Nestlé is really threatening," he said. "They want it for [their] own. They can make money because they have money to market. . . . I think the industry will grow forever. Eventually the Australians will start growing it if necessary." He mentioned a foreign camera crew that had passed through his community the day before to ask about other countries' growing rooibos, but he did not want to talk about it. "I am very upset," he said and left it at that.

Hansie and Diederik lived in the mountainous heart of the rooibos area. To reach the region, you take a relatively flat road from Cape Town until you hit Piekenierskloof Pass. There, a steep, windy road makes its way up and then down the mountains, marking the passage from the wheat fields of the area known as the Swartland to the dusty shrubs of the Cederberg's fynbos. *Swartland* is Afrikaans for "black land." The area got its name, a local farmer said, from the dark, rich soil and indigenous plants that settlers found when they made their way to the area. Environmental workers in the Swartland now talked about how the soil had become "used up" by centuries of "overuse" as a breadbasket for Cape Town. Construction often closed Piekenierskloof Pass for more than an hour each day, and I would have to sit in my car waiting for it to open in what felt like a liminal zone between the rush of Cape Town and the rooibos world. After living in the area for a few months, however, I learned that some farmers on the Swartland side of the pass had begun farming with rooibos.

When I inquired about these farmers, someone in the industry directed me to Christo, an Afrikaner who resided on a large-scale commercial farm. I drove over the pass to reach his Swartland farm, which consisted of a sizable modern-looking house and a metal barn. Since it was not rooibos harvest season, many of the farms in the Cederberg were relatively quiet. Christo's farm, however, was teeming with activity, as coloured and black workers loaded crates into a large truck. Christo, like many of his neighbors, only dabbled in rooibos, planting some bushes when the price for tea was high and focusing on wheat when the rooibos price was low. Because the price was low in 2010, he was not currently planting any tea. "My neighbor was the first guy to do it here. We saw it worked. To produce rooibos is not difficult. He could tell me in fifteen minutes what to do. There is not a lot of technical knowledge if you do it as a sideline. Fifteen minutes was enough for us," he said. "We would grow it again if the price was good. Rooibos is a good industry. Tea is a healthy drink. It is an honest industry." He paused, "Actually I put 'honest' in quotes. They want to protect the industry by saying their area is the best. I think it can be grown almost anywhere. It's competition for them. They can manage the price if it's close to them." I interrupted, "But what about the quality of the tea? Everyone tells me that you need certain soil and rainfall to produce A-grade rooibos." He shook his head and blew air slowly out of his heavily bearded mouth: "We get a good flavor. They say we can't make quality tea, but we have better soil and more rain." Christo claimed that his land not only could produce rooibos but could produce *better* rooibos than its indigenous ecosystem.

Afrikaans farmers south of the pass were not the only people experimenting with rooibos. A coloured community in the Southern Cape, not far from the southernmost tip of Africa, had started growing rooibos a few years prior. I spent the Easter holiday with one of the farmers in the area. After attending my fourth church service of the weekend in the packed pews of the town's Moravian church, we drove from farm to farm to visit various people in the community. The landscape was relatively flat and green, as it received far more rainfall than the traditional growing area. Here, farmers seemed significantly wealthier than coloured farmers in the Cederberg Mountains. Most of them owned their own land, and we drove in separate cars, forming a caravan—something I never experienced among the coloured farming community in the Cederberg, where I was often the only one with a car.

We sat in a rooibos farmer's large, modern home and shared a buffet family dinner. The conversation turned to the rooibos industry up north in the Cederberg. "They don't like us growing rooibos here. It grows massive in less than a year. We can replant it every year," Werner said between bites of curried fish. "Rooibos isn't central here, but we want to expand it. I never planned to be a rooibos farmer." We drove on to the next farm for still more curried fish. The family chatted and caught up about this or that cousin, debated the latest successes of their favorite rugby team, and joked about the notoriously out-of-tune church choir ("At least they sing their praises loudly!"). While they discussed the morning services, I sat at a table with another farmer, Carin. "The soil here is better for agriculture than the Cederberg," she said, echoing Christo's and Werner's claims. "It's not so hard to work on rooibos." Through such conversations, Christo, Werner, Carin, and other farmers growing rooibos outside of its traditional area undermined both the localness of the plant and the skill involved in growing it. They seemed to believe that rooibos could actually grow better if it was liberated from its native ecosystem. Yet the tea's belonging in the Cederberg was also central to marketing campaigns. Tea box after tea box and marketing pamphlet after marketing pamphlet contained the words, "Grown only in the Cederberg Mountains." Could marketers take that position if farmers such as Werner began growing the tea in significant amounts? Could coloured and white residents of the traditional growing region claim a rooted sense of belonging in relation to a plant that seemed to thrive as it moved southward?

Uprooting Indigeneity

"Climate change will make a difference. It is happening, and it's difficult to quantify," Le Roux, who owned one of the region's biggest commercial rooibos farms, said. "You are speaking about more or less rain, rain that is erratic and more violent. Perhaps a two-degree temperature change. Who knows what's going to happen? If it gets hotter, marginal guys . . . will hurt, never mind the rainfall." He paused. "But market forces will push it. Look at agriculture worldwide." Le Roux moved quickly between two seemingly unstoppable global forces: climate change and agribusiness. For him, the power of the nonhuman climate merged with the power of capital. Farms needed to become bigger, he continued, to fight both of these global threats.

Compared with producers in local industries such as grapes or citrus, many rooibos farmers still used a "family farm" model, even if for commercial farmers that model might include several, or even hundreds, of coloured and black workers. The use of the label "family farm" in this context implied multiple meanings of "family." Typically, a "family farm" meant that the farm was owned by a white man who lived and worked with his relatives, often with the help of his wife or daughters as bookkeepers and his son or sons as managers. The idea of family was not negated by the presence of workers in part because of the tradition of paternalism in the region: White farmers often considered workers childlike and needing supervision.

I mentioned to Le Roux that many farmers celebrated the "family farm," and he responded, "One tends to see these time frames that are too short. The rooibos farmer is an ultraconservative person who can survive on very little. They have sheep and rooibos. . . . Now you have to have DSTV (cable) and pay the bill every month. You need a truck, a cell phone." With these new desires, he continued, "The children won't come back." I asked him whether he thought family rooibos farms would start to fade away. "If you look at the relevance of some of the smaller farms," he replied, "twenty years ago they were big players." Le Roux described his idea of the stereotypical rural farmer, tempted by the desire for global consumer goods but attached to a mode of farming no longer sustainable in a world affected by economic globalization and climate change.

Throughout this book, I have attempted to de-emphasize one-to-one connections between people and place. In this section, however, I turn my focus back to place as it relates to both climate change and commodification. Farmers, residents, and scientists feared that a changing economic and ecological climate might deprive rooibos of its indigenous, rooted identity. Climate change—in concert with political and economic shifts—unsettled not just livelihoods, land rights, and ideas of private property, but also cosmologies. If rooibos's growing range shifted southward, how would it affect farmers' descriptions of rooibos as an inalienable part of their existence?

In the Cederberg region, rooibos researchers asserted that droughts and erratic rainfall over the past ten years had negatively affected cultivation. The rooibos plant, and thus the industry, relied on certain indigenous species of bees and wasps for pollination. Scientists observed that the changing climate was threatening these insects, as well as fungi and bacteria in the soil. Thus, the symbiotic relationship among natural plant, indigenous insect, and dependent farmer appeared to be under threat. "Exports are going up. Everything is positive," one white farmer said. "But the climate is not cooperating." And while vast social and economic differences divided coloured and white farmers, coloured farmers were struggling with the same climatic changes. "We have to listen to what the weather says," a coloured farmer stated. "We have no choice." The use of the word "cooperate" by the white farmer and "choice" by the coloured farmer seemed telling. For the white man, the environment was refusing to work in harmony with his needs. For the coloured man, climate change seemed to be undermining his hard-fought agency as an independent farmer.

Most—though not all—farmers felt that human-caused climate change was a factor in rooibos farming.[6] What varied from farmer to farmer, however, was the degree to which people believed that climate change would affect them. In these discussions, finance and climate often came together. Some of the larger, wealthier farmers in the area seemed less worried than smaller-scale farmers. One large-scale commercial farmer scoffed at the concerns: "I've noticed the climate changing, but I'm not worried. We can adapt to it." He believed that he could surmount any problem with technology, such as fertilizers. A climate specialist lamented, "There is quite a lot of knowledge [the commercial farmers have] been sitting on about climate change and adaptation from five generations on the same farm, but they don't want to share the information."

Instead of sharing, some farmers felt their knowledge could give them a competitive advantage in the industry. Commercial farmers' economic resources and technical know-how made them feel better equipped to work with (and against) nature to survive climatic shifts.

In adjusting to the changing ecological and economic climate, wealthier farmers used their resources to shore up land and power, while others—both coloured farmers and less well-off white farmers—struggled. In response, scientists and economists came to the region to teach local people technical skills to cope with climate change. They held workshops that combined tactics for adapting to shifting climate conditions and new agricultural market conditions. "You have to put all the pieces together," someone involved in training said. "If you don't know, you are in a race to losing." Another trainer used language that invoked classic neoliberal tropes, even describing his "pitch" to farmers as "selling climate change." He explained, "We use words like 'risk,' 'insurance,' and we sell things in rands and cents. Not just 'Wetlands Are Important.' We make an economic argument; functionality costs." At one such workshop, he preached this message while small-scale farmers politely listened, only to chuckle and shake their heads as they huddled outside during a cigarette break.

The idea of adapting simultaneously to ecological and economic changes did, however, have traction for many farmers. The website for the Heiveld Cooperative, a group composed mostly of small-scale coloured farmers in the Northern Cape, includes a section titled "Adapting to Climate Change." The page begins with a historical narrative: "In 2003 the winter rains arrived 3 months late. After a single rain event in August which did not provide enough rain to replenish the ground water, drought set in and held the Suid Bokkeveld [region] in its grip for 3 years. The drought caused rooibos plants to die, and springs to dry up. Animals went hungry. No-one could remember such a severe drought, or such hardship."[7] Weaving climate change adaptation into its marketing narrative, the website goes on to explain the steps taken by farmers since the 2003 hardship. "Place your tea order here," the bottom of the page reads, with a phone number and links to sales information. Using the fight against climate change as a selling point, Heiveld members brought together economics and climate in ways that showed their attempts to combat the seemingly uncontrollable forces. They adapted to the changing agricultural market by representing their tea as "niche" through an emphasis on environmental sustainability, an emphasis that informed their newly designed tea boxes. The boxes depicted images of indigenous plants and flowers rather than images of farmers. I discussed the switch from people to plants with a member of the group, wondering whether it signaled an erasure of human labor. "We've changed our information not to say to the consumer ... we're fair trade; we're poor. With the picture [of a flower] on the box, we're trying to make it feel that this is a part of nature." She discussed new farming practices alongside the marketing adjustment: The Heiveld farmers were attempting to adapt to the changing climate by creating windbreaks to stem erosion, keeping detailed climate diaries, and removing "water-hungry" invasive plant species.

Embodied Adaptation

As I described in earlier chapters, the relationship between farmers and the rooibos landscape was deeply embodied, making the possibility of losing rooibos to climate change more than just an issue of livelihoods. The idea of embodied adaptation draws from historical connections between people and land in South Africa. Early settler colonists saw the body as merging with the environment through acclimatization. For Afrikaans farmers, their formerly "European" bodies became "indigenized" through exertion in the rooibos soil. According to local lore, British settlers could not adjust to the harsh local climate, and many died or moved to other parts of the country, their absence marked not only by oral histories but also by their tombstones, which were still present in the graveyards of local churches. A Clanwilliam history book describes the brief stay of these "1820 Settlers": "The local population was greatly increased for a short time with its first British folk, the 1820 Settlers.... The settlers found the dry conditions very different from their ultra-rainy homeland. And drought was prevailing over many parts of the Cape Colony ... the great majority therefore left for the Eastern Cape almost immediately" [Langham-Carter 1993: 6]. Afrikaans farmers' bodies, however, were seen as better adapted to the area. They (along with their workers) molded the landscape into the place it is today, just as the landscape molded them.

The positive associations with adaptation expressed by Afrikaners were quite different from the negative associations given to the Khoisan. As described in chapter 2, Jan Smuts depicted nature as having mentally underdeveloped and physically dwarfed the Bushmen. Smuts insisted that Bushmen could not acclimatize to the environmental and economic changes brought on by colonial settlement. The current need to adjust to climate change seemed to signal a fresh anxiety—a fear that the Afrikaans body, like that of the Khoisan who came before him, could not adapt to the new economic and ecological climate.

Piet, an Afrikaans farmer, reflected these concerns. I sat in his farmhouse kitchen in early autumn. He had invited me for lunch, and Piet and I talked as his wife sliced a warm loaf of bread to add to the meats and vegetables spread across the long wooden table. Piet had inherited the farm from his father, who had recently moved to a "retirement farm" he purchased from a farmer who had moved to Australia. "Farming in this area is not a very lucrative business," Piet explained as he made himself a sandwich. "There are periodic droughts." Piet had rainfall data on the farm since 1932, diligently maintained by his grandfather, then his father, and now himself. He showed me the handwritten charts. "You can see how the weather changes with the earth warming," he said as he pointed to the peaks and valleys of lines carefully drawn on pieces of paper. "The temperature is bouncing up and down. The weather is less predictable. You have to change your approach." He worried about the altering plant composition. "Floods are also worrying. The river is dry right now," he said, sighing.

Anxieties crossed racial boundaries, but with differences that were central to coloured attempts to escape white dominion. Oscar, a coloured rooibos farmer, worked at a rooibos processing plant to earn additional income. We sat on the edge of a concrete drying yard and watched other workers spread rooibos cuttings with large broom-like sticks made from local plants as they sang Justin Bieber's latest pop song. Oscar discussed the environmental changes he had witnessed during his decades of working with the tea. I mentioned that some commercial farmers were not as interested in climate change as he was. "It's because they are not farmers," he scoffed. "They just have the money and pay people to farm." For him, farming rooibos and understanding climate change's effect on the industry was tied up with independence from white farm owners. "Commercial farmers are hating us now because we are self-sufficient. I was born on my 'heritage' farm. My dad farmed it." But now, he said, climate change was decreasing the rooibos yield. Oscar spoke of the farm as his heritage, integral to his identity as a farmer and a son. He had managed to piece together a livelihood free from laboring on white farms; yet, the climate seemed poised to betray him and undermine his hard-fought freedom. For poor farmers on land with few nutrients and little access to water, rooibos was what allowed them to survive financially and to stave off the feared encroachment of corporate agribusinesses.

"Wild Plants to the Rescue!"

"With climate change," a farmer said, "I think [we] will have a slow death in rooibos ... because most of the area will be drier." In the passage from wild to cultivated, rooibos seemed to risk losing its ability to subsist without human care, such as irrigation and pruning. Most conservationists and climate experts did not think that people alone could solve the problem. In an article supported by the Climate and Development Knowledge Network, Rhoda Malgas, a scientist at the University of Stellenbosch, warns that climate change will negatively affect rooibos "because of the plant's geographic limitation, but also because there exists only one species of Rooibos. If it gets wiped out, that's it" (quoted in Palitza 2011). What, then, is the solution? A number of scientists have proclaimed that the solution could be "wild bushes to the rescue." Because wild rooibos ecotypes are adapted to a wide range of rainfall regimes, many can survive extreme drought conditions. The pure, wild tea could be harnessed to save the cultivated tea—it would become the tea of salvation.

At the beginning of the Enlightenment, Harriet Ritvo (1987) argues, people believed that they were at the mercy of natural forces. By the end, she contends, a shift occurred.[8] Science and engineering appeared to make nature susceptible to human control. Recent years have marked another shift. In 2000, the atmospheric chemist Paul Crutzen and the biologist Eugene Stoermer argued that, starting with the industrial revolution, human impact on the climate had become so dramatic as to usher in a new epoch: the Anthropocene (Crutzen and Stoermer 2000). Drawing on this work, Eben Kirksey and Stefan Helmreich (2010) assert that in the Anthropocene, human action, such as deforestation and fossil fuel emissions, has become a force of nature. Echoing this perspective, a number of researchers involved with rooibos have expressed fear that cultivated rooibos has lost its ability to withstand extreme human-caused weather changes through years of farmers' seed selection and adaptation. Jake Kosek (2010: 651) argues that human-nonhuman relations require "an epidemiology mindful of how human interests, fears, and desires have become part of the [animal or plant's] material form." He describes how the honeybee's very exoskeleton has been transformed in relation to its connections to the human, evolving to be more than twice as thick as its predecessors' just a hundred years ago. Like the exoskeleton of the bee, the biology of rooibos plants had altered over time through a phenotypic plasticity, in which the plants' morphology has transformed in response to environmental changes (Scheiner 1993).

While locals had been harvesting wild rooibos for centuries and white and coloured farmers began domesticating it in the early 1900s, it was not until the 1920s and 1930s that a group of farmers started explicitly experimenting with seed selection. They focused on the commercial priorities of farmers at that time: growth rate, seed production, and taste. These experiments produced the rooibos most often used for cultivation today, the Nortier type (Morton 1983). But Nortier is not the only varietal of rooibos. Wild tea variants include

Boomsoort, Langbeentee, Bossietee, and Rankiestee. These variants could hold the secret to preserving rooibos against unknown climatic fluctuations.

Throughout this book, I have described how the biology and existence of both wild and cultivated rooibos were linked to and determined by human husbandry, seed selection, fertilization, the presence of invasive plants and insects, and shifts in temperature and precipitation. Some people saw wild rooibos plants—*and not necessarily farmers' actions*—as a potential actant in the Latourian sense, an actant that might keep the growing region from moving south (Latour 2004 [1999]). Latour uses the word "actant" rather than "actor" to avoid the human connotations of the latter term. In other words, actants do not have to be conscious beings but can include nonhuman "actors" such as plants. Malgas states that wild tea's cultivated cousin has changed over years of genetic selection for ease of farming. "It would be wise to start building seed banks," she says. "If you conserve wild Rooibos, you can conserve the genetic material from which the cultivated Rooibos tea is derived" (quoted in Palitza 2011). The *Right Rooibos Handbook* echoes this claim in its directive to farmers: "All types of wild rooibos must be protected at all costs because they may contain the genetic code that will enable new, improved cultivars that can better cope with climate change in the future" (Pretorius et al. 2011: 104). The language is tinged with urgency: "*must*" and "*at all costs.*"

With the focus on wild varietals, the tea's indigenous heritage became explicitly future-oriented. People were hopeful that we might find the answer to climate change in the plant's genes and thereby redeem our environmental sins through as yet undiscovered technology. At the same time, people were future-affirming in ways that were not just about beliefs in technology and progress but also about a continued spiritual and material relation between farmer and plant.

Conclusion

The rooibos industry plays a very big role in the economy of Clanwilliam.
When the prices are low, the shops feel it in their sales. People don't buy cars.
If the price is up, the mood is up. —ROOIBOS FARMER

"What are the major issues in the rooibos industry today?" a moderator asked the group of farmers, marketers, and industry personnel sitting on folding chairs in a massive metal barn owned by a commercial rooibos producer. We were participating in "Rooibos Biodiversity Day," an industry meeting with more than a hundred people in attendance. The day started with a few scheduled talks about economic and environmental sustainability. After the lunch break, however, the mood changed dramatically when farmers began to express their concerns about the industry more generally. Frantically scribbling on an outsize piece of paper on an easel at the front of the room, the moderator began to make a list of *kwessies* (issues) as farmers responded to her question: "distrust," "market and price," "climate," "competition," "quality," "strengthening producer representation," "levies," "fear of change." I wrote down the answers in the Afrikaans spoken by the farmers, careful to double-check my translations when I returned to my room.

I had given several coloured farmers a ride to the meeting. As we made our way off the pavement and onto the maze of dirt roads that wove through the mountains and connected the region's farms, one of the farmers pointed to a commercial rooibos farm where he had labored for a small wage before gaining access to his own land and transitioning from "worker" to "farmer." His journey from being one of thousands of mute laborers to a person who might be included in an industry meeting seemed to signal an end to one form of alienation.

In this chapter, I linked residents' anxieties about the future of the rooibos-growing region to their fears that their kinship with rooibos might be ruptured by forces deemed unstoppable: the changing global agrarian market, changing political dynamics, and climate change. I showed how other, mostly coloured, residents feared that nothing would change. Conditions for workers would remain poor—or worse, workers might lose their jobs—and land would remain in white hands. At the "Rooibos Biodiversity Day" meeting, I watched as tensions rose. Some farmers' voices seemed to break as they shook their fists and lamented the industry's major "issues."

Attempting to end the meeting on a more positive note, the moderator changed the topic. What, she asked in Afrikaans, would constitute "success" in the rooibos region? At first, the list seemed to be a continuation of kwessies. Some farmers mentioned powerlessness and desperation. I was unsure what that had to do with success. Others asked for more reliable market information, sufficient funds, and collaboration among producers. Eugene, an Afrikaans farmer I knew, stood up and loudly proclaimed: "*Produsente moet tande kry*" (Producers must be teething). He clarified his statement, and the moderator wrote the following in parenthesis on the easel: "*Spiere bou, rug*" (Producers must build muscle, back). Eugene seemed to measure success in terms that were at once neoliberal and linked to Afrikaans ideas of bravado and masculinity. Farmers needed to stop being babies and start "teething." To Eugene, uncertainty was an intractable part of the new economy, not something to resist. He felt that Afrikaans farmers must use their cultural resources—strength and rugged independence—to adapt. The meeting began to wrap up. "*Hoop vir die beste!*" (Hope for the best!), the moderator wrote at the bottom of the list. It seemed to signal a plea or a prayer more than a reflection of farmers' feelings about success.

During moments such as the rooibos meeting, I noticed how many people referred to Afrikaans farmers as a sort of anthropological specimen. "You see, the thing about the Afrikaners," I was often told, followed by various insights into his (and always *his*) character. Even Afrikaans farmers used this language, "We Afrikaners, we don't think very wide." Or "We Afrikaners are just farmers." The habit of speaking about themselves in the third person was common— identifying wholly yet also distancing. The idea of a bounded Afrikaans cultural history linked inextricably to the rooibos landscape was reinforced through these statements. Yet in the postapartheid context, the discursively and geographically bounded identity of the white rooibos farmer was no longer safeguarded by nationalist dogma, state protections, or a marketing board. Without protections, residents worried that some rooibos farmers would be led astray and follow the country along a path of corruption and greed. Or worse, they feared that they would lose their farms to global agribusinesses or their rooibos to climatic shifts. Production, consumption, and exchange were not merely economic or technocratic issues. They were rooted in a moral connection to the rooibos landscape through which ideas of indigeneity and inalienability were linked by the professed symbiotic relations between people, plant, and ecosystem. Shifting climatic patterns and global commodity market trends seemingly undermined these entanglements by uprooting the tea's localized geography.

Drawing on the existential anxieties that arose from rooibos's potential estrangement, some farmers attempted to adapt to uncertainty (as Eugene described), while others tried to control it (as Awie, the environmental worker, explained), and still others sought to find a "life" in it (as a farmworker implored). For many farmers and scientists, technological progress could take the form of mapping rooibos to affirm its place-based indigeneity or espousing a unique relationship to its cultivation to affirm their rightful ownership. Thus, the goal of mapping rooibos's "proper" place emerged as more than just an issue of cartography. The desire to map the tea stemmed from a fear that rooibos itself will move southward, abandoning its indigeneity.

Senses of both aspiration and fear coalesced around agricultural research and climate models that employed technologies such as GIS, remote sensing, and genomics. How, I asked, has the idea of "place" emerged for residents as not only unstable, mutable, and precarious but also filled with both the dread of *and* hope for the unknown? How do ecological and demographic changes—and their attendant affective dimensions—become mapped onto the landscape? In the rooibos region, intersections between social and ecological imaginaries grew out of an increased emphasis on plant genomics and human DNA ancestry. As they faced changing climatic conditions, many farmers looked to wild rooibos for salvation. Farmers and scientists explored how elements of place could be disaggregated in a single seed: Some varieties of wild rooibos are adapted to a range of rainfall regimes and others to a range of temperatures (Hawkins et al. 2011). Scientists advised building wild seed banks to conserve these genetic building blocks. At the same time, farmers, farmworkers, and other residents showed increasing interest in their own "genetic building blocks" as a way to understand and claim their heritage in the region, such as Paul's interest in DNA testing. Yet while many residents focused on harnessing human and plant genetic technology in an attempt to preserve or cultivate a rooted social imaginary, the responses of others to climate change hinted at the emergence of new social imaginaries. In their awareness that even "rooted" beings were in flux, some began to question their own identities and emplacements.

Conclusion

"ALTHOUGH THERE IS

NO PLACE CALLED ROOIBOS"

As I began writing this book, a fire raged in the Cederberg, destroying homes, farms, and wide swaths of uncultivated land. People posted images on Facebook of bright-orange flames and dark-gray smoke billowing over the mountains. Others shared photographs of burned houses with nothing but bedframes remaining in sooty shells of buildings. One image showed a farmhouse surrounded by a small patch of green among the immensity of the blackened landscape. Firefighters and volunteers had managed to save the farm and its lawn by dousing it in water. The workers' homes, people said, had not been spared. Many residents mourned a local white man who died fighting the blaze, while others celebrated the fact that there had been "only one casualty." Still others decried the deaths of animals by showing their burned corpses, twisted and brown in the coal-charred soil.

"Thank goodness only one person died," I mentioned when I visited the region in 2013. "It's true. Thank God," Gert, an Afrikaans resident, said. "Oh, and I think a couple of coloured guys might have died, too." Susan, a neighbor, commented that the fire was both a miracle and a tragedy, despite the harshness of the burned landscape and the apparent dismissal of coloured deaths. Many indigenous plants rely on fire for germination. The fynbos biome is a fire-driven ecosystem, and wild rooibos seedlings are among the first to emerge after fire events. Susan hoped that the fire would mean an abundance of wildflowers in the spring. Gert's and Susan's comments, and the many photographs of the fire, illustrated a highly racialized cycle of life and death.

After the fire passed, a rooibos battle of a different sort began brewing. A French company was trying to trademark the word "rooibos," an incident that brought back memories of a similar situation in the United States years before. Once again, it seemed that rooibos, its indigenous charisma, and its place as "South Africa's National Beverage" were under threat from global agribusinesses. In 2013, South African newspapers, rooibos industry leaders, and the South African Department of Trade and Industry (DTI) responded forcefully. "The DTI stands ready to defend South Africa's trade and intellectual property interests vigorously," said Minister Rob Davies.[1] The issue took on diplomatic proportions as the DTI and the Department of Agriculture, Forestry, and Fisheries raised objections with the French Embassy in South Africa and with the European Commission Delegation. In this instance, law experts offered the following opinion:

> The plant that rooibos tea is derived from is only to be found in a particular region of the Western Cape, which means that, *although there is no place called Rooibos*, the word does have a certain geographical significance. . . . South African law, however, does not have any protection for geographical indications. As a result . . . foreign authorities like those in the [European Union] won't grant protection to South African names like rooibos. This problem, says the government, will be solved once the Intellectual Property Laws Amendment Act 2007—or the "Traditional Knowledge Act" (TKA) . . . becomes law. . . . It is worth noting that the TKA makes provision for the protection of a "geographical indication," which is defined as "an indication which identifies goods as originating in the territory of the Republic or in a region or locality in that territory, and where a particular quality, reputation or other characteristic of the goods is essentially attributable to the geographic origin of the goods, including natural and human factors." (Forster 2013; emphasis added)

"Although there is no place called Rooibos," the experts offered. The lawyers' opinion brought together ideas about human and nonhuman, South African identity, threats from outsiders, and the idea of traditional knowledge—all within the framework of geography. Although there is no place called rooibos, the tea represents distinctly spatialized ideas of cultural belonging that merged traditional knowledge with national identity and ecologically specific geographical indications.

The issue of French appropriation appeared to be resolved in 2014 after an agreement with the European Union put a halt to France's attempts at trademarking. The idea of traditional knowledge, however, became still more fraught by 2015. A few years earlier, the South African San Council had approached the Department of Environmental Affairs (DEA) "expressing concerns about inadequate acknowledgement, recognition and protection of their interest in relation to the ownership of traditional knowledge associated with the rooibos" (Department of Environmental Affairs 2015a). As a result, the DEA undertook a study to determine whether the council's claims were valid. The DEA released its official findings:

> The fact that these species are endemic in areas where the species are in abundance, combined with the fact that the San and Khoikoi populations were resident in these areas for centuries before the arrival of the settlers and that the industry has evolved and expanded in these particular areas does largely support the communities['] perception that the TK [traditional knowledge] for rooibos and honeybush rests with the communities who originate in these areas. There is no evidence that disputes that the Khoi and San as holders of TK for these species. (Department of Environmental Affairs 2014: iii)

The reaction in the rooibos-growing community was confusion and disbelief. The San Council describes itself as working on behalf of the "first" Indigenous peoples of Africa. But who, residents wondered, made up the San Council, and whom did they represent? Would people receive money for their "traditional knowledge"? Would these people include coloured residents who live in the region and who hold generations of knowledge about the plant? If so, would they have to prove a Khoisan indigeneity through DNA (an identity, I have argued, that few explicitly claimed)? These answers remained elusive and unsettling to many in the region and seemed to confirm coloured residents' struggles against ideas of authenticity and placelessness.

Through intensely personal narratives, the "tea stories" told by coloured and white farmers, farmworkers, marketers, scientists, and politicians resonated with issues of globalization and isolation, neoliberal economic reforms, and post-apartheid politics. As residents grappled with questions relating to traditional knowledge and climate change, however, they focused more on the intimate relations among the plant, ecosystem, and themselves than on connections to foreign consumers. Local concerns revolved around securing livelihoods and navigating a political, economic, and demographic landscape that seemed to be both changing beyond their control and remaining frustratingly the same. Residents worried over adapting to climatic shifts and—at the core—negotiating their contested claims to belonging with an indigenous ecosystem.

These concerns were magnified by residents' uncertain connections to indigeneity. Afrikaners claimed a kind of white African indigeneity that was fiercely contested by black and coloured South Africans, not to mention groups such as the San Council. And in contrast to pervasive narratives of pure, ecologically indigeneous rooibos, coloured people were sometimes deemed the mixed-race offspring of "extinct Bushmen" and at other times labeled as possessing a "false identity," indigenous to nowhere. Ecological, economic, and political precarity merged with racial precarity. This precarity could be all-consuming, particularly for coloured residents who desired a "life" amid profound structural inequalities. Yet the ways in which residents connected to the ecological—to rooibos—potentially opened up claims to belonging that operated outside preexisting power structures, speaking instead to Anna Tsing's (2015: 135) "alternative politics of more-than-human entanglements." As rooibos's economic value increased, contestations around cultural ownership similarly increased. At stake for local residents was not the established scholarly concept of indigeneity—as a relationship between people and place—but, rather, a new kind of claim to indigeneity based on a relationship among people, place, and plant. The plant-human connections were inextricably tied to the violent racial histories mapped to the ecosystem. Rooibos was unquestionably indigenous, its naturalness supposedly outside politics; yet this naturalness was the source of its economic, cultural, and spiritual value and engendered its politicization.

Emerging from this racially charged environment was something potentially hopeful. "Through rooibos, we are getting our dignity back," a coloured farmer said. "We are able to make a life." "Our farmers will not be small farmers forever," another farmer stated. "We will grow big." With the cultivation of rooibos viewed as more than just a livelihood, coloured farmers used their connections to the plant to reframe their heritage and put forth an alternative politics of recognition. Their understanding of belonging with rooibos enabled something more encompassing, flexible, and potentially emancipatory. They defied the country's history of incarcerating and essentializing ethnicity and challenged the apartheid government's use of primordial attachments to land to justify the spatial control of nonwhite people. Coloured residents oriented this politics of recognition less around legal and political recognition than around a "self-fashioning" that seeks to "*prefigure* radical alternatives to the structural and subjective dimensions of colonial power" (Coulthard 2014: 18). They redefined heritage not only as a claim to a "traditional" past, but also as a potential for the future.

What will the future bring to the region's social and ecological relations? Will coloured residents gain access to more land? Will climate change uproot rooibos and the lives and livelihoods that come with it? Some farmers seemed to be thriving. They leveraged their social and economic capital to negotiate the new political, economic, and climatic environment. A number of large-scale rooibos producers bought their neighbors' farms, consolidating land and expanding their influence. Other farmers made use of fair trade certifications and Black Economic Empowerment programs to sell their tea at a premium. Bertie, a local coloured man who worked odd jobs around town, said that he had recently obtained access to land for the first time. His business was progressing slowly, but he was optimistic and wanted to name his rooibos after Khoisan terms for "red" and "bush." He consulted with a linguist to determine the correct words but could not find the symbols on his computer to write the name for me.

Many farmers, however, were suffering, unable to compete with large-scale farms and meet the challenges of a shifting climate. Some white commercial farmers were reluctantly leaving the area. And despite Bertie's success, most coloured residents remained unable to access land. Farmworkers' lives were also uprooted, with jobs becoming more casual and temporary and housing increasingly not provided on farms due to evictions, among other reasons (Ewert and du Toit 2004; Visser and Ferrer 2015). The shift in living and working practices seemed primed to alter relations between workers and farm owners, as well. In other South African agricultural industries, researchers have noted how paternalism has given way to obligations based on contracts rather than on history and place (Bolt 2013; Rutherford and Addison 2007). In the short term, workers spoke of a more tenuous life in which they faced insecure jobs and housing. What these changing labor relations might mean for the rooibos region in the long term is still unclear. Could the upending of paternalistic farm dynamics help overturn apartheid legacies that rendered coloured workers "children"—or, worse, "animal"? Or will the deregulation of the postapartheid era combine with an increasingly neoliberal global trade regime to consolidate rooibos land in the hands of a (white) few and shift power downstream away from producers to processors and retailers (Visser and Ferrer 2015)?

During my trip to the region in 2013, a government employee seemed defeated. "We haven't gotten any new land [for coloured claimants] since 2010," he said. He was taking graduate school courses online at night to try to find another line of work so he could leave the region. "It's bad," he said. "Nothing is happening." I learned that one of the area's coloured ministers had moved back to Cape Town. "He just got frustrated," his friend explained. "He felt like he couldn't make a difference with the people." Another resident said, "I've been applying for jobs overseas. I just don't know what is going to happen here." Others considered moving to Cape Town for work but found few opportunities in urban areas and worried about losing the support of their kin networks. The majority of people, however, did not have the option to leave. Poor and lacking education, most coloured residents, many black migrants, and even a number of Afrikaans farmers were bound to the region. In these instances, connections to the area served as a trap, not a redemptive form of belonging.

A few farmers worried about the rooibos industry's success. Diedrik, an Afrikaans farmer, explained, "Our biggest fear is that being so small an area if the world starts asking and you get a drought you won't be able to supply." Apprehensive about the ambiguity of the present moment, he wanted to return to the stasis of apartheid-era protections, to a time when he was not concerned about global supply, the presence of agribusinesses, the effects of climate change on rainfall, and the loss of white political power. Yet his statement also contained a subtly hopeful quality informed by his belief in rooibos's miracle-like qualities and its unquestioned value. His biggest fear was that the world would want too much rooibos, not that the industry would not survive.

When I discussed questions about the future with farmers, farmworkers, residents, and migrants, one theme kept emerging: the idea of "generations." The invocation of generations referred to the future, whether it was white farmers' anxieties that their children's "rightful" land would be stolen by the government or coloured workers' fears that they would remain subjugated forever. People across racial divides discussed concerns that future generations would be unable to control the climate. "How can a small farmer survive?" a young coloured farmer shook his head. The idea of generations also referred to the past, whether it was generations of white farmers working the rooibos land or generations of coloured workers unable to claim ownership of their homes or livelihoods. In their research on South Africa, John Comaroff and Jean Comaroff (2000: 17) link generations to socioeconomic class: "As the expansion of the free market runs up against the demise of the welfare state, the modernist ideal in which each generation does better than its processor is mocked by conditions." Class dynamics were undoubtedly a central factor in local concerns about the future and in the ability to navigate the rooibos region's "conditions." Yet some people did retain hope. While the majority of people who were able to improve their circumstances were the owners of capital— large-scale farmers and the wealthy *inkomers*—some small-scale farmers were finding a niche, selling their rooibos at a premium. Although many poor and middle-class residents appeared to be worse off economically than previous generations, an interesting paradox emerged: Because of rooibos's financial success, a new sense of belonging was seemingly made possible through connections to the charismatic plant.

In this context of hope and fear, I turn back to the idea of rooibos as "a gift from nature" to show the entangled sociality of rooibos's human-nonhuman world. The geographers Soren Larsen and Jay Johnson (2012: 639) assert that "every human and nonhuman 'being' is ineluctably connected to every other . . . a sociality of dwelling together amid the common condition of a meaningful but finite existence." They insist that this sociality opens up a place for compassion. In all the violence and seemingly intractable segregation and inequality in South Africa, it was hard to imagine a "sociality of dwelling together." But perhaps this sociality—rather than a continuation of conflict—could emerge through the cross-racial love of rooibos and its ecosystem.

Nevertheless, a danger persists in being celebratory about the plant and its indigeneity—or even in affirming links among people, plant, and place. Connections between the "natural" love of the land and the "natural" racism endured. Too often in South African history, people with economic and political power have treated plants like moral subjects, while coloured and black humanity remained uncertain. After the recent fires, many white residents mourned the burned landscape, mangled animals, and death of a white volunteer firefighter. They celebrated the potential for new plant life. Only as an afterthought did they mention, "I think a couple of coloured guys might have died, too." Hopeful forms of belonging remained tempered by worrying continuities of race-based exclusions. Yet the future was not necessarily bleak for "coloured guys." They were not only victims. With its changing demographics, they could also be the people who inherit the region in the long term. While life on a rooibos farm may have been measured by the cycles of the seasons, the future looked to be more than just the eternal repetition of the same.

Notes

PREFACE

1 Cedarburg is the English translation of Cederberg (the Afrikaans for the words "cedar" and "mountain"). In South Africa, the region is spelled Cederberg, which is why I use that spelling. However, many marketing materials/tea boxes use the "English" spelling.

INTRODUCTION

1 Increasingly, journals such as the *International Journal of Indigenous Health* and media organizations such as the Canadian Broadcasting Corporation have begun changing editorial guidelines in relation to the capitalization of "Indigenous," much as English, Afrikaans, or South African would be capitalized. The people of the rooibos-growing region use the concept, "indigenous," in different and contested ways. Indeed, they typically rejected affiliation with international Indigenous movements. As such, I will not capitalize "indigenous" when referring to ecology or when referring to indigeneity in the rooibos region. However, I will capitalize the word when referring to Indigenous People or facets of their culture in a broad context.

2 I use the South African spelling of the word "coloured" to underscore the term's particular location in South Africa and to differentiate it from its usage in other contexts, such as the United States.

3 Language in the rooibos-growing area and in South Africa as a whole is simultaneously political and banal. Certain words, such as "Khoisan" and "Bushmen," were both controversial and used without thought. Common terminology constructed sets of categories that challenge binary thinking about race, nativity, and foreignness and even about what it means to be a farmer. Most anthropologists agree that people who speak Khoisan languages inhabited the region before white colonization. However, "Khoisan" is a problematic label, as no singular precolonial group existed. Rather, "Khoisan" is a unifying name for ethnic groups in South Africa who shared physical and linguistic characteristics distinct from the Bantu (or black) majority

(Adhikari 2010a; Barnard 1992; Wilson 1986). Often, scholars divide the Khoisan into the "foraging" or hunter-gatherer San and the pastoral Khoi (or Khoe, Khoe-Khoe, KhoiKhoi). Even these distinctions fall apart on closer inspection, as groups blended together and practiced multiple forms of subsistence, often combining hunting and gathering with herding depending on the time of year (Gordon 1992; Penn 2005; Wilmsen 1989). Colonists sometimes labeled the Khoi "Hottentot" and the San "Bushmen," words now generally considered derogatory. Residents used a variety of these terms interchangeably to describe a group considered "extinct" in the rooibos region. I will use the term "Khoisan" to refer to a general idea of the preco-lonial people who lived in the rooibos-growing area, as this was the term most often employed by residents.

4 I have changed all names and kept some biographical details vague to protect infor-mants' anonymity.

5 The word "farmer" is highly emotive and politicized in the rooibos region. So in-timately is it linked to Afrikaans identity that its Afrikaans translation, *boer*, is also another word for Afrikaner. In this linguistic context, coloured farmers were almost always labeled small-scale farmers or emerging farmers—or *klein boere* (in Afrikaans, literally translated as "small farmers"). This terminology had practical implications. With little access to land, most coloured farmers operated by necessity on a small scale. But as one farmer said, "I am not a small-scale farmer. A small farmer chooses to be small. I am only a small farmer because I have limited access to land." Another coloured farmer laughed at the term "emerging," a euphemism for coloured farmer. "Emerging into what?" he asked. In a more serious tone, an older farmer asserted, "I prefer 'small scale' because my family has been farming for generations. [I am not] emerging." By contrast, white farmers were almost always called commercial farmers. They often used this term—and the term "farmer"—proudly, unlike many people involved in the nearby wine and citrus industries, who preferred the term "producer" because it sounded more "sophisticated" and did not carry with it the burden of the stereotypical Afrikaans farmer identity. But the size of farms had concrete effects that went beyond terminology. In a comprehensive study commissioned by the South African Rooibos Council (Sandra Kruger and Associates 2009), small-scale farmers were defined as cultivating fewer than ten hectares. Large-scale commercial farmers were defined as cultivating more than one hundred hectares. Using figures from farms sampled for the study, Kruger and Associates found that commercial farms larger than ten hectares produced 97 percent of harvested rooibos, or twenty-eight times more harvested rooibos than did small-scale farms (Sandra Kruger and Associates 2009: 57). White farmers also tended to have a diverse farming portfolio that included livestock or fruit cultivation in addition to rooibos. Small-scale co-loured farmers, however, tended to be reliant on rooibos and used nearly all of their available land for its cultivation. Consequently, they were far more dependent on rooibos's economic market and climatic conditions than many white farmers were.

6 Statistics South Africa, 2012, http://www.statssa.gov.za.

7 When speaking in English, residents frequently used the word "endemic" inter-changeably with "indigenous," and readers will see that usage reflected in my writing.

In broad terms, "endemic" means ecologically unique to a specific geographical location. Rooibos is endemic to South Africa's Western and Northern Cape. Yet the word also has epidemiological usages that complicate its positive connotations. Endemic is an infection maintained in a population without the need for external inputs. In other words, it is an infection in a self-contained group. Anna Tsing (2012: 19) describes: "As long as the relevant other species are found—at least sometimes—inside the human body, we can study them in relations of co-habitation and dependency. If the other species is outside the human body, that is, part of the 'environment' for humans, analysis suddenly switches to a discourse of human impact, management, and control." In the rooibos-growing area, the term was undeniably positive. Any "infections" did not stem from the local population; they came from outsiders. Unlike "endemic," the term "indigenous" could have multiple and shifting connotations in the region. Indigenous plants were "good" and should be protected on moral and economic grounds. For coloured people, claiming indigeneity had both positive and negative implications. It could redeem their liminality and give them the right to make land claims or it could relegate them to a state of extinction or even negate their land claims by rendering them nomadic.

8   United Nations Educational, Scientific and Cultural Organization, "Cape Floral Region Protected Areas," 2011, http://whc.unesco.org/uploads/nominations/1007rev .pdf.

9   World Bank, "GINI Index," 2013, http://data.worldbank.org/indicator/SI.POV. GINI. The GINI index measures the extent to which the distribution of income or consumption expenditure among individuals or households within an economy deviates from a perfectly equal distribution. A recent working paper by scholars at the University of KwaZulu-Natal argues, however, that the World Bank does not take into account the South African government's welfare policies (Bosch et al. 2010). They recalculated the GINI coefficient to include social security grants, as well as pensions from previous employment and annuities from investments, making South Africa "more equal" than the World Bank's measurement. This claim, however, is debated.

10 United Nations Department on Drugs and Crime, "Homicide Statistics, 2012, https://www.unodc.org/gsh/en/data.html.

11 Statistics South Africa.

12 I spoke with a government employee who was supposed to interact with farmworkers as part of his job, but he said, "It is not easy to reach the workers." White farmers, he explained, controlled workers' housing and most aspects of their lives. "You first need to contact the owners. The locals and the foreigners [stay there]. They are not easy to access." With the exception of workers who lived off the farm or also cultivated rooibos as part of a cooperative, I had similar difficulties. Initially, because workers lived and spent most of their time on farm owners' private property, I tried speaking with some after getting permission from the farm owner. Not surprisingly, these interviews tended to be awkwardly brief. Despite my explanations about who I was and the anonymity I would provide, I was never sure that the workers believed that I was not working on behalf of the farm owner. I abandoned that strategy and

instead tried multiple other avenues to reach workers: through church activities, labor-related meetings, political events, and so on. These interviews and casual conversations proved far more candid. However, I likely never reached some of the most isolated workers—workers whom people joked did not know apartheid was over. Their voices remain silent in my narrative. My analysis of workers' heterogeneous experiences should keep these limitations in mind.

13 Hodgson (2011) pluralizes Li's (2000) idea of positioning to recognize the multiple, dynamic, and sometimes contradictory ways in which a group self-identifies or mobilizes its self-identification. This multiplicity was reflective of the ideas of indigeneity in the rooibos-growing region.

14 Audra Simpson and Andrea Smith discuss relationships between indigeneity and ethnicity. They ask whether the term "ethnic" assimilates "indigenous" and makes it just another racial minority instead of a sovereign people. Ultimately, they argue that ethnic studies should not be "a melting pot but a 'coalitional intellectual project'" (Simpson and Smith 2014: 13). Coloured residents envisioned themselves as part of a racial group and spoke of their "cultural heritage" rather than any idea of sovereignty. Yet their claim to rightful belonging in the land because of their cultural ownership of an *indigenous* plant speaks to Simpson and Smith's idea of a coalitional project undeterred by sharp lines between indigeneity and ethnicity.

15 United Nations, "Indigenous People, Indigenous Voices: Factsheet," 2013, http://www.un.org/esa/socdev/unpfii/documents/5session_factsheet1.pdf.

16 Significantly, scholars such as Wilma Dunaway (2014) have critiqued commodity chain analyses for their lack of attention to gender. While I do not focus on gender as the axis of my analysis, I incorporate discussions of gender as they intersect with race and class in the rooibos region. These discussions range from examinations of the complicated masculinities expressed by male Afrikaans farmers to the role of women in coloured farming cooperatives and the ways in which my own gender influenced how people viewed and interacted with me in the region. Part of Dunaway's critique advocates moving beyond a separation between the market and the home and bringing households into commodity analyses. This critique resonates with my research in ways that extend beyond seeing the informal or non-wage contributions of women who are not actively involved with farm labor (though many coloured women did work in the fields). Through the intimate, racialized, gendered, and highly unequal notions of "family" that inform the rooibos "family farm," I explore how patriarchal ideas of nurturance undergirded commercial farming practices. But I also show how nurturance extended to the plant and soil in ways that complicate notions of women as close to nature and men to culture (Ortner 1974).

17 As an indigenous plant and herbal tisane, rooibos's commodity history differs from that of black teas such as those from Darjeeling. Indeed, rooibos's history differs from that of many African commodities as well. These commodities, such as rubber or gold, helped to consolidate colonial power and connect the colony to the metropole through dependence on export-oriented trade networks. However, rooibos did not become a globalized commodity until the late twentieth century.

18 Other scholarship on agricultural commodities in the postcolonial context has

focused on connections between people across space. In *The Modern World-System* (1974), Immanuel Wallerstein famously described the relationship among capitalism, agriculture, and the origins of the world economy. Building on the idea of a network, Ian Cook and Philip Crang (1996) describe food not only as emplaced cultural artifacts, but also as displaced practices and materials that cross boundaries. Beginning in the 1980s, consumers began showing an increased interest in the origins of their food and beverages (Fischer and Benson 2006; Guthman 2009; Sen 2014). Cook and Crang use the concept of the "double-fetish" to argue that producers attempt to limit consumers' knowledge while simultaneously emphasizing the idea of "geographical knowledge" to "re-enchant" certain foods and distinguish them from standardized food and tastes. With the exception of a brief discussion of tea boxes and geographical indications, I will not focus on rooibos consumption outside the growing region. However, I will show how this enchantment not only acted on consumers but also informed residents' own understandings of the tea.

CHAPTER I. CULTIVATING INDIGENEITY

1 See, e.g., United Nations, "Declaration of the Rights of Indigenous People," 2008, http://www.un.org/esa/socdev/unpfii/documents/DRIPS_en.pdf.

2 Wiedouw Estate Rooibos Tea, 2013, http://www.wiedouw.co.za/rooibos_detail.php.

3 The terms "coloured" and "mixed race" should not be used interchangeably. In South Africa, the coloured community—though composed of people from different backgrounds and religions—was cemented into one group under apartheid. It became its own racial category, and because it was a racial category, being coloured meant that one could legally live, marry, and move freely only among other coloured people.

4 Statistics South Africa, 2012, http://www.statssa.gov.za.

5 Vast diversity exists among the coloured population. Approximately two-thirds of the population lives in the Western Cape and 40 percent in the Cape Town area (Adhikari 2005). Perhaps because of this concentration, the majority of researchers who address coloured history and identity focus on Cape Town and its surrounding areas (see, e.g., Jensen 2008; Ross 2010; Salo 2003; Trotter 2009; Western 1996). Many cross-regional similarities about the concept of colouredness and its fraught history exist. However, experiences of colonialism, livelihoods, relationships to land, and contemporary understandings of colouredness differed in the rural rooibos region from those in Cape Town—a city where most coloured farmworkers, small-scale farmers, and residents had never traveled.

6 Clanwilliam Living Landscape Project, Living Landscape website, 2011, http://www.cllp.uct.ac.za/index.htm.

7 Clanwilliam Living Landscape Project, "Living Landscape Pamphlet," 2011.

8 Wilcocks Commission, *Commission of Inquiry Regarding Cape Coloured Population of the Union*, UG 54 (1937), Pretoria.

9 South African Land Claims Court, 2011, http://www.justice.gov.za/lcc/index.html.

10 In 2015, Rural Development and Land Reform Minister Gugile Nkwinti delivered

an opening address at the National Dialogue on exceptions to the cutoff date in the Natives Land Act of 1913. The dialogue set the stage for allowing exceptions with the aim of "achieving reconciliation and address[ing] landlessness among Khoi San people" (Department of Rural Development and Land Reform 2015). This discussion had not begun during my fieldwork, and at the time of writing it was unclear how it might affect coloured people in the rooibos-growing region.

11 Congress of the People, "South African Freedom Charter," Kliptown, South Africa, 1955, http://www.anc.org.za.

12 According to a report by the Surplus People Project and the Legal Resources Centre (2000: 1), "The relationship between the inhabitants of this land and the Church as registered owner of the land has, since the outset, been fluid. It is this relationship that determines the respective rights of the Church and the occupants. These rights have been, and continue to be, reinterpreted and contested." In other words, the relation between church as "owner" and resident as "tenant" is not straightforward, an issue that I address later in the book.

13 Wupperthal website, 2011, http://www.wupperthal.co.za.

14 If you speak to many South Africans today, they associate Wupperthal with Christianity, rooibos, and shoemaking, a craft initiated by the German missionaries. I engage more with ideas of spirituality in chapter 2 and with contemporary community dynamics in chapter 4. The Moravian Church has a fascinating history in relation to farming in South Africa. Michael T. Bravo (2005) explains this history in his work on mission gardens. Moravian missionaries first came to the Cape of Good Hope in 1737. They purchased land from the colonial government to gain some autonomy. As unpaid volunteers for the church, missionaries supported themselves through labor, such as small-scale collective agriculture aimed at self-sufficiency. The gardens, Bravo explains, were "place-responsive." In other words, they were the sites where "missionaries and indigenous botanical traditions intersected, as though they were a practical space where the incommensurability between cultures could be overcome" (Bravo 2005: 51). Missionaries viewed artisanship, such as making shoes, and natural knowledge as tools for their ultimate goal: "non-coerced conversion." In their gardening practices they believed that "the natural world was tamed and made virtuous through skilled labor" (Bravo 2005: 53). Church rhetoric was full of visions of natives and missionaries working side by side. However, mission lands also became a form of incarceration, as loss of mobility and personal freedom were often conditions at mission stations. Thus, missionaries helped to formalize the economic structures of the colony.

15 Redbush Tea Company, 2016, https://www.redbushtea.com/.

16 The publicizing of Nelson Mandela's DNA prompted discussions in the news about South Africa's racial background, including findings in the 1980s that Afrikaners have an average of 7 percent black blood. In 2011, the journalist Max Du Preez asked, "Are We All Coloured?" News24, September 3, 2011, http://m.news24.com /news24/Columnists/MaxduPreez/Are-we-all-coloured-20110309. He put forward problems associated with racial labels: (1) Most South Africans have some mixed-race heritage; and (2) the term "coloured" does not adequately encapsulate the fact

that many coloured people are partially descended from the Khoisan. Du Preez himself was labeled "European" under apartheid categories but says he does not consider himself European. "I had my DNA tested at the National Health Laboratory. They tell me from my father's side I'm in the E1b1b1c1 haplogroup—23% of Ethiopians belong to this small genetic group," he wrote. Notably, while he seems to celebrate a mixed ancestry, he cites a genetic connection not to black South African heritage but to an Ethiopian one far removed from South Africa's racial politics.

17 Origins Center website, 2011, http://www.origins.org.za.

18 These ideas of primitivity mirror Laura Graham and Glenn Penny's (2014) discussion of indigeneity. They argue that self-conscious, reflexive performances of indigeneity became more common in the second half of the twentieth century. While these performances "are critically important in global politics today" (including politics of recognition in relation to land claims), they also have potential pitfalls (Graham and Penny 2014: 1). When groups are not able to control "the means and forms of their representation," they can fall into romanticized ideas of indigenous peoples (Graham and Penny 2014: 7).

19 The scientist was referring to *The Medicinal and Poisonous Plants of Southern Africa* (Watt and Breyer-Brandwijk 1932). The book lists rooibos as a medicinal plant but does not indicate specific applications.

20 A difference existed between farmers' discourse and the discourse of some residents who lived in town. Despite the region's small population, it held many concerts and festivals. While Afrikaans folk, pop, and Christian singers dominated most of these events, a number of festivals featured people from the coloured community. The Cederberg Fees, a major festival sponsored in part by Rooibos Ltd., included a diversity of events. On the last day of the 2011 festival, a sold-out play featuring two famous coloured soap opera stars caused much thoughtful conversation in town. The play, *My Name Is Ellen Pakkies*, describes the true-life story of a mother who murdered her drug-addicted son.

21 Chris Kilham, "Red Tea: Even Better for You than Green Tea?" Fox News, March 27, 2012, http://www.foxnews.com/health/2012/03/27/red-tea-even-better-for-than-green-tea.

22 Statistics South Africa.

23 United Nations Educational, Scientific and Cultural Organization, "Cape Floral Region Protected Areas," 2011, http://whc.unesco.org/uploads/nominations/1007rev.pdf.

CHAPTER 2. FARMING THE BUSH

1 Scholars have worked to unpack and politicize distinctions between the human and nonhuman in relation to commodities and to plants and animals. Theories of materiality explore the tensions in the dialectic between people and things (Meskell 2004; Miller 2008). Donna Haraway (2008: 11) critiques anthropocentrism by describing the "culturally normal fantasy of human exceptionalism, or the 'foolish' idea that humanity alone is not a spatial and temporal web of interspecies dependencies."

The nonhuman emerges not as the "other" against which humanity defines itself, but as a "constitutive ground on which humanity is enacted" (Feldman and Tickin 2010: 19). Some scholars have critiqued the use of the term "nonhuman" as maintaining the centrality of the human and making plants, animals, and objects merely that which is not human (Kirksey and Helmreich 2010). While I accept these critiques, echoing Eduardo Kohn's (2007) work on forests and humans, I want to open up the human and shatter the self-referential current, not do away with the human.

2 South African Rooibos Council, "The Official Site of South African Rooibos," 2011, http://www.sarooibos.org.za.

3 Many theorists have addressed the connections between capitalism and changing ideas about nature. For example, Stephen Mrozowski (1999) explores the relationship between colonization, the rise of capitalism, and the commodification of nature in South Africa and Virginia through the construction of "abstract space" and the need for colonizers to classify and organize the "natural" people and plants they observed. However, Afrikaners in the rooibos region did not fall easily into generalized conceptions of Europeans' views of nature. Similarly, I am wary of conflating Afrikaner and "European" notions of capitalism. (Certainly, apartheid's economic policies counter any straightforward comparisons.) Max Weber's *Protestant Ethic* (2003 [1905]) reflects connections between spirituality and the economy in a Calvinist tradition. In this influential work on the cultural origins of capitalism, Weber implies that Protestantism affected the growth and formation of capitalism. Religious residents of the rooibos region were almost exclusively Protestant. Again, however, I will stop short of making direct comparisons because of the specific role and history of the Dutch Reformed Church in South Africa, as well as the other prominent religions in the area, such as the Moravian Church.

CHAPTER 3. ENDEMIC PLANTS AND INVASIVE PEOPLE

1 During the sweep of xenophobic attacks in 2008, almost a third of those targeted were actually black South Africans. As a result, "naming" the violence became a site of contention. Was it xenophobia or criminal activity? Or, as former President Thabo Mbeki charged, were criminals merely using the garb of xenophobia to justify their contempt for the law? Whatever the cause, most observers assert that the victims were attacked because of mistaken identity—their darker skin or spoken languages made people believe that they were from countries such as Zimbabwe (Worby et al. 2008).

2 Proudly South African website, 2012, http://www.proudlysa.co.za.

3 It is easy to romanticize the organic mode of farming employed by small-scale coloured farmers. In fact, a number of both coloured and white farmers technically farmed organically but lacked the money or bureaucratic wherewithal to obtain organic certification. Organic farming did not require the high input costs of chemicals (money that most small-scale farmers did not have), and the small size of their land made the labor-intensive process of organic farming more feasible.

4 According to Margareet Visser and Stuart Ferrer (2015), more than 90 percent of

people in Western Cape agricultural areas were South African citizens, confirming that "immigrants" from other countries were not predominant. However, Visser and Ferrer add that much of the available information on migrants in rural areas is anecdotal.

5 "All Pay" refers to the social grant system in South Africa. These grants covered more than 44 percent of the population in 2010: Statistics South Africa, 2016, http://www.statssa.gov.za. The grants are "means tested," denoting that eligibility depends on income and assets falling below a certain threshold. Grants are dispersed monthly, and the amount received depends on the type, with, for example, 350 rands per month per child for the Child Support Grant and approximately 1,500 rands per month for the Old Age Pension: South African Social Security Agency website, 2016, http://www.sassa.gov.za.

6 When they arrived in the region in the seventeenth and eighteenth centuries, white farmers brought with them new techniques for farming and earning a livelihood off the land. Colonists often attempted to reconstruct nature from "the ground up." The core reason that the Dutch East India Company initially founded the Cape Colony was to cultivate foreign crops and animals to resupply its ships.

7 Many South Africans considered the Independent Democrats the political party of coloured South Africans when it was founded in 2003, because its leader, Patricia de Lille, was coloured. In 2010, however, the party merged with the Democratic Alliance.

CHAPTER 4. THE POLITICS OF NARRATION

1 Whether or not rooibos stimulates or suppresses appetites depends on the marketing campaigns of specific rooibos products. Rooibos was simultaneously advertised as a weight-loss tool and a weight-gain tool.

2 For a detailed account of Wupperthal from 1830 to 1965, including a discussion of class formation, the ethnic composition of Wupperthal's coloured community, and its growing coloured "consciousness" at the beginning of the twentieth century, as well as a literature review of other Wupperthal histories, see Bilbe 2009. For a detailed discussion of how the church acquired land in Wupperthal and its surrounding areas, see Surplus People Project and Legal Resources Centre 2000.

3 South African Council of Churches website, 2012, http://www.sacc.org.za.

4 With the help of two organizations—the Surplus People Project and the Legal Resources Centre—a group of coloured residents in the Cederberg region launched a claim to obtain rights to land in the 1990s. In 2000, the Surplus People Project and the Legal Resources Centre also made a case that all mission station inhabitants should be "entitled to State assistance for the purpose of securing their tenure" (Surplus People Project and Legal Resources Centre 2000: 3). These claims brought out so many emotions and tensions—and even a rumored suicide—that few people wanted to discuss them. In 2016, disputes and animosities surrounding church land were ongoing. Because the issue was so divisive, numerous people specifically asked me not to raise the claims in interviews in Wupperthal and other former mission

lands. History helps to explain the divisions. Between 1832 and 1855, the Rhenish Missionary Society acquired considerable land in the Cederberg. The society paid for some of the land, while other land was "'gifted' from colonial authorities who did not regard the area's indigenous peoples, denigrated as 'half-castes' or 'bastards' during this era, as having any legal rights to the lands they worked" (Coombe et al. 2015: 229). Wupperthal and its surrounding outstations became part of the Moravian Church in 1965. Land acquired by the Dutch Reformed Church followed a similar history, although much Dutch Reformed Church land was sold to white farmers in the mid-twentieth century rather than turned over to the Moravian Church. According to Lungisile Ntsebeza (2005), policies involving mission land were unclear after 1994. The Genadendal Accord of 1996 attempted to promote tenure security at mission stations and address other land-related problems. However, Ntsebeza argues that the accord did little to provide straightforward guidelines. Ntsebeza's research on other mission stations reflects unresolved questions: Should churches sell or lease land? Or should they give land to those who worked and paid taxes on it for years? Many residents have fought for restitution, but Ntsebeza found that a minority of residents were "grateful to the church" for protecting them from apartheid evictions, and while they acknowledge that "there was/is 'racism in the church,' they felt that the *status quo* is much better than land reform" (Ntsebeza 2005: 69). Jennifer Keahey, a sociologist who works on sustainability initiatives in the region, also speaks to these questions (Keahey and Murry 2017). She states that because much of the land around Wupperthal is designated for conservation, insufficient acreage remains to support hundreds of farmers, regardless of land reform outcomes.

5 The DA regained the majority in the 2016 election as part of a major shift in the country away from the ANC due to a number of factors, including dissatisfaction with ANC President Jacob Zuma. While the ANC retained more than half the country's votes, it lost ground in major cities across the country.

6 For an in-depth discussion of emerging farmers and fair trade certifications, see Keahey 2013.

CHAPTER 5. PRECARIOUS LANDSCAPES

1 "Farmworker Shot in Face as Strike Turns Riotous," SABC News, January 10, 2013, http://www.sabc.co.za/news/a/3bd7c7804e21b1968f39bff251b4e4e2/Farmworker -shot-in-face-as-strike-turns-riotous.

2 Central to Hegel's idea about consciousness is man's relation with the external object. He argues that people attempt to reincorporate the other and the external object into the subject, forming new collective forces such as societies through a dialectical flow of relations in which we make the world and in doing so make ourselves (Hegel 1977 [1807]; Hodder 2012). In this matter, Hegel implies his own kind of inalienability between humans and nonhumans.

3 Hantam Municipality website, n.d., www.hantammunicipality.co.za.

4 As described earlier, land *restitution* was not a major factor in the rooibos region, as

most land was in white hands long before the 1913 cutoff date. Rather, transfers of land would more likely fall under land *redistribution*. According to the South African Institute of Race Relations, about 95.6 percent of restitution claims had been resolved nationwide: see http://www.sairr.org.za/services/publications/south -africa-survey/south-africa-survey-2012. When it comes to redistribution, however, South Africa had reached only 15.5 percent, or approximately four million hectares of the total 25.9 million hectares of land. The Western Cape had redistribution rates of only 4.5 percent, the lowest in the country. I asked a white rooibos farmer who had lost a farm in another part of the country as a result of a successful land claim whether he worried that the same thing might happen in the rooibos-growing area. He responded, "I don't worry about land claims here. When I moved, I went to the land claims office and asked. He showed me the title deed. The land had been given to whites [by the colonial government] in the 1700s, so we are fine." That said, it is possible that restitution could play a role in the future with the government's revisiting of the 1913 cutoff date (see Department of Rural Development and Land Reform 2015).

5 A local ANC branch helped Arend's group gain access to rented land through the Nieuwoudtville Municipality after the previous tenant's contract expired. According to Jennifer Keahey (2013: 174), "The group formed in the late 1990s to help retired farm laborers hold onto their sheep as 'they were kicked off' their commercial farms when they became 'too old to work' and wished to retain their sheep after relocating to low-income housing in town. . . . [The group also] recently received funds from the Department of Trade and Industry to assist in small cooperative formation." Because the group does not own the land, however, Arend was not certain that it would be able to continue farming when its contract expires. "We don't have our own land. The municipality wants to kick us off," Arend told me. "We went to the high court of Kimberly, and they lost the case. They have to honor their five-year agreement."

6 The impact of climate change in the region—and on the rooibos industry in particular—has been researched extensively (Archer et al. 2008; Lötter and Maitre 2014). South Africa's Long Term Adaptation Scenarios (Department of Environmental Affairs) state that the fynbos biome is "significantly threatened by climate change" (Ziervogel et al. 2014: 608). For example, negative trends in winter rainfall have already been accompanied by increases in the length of dry spells. Winter rainfall is particularly important for rooibos germination and establishment, while occasional summer rainfall enables young seedling to survive dry, hot months. The idea that rooibos cultivation might spread to areas outside rooibos's "natural" growing area could "threaten the genetic integrity of different wild types and cause homogenization of the species" (Lötter and Maitre 2014: 1219).

7 Heiveld Cooperative website, 2013, http://www.heiveld.co.za.

8 It is important to note that Ritvo is discussing European Enlightenment thinking about nature and science. Through the book, I have discussed understandings of nature and people's relations to nature that are specific to the rooibos region and

challenge aspects of Enlightenment thinking. That said, ideas about control and understandings about the role of science in the rooibos-growing area largely mirrored those expressed by Ritvo.

CONCLUSION

1 Government News Agency, Republic of South Africa, "DTI Responds to French Rooibos Trademark Matter," February 22, 2013, http://www.sanews.gov.za/world /dti-responds-french-rooibos-trademark-matter.

References

Adams, Jonathan, and Thomas McShane. 1992. *The Myth of Wild Africa: Conservation without Illusion*. Berkeley: University of California Press.

Addison, Lincoln. 2014. "Delegated Despotism: Frontiers of Agrarian Labour on a South African Border Farm." *Journal of Agrarian Change* 14, no. 2, 286–304.

Adhikari, Mohamed. 2005. *Not White Enough, Not Black Enough: Racial Identity in the South African Coloured Community*. Africa Series, 83. Athens: Ohio University Press.

———. 2010a. *Anatomy of a South African Genocide: The Extermination of the Cape San Peoples*. Athens: Ohio University Press.

———. 2010b. "A Total Extinction Confidently Hoped For: The Destruction of Cape San Society under Dutch Colonial Rule, 1700–1795." *Journal of Genocide Research* 12, nos. 1–2, 19–44.

Agamben, Giorgio. 1998. *Homo Sacer: Sovereign Power and Bare Life*. Stanford, CA: Stanford University Press.

Alfred, Taiaiake, Glen Coulthard, and Deborah Simmons, eds. 2006. "Indigenous Radicalism Today." *New Socialist* 58:2.

Anderson, Kay. 2000. "'The Beast Within': Race, Humanity, and Animality." *Environment and Planning D: Society and Space* 18, no. 3, 301–20.

Appadurai, Arjun, ed. 1986. *The Social Life of Things: Commodities in Cultural Perspective*. Cambridge: Cambridge University Press.

———. 1988. "Putting Hierarchy in Its Place." *Cultural Anthropology* 3, no. 1, 36–49.

Archer, Emma R. M., Noel M. Oettlé, Rhoda Louw, and Mark A. Tadross. 2008. "'Farming on the Edge' in Arid Western South Africa: Climate Change and Agriculture in Marginal Environments." *Geography* 93, no. 2, 98–107.

Arendt, Hannah. 1958. *The Human Condition*. Chicago: University of Chicago Press.

Ashton, Glenn. 2010. "Lessons from Rooibos." South African Civil Society Information Service, June 9. http://sacsis.org.za/site/article/495.1.

Austin, John L. 1962. *How to Do Things with Words*. Cambridge, MA: Harvard University Press.

Badroodien, Azeem, and Steffen Jensen. 2004. "Fragments of a Coloured History:

Migration, Governmentality and Race in Cape Town": Paper presented at Township Now Conference, Wits Institute for Social and Economic Research, Johannesburg, June 9–11.

Barchiesi, Franco. 2011. *Precarious Liberation: Workers, the State, and Contested Social Citizenship in Postapartheid South Africa.* Albany: State University of New York Press.

Barnard, Alan. 1992. *Hunters and Herders of Southern Africa: A Comparative Ethnography of the Khoisan Peoples.* Cambridge: Cambridge University Press.

———. 2003. "Diverse People Unite: Two Lectures on Khoisan Imagery and the State." Occasional paper no. 94, Centre of African Studies, Edinbourgh University.

———. 2007. *Anthropology and the Bushman.* Oxford: Berg.

Bauer, Nickolaus. 2012. "Malema Promises to Fight for Land Reform—At Any Cost." *South African Mail and Guardian*, February 26. http://mg.co.za/article/2012-02-26-malema-slams-zumas-land-reform-approach.

Bauman, Zygmunt. 1990. "Modernity and Ambivalence." In *Global Culture: Nationalism, Globalization and Modernity,* ed. Mike Featherstone, 143–70. London: Sage.

Beck, Ulrich. 2000. "The Cosmopolitan Perspective: Sociology of the Second Age of Modernity." *British Journal of Sociology* 51, no. 1, 79–105.

Beinart, William, and Karen Middleton. 2004. "Plant Transfers in Historical Perspective: A Review Article." *Environment and History* 10:3–29.

Beinart, William, and Luvuyo Wotshella. 2011. *Prickly Pear: The Social History of a Plant in the Eastern Cape.* Johannesburg: Wits University Press.

Benjamin, Walter. 1986. "The Work of Art in the Age of Mechanical Reproduction." In *Illuminations,* ed. Walter Benjamin and Hannah Arendt, 217–52. New York: Schocken.

Bennett, Jane. 2001. *The Enchantment of Modern Life: Attachments, Crossings, and Ethics.* Princeton, NJ: Princeton University Press.

———. 2010. *Vibrant Matter: A Political Ecology of Things.* Durham, NC: Duke University Press.

Bernstein, Henry. 1996. "How White Agriculture (Re)Positioned Itself for a 'New South Africa.'" *Critical Sociology* 22, no. 3, 9–36.

Besky, Sarah. 2014. *The Darjeeling Distinction: Labor and Justice on Fair-Trade Tea Plantations in India.* Berkeley: University of California Press.

Besten, Michael. 2009. "'We Are the Original Inhabitants of This Land': Khoe-San Identity in Post-Apartheid South Africa." In *Burdened by Race: Coloured Identities in Southern Africa,* ed. Mohamed Adhikari, 134–55. Cape Town: UCT Press.

Bilbe, Mark Charles. 2009. *Wupperthal: The Formation of a Community in South Africa, 1830–1965.* Cologne, Germany: Rüdiger Köppe.

Boddy, Janice. 1989. *Wombs and Alien Spirits: Women, Men, and the Zar Cult in Northern Sudan.* Madison: University of Wisconsin Press.

Bolt, Maxim. 2013. "Producing Permanence: Employment, Domesticity and the Flexible Future on a South African Border Farm." *Economy and Society* 42, no. 2, 197–225.

Bosch, Adel, Jannie Rossouw, Tian Claassens, and Bertie du Plessis. 2010. "A Second Look at Measuring Inequality in South Africa: A Modified Gini Coefficient." Working Paper no. 58, School of Development Studies, University of KwaZulu-Natal.

Bravo, Michael T. 2005. "Mission Gardens: Natural History and Global Expansion, 1720–1820." In *Colonial Botany: Science, Commerce, and Politics,* 2nd ed., ed. Londa L. Schiebinger and Claudia Swan, 49–65. Philadelphia: University of Pennsylvania Press.

Breytenbach, Breyten. 1996. *The Memory of Birds in Times of Revolution: Essays on Africa.* New York: Harcourt Brace.

Brosius, Peter. 1999. "On the Practice of Transnational Cultural Critique. *Identities* 6, nos. 2–3, 179–200.

Brown, Bill. 2001. "Thing Theory." *Critical Inquiry* 28, no. 1, 1–22.

Burke, Timothy. 1996. *Lifebuoy Men, Lux Women: Commodification, Consumption, and Cleanliness in Modern Zimbabwe.* Durham, NC: Duke University Press.

Carruthers, Jane. 2006. "Tracking in Game Trails: Looking Afresh at the Politics of Environmental History in South Africa." *Environmental History* 11 no. 4, 804–29.

Cason, Chris. 2004. "Rooibos Tea." http://www.teamuse.com/article_040501.html.

Cerwonka, Allaine. 2004. *Native to the Nation: Disciplining Landscapes and Bodies and Australia.* Minneapolis: University of Minnesota Press.

Chalfin, Brenda. 2004. *Shea Butter Republic: State Power, Global Markets, and the Making of an Indigenous Commodity.* New York: Routledge.

Chari, Sharad. 2008. "The Antinomies of Political Evidence in Post-Apartheid Durban, South Africa." *Journal of the Royal Anthropological Institute* 14, no. s1: S61–76.

Chatterjee, Piya. 2001. *A Time for Tea: Women, Labor, and Post/colonial Politics on an Indian Plantation.* Durham, NC: Duke University Press.

Clark, Nigel. 2002. "The Demon-Seed: Bioinvasion as the Unsettling of Environmental Cosmopolitanism." *Theory, Culture and Society* 19, nos. 1–2, 101–25.

Clifford, James. 1988. *The Predicament of Culture: Twentieth-Century Ethnography, Literature, and Art.* Cambridge, MA: Harvard University Press.

Coetzee, J. M. 1988. *White Writing: On the Culture of Letters in South Africa.* New Haven, CT: Yale University Press.

———. 1997. *Boyhood: Scenes from Provincial Life.* New York: Penguin.

———. 1999 [1980]. *Waiting for the Barbarians.* New York: Penguin.

Collins, Jane. 2014. "A Feminist Approach to Overcoming the Closed Boxes of the Commodity Chain." In *Gendered Commodity Chains,* ed. Wilma Dunaway, 27–37. Stanford, CA: Stanford University Press.

Comaroff, Jean. 1980. "Healing and the Cultural Order: The Case of the Barolong Boo Ratshidi of Southern Africa." *American Ethnologist* 7, no. 4, 637–57.

Comaroff, John L., and Jean Comaroff. 1999. "Alien-Nation: Zombies, Immigrants, and Millennial Capitalism." *CODESRIA Bulletin* 3–4:17–26.

———. 2000. "Millennial Capitalism: First Thoughts on a Second Coming." *Public Culture* 12, no. 2, 291–343.

———. 2001. "Naturing the Nation: Aliens, Apocalypse and the Postcolonial State." *Journal of Southern African Studies* 27, no. 3, 627–51.

———. 2009. *Ethnicity, Inc.* Chicago: University of Chicago Press.

Conservation South Africa. 2011. "Rooibos: GreenChoice Producer Initiative." http://www.conservation.org/global/ci_south_africa/our-initiatives/food-security-land-reform/greenchoice/pages/rooibos.aspx.

Cook, Ian, and Philip Crang. 1996. "The World on a Plate." *Journal of Material Culture* 1:131–53.

Coombe, Rosemary J., and Nicole Aylwin. 2011. "Bordering Diversity and Desire: Using Intellectual Property to Mark Place-Based Products." *Environment and Planning A* 43, no. 9, 2027–42.

Coombe, Rosemary J., Sarah Ives, and Daniel Huizenga. 2015. "The Social Imaginary of Geographical Indicators in Contested Environments: The Politicized Heritage and the Racialized Landscapes of South African Rooibos Tea." In *The Sage Handbook of Intellectual Property*, ed. Matthew David and Debora Halbert, 224–37. London: Sage.

Coulthard, Glen Sean. 2014. *Red Skin, White Masks: Rejecting the Colonial Politics of Recognition*. Minneapolis: University of Minnesota Press.

Crapanzano, Vincent. 1985. *Waiting: The Whites of South Africa*. New York: Random House.

Crutzen, Paul J., and Eugene F. Stoermer. 2000. "The Anthropocene." *Global Change Newsletter* 41:17–18.

Deleuze, Gilles. 1988 [1970]. *Spinoza: Practical Philosophy*. San Francisco: City Lights Books.

Delgado-P, Guillermo, and John Brown Childs, eds. 2012. *Indigeneity: Collected Essays*. Santa Cruz, CA: New Pacific Press.

Department of Agriculture, Forestry, and Fisheries, Republic of South Africa. 2011. *A Profile of the South African Rooibos Tea Market Value Chain*. Arcadia, South Africa: Directorate Marketing. http://www.daff.gov.za/docs/AMCP/RooibosTea MVCP2010–2011.pdf.

———. 2014. *A Profile of the South African Rooibos Tea Market Value Chain*. Arcadia, South Africa: Directorate Marketing. http://www.nda.agric.za.

Department of Environmental Affairs, Republic of South Africa. 2014. *Traditional Knowledge Associated with Rooibos and Honeybush Species in South Africa*. Lynnwood: Siyanda Samahlubi Consulting. https://www.environment.gov.za/sites/default/files /reports/traditionalknowledge_rooibosandhoneybushspecies_report.pdf.

———. 2015a. "Report of the Study Conducted on the Traditional Knowledge Associated with the Rooibos and Honeybush Species in South Africa." Media release, May 19. https://www.environment.gov.za/mediarelease/report_rooibosandhoneybushspecies.

———. 2015b. "Working for Water." https://www.environment.gov.za/projects programmes/wfw.

Department of Labour, Republic of South Africa. 2016. "Sectoral Determination 13: Farm Worker Sector." http://www.labour.gov.za/DOL/legislation/sectoral -determinations/sectoral-determination-13-farm-worker-sector.

Department of Rural Development and Land Reform, Republic of South Africa. 2015. "Minister Gugile Nkwinti on National Dialogue on 1913 Natives Land Act Cut-Off Date." Media statement, November 20. http://www.gov.za/speeches/minister -nkwinti-officially-opens-national-dialogue-exceptions-1913-natives-land-act-cut.

Department of Social Development. 2012. "Substance Use and Abuse in South Africa: A Presentation by the Central Drug Authority to the National Mental Health Summit." April 12.

Derrida, Jacques. 1981. *Dissemination*. Chicago: University of Chicago Press.

Dlamini, Jacob. 2013. "Edward Tsewu and the Struggle for African Property Ownership: Rethinking the Prehistory of the 1913 Natives Land Act." Paper presented at the Land Divided Conference, Cape Town, March 22.

Donnelly, Mary. 2012. "A Treasure Traded as a Commodity." *South African Mail and Guardian*. April 20: http://mg.co.za/article/2012–04–20-a-treasure-traded-as-commodity.

Douglas, Mary. 1970. "Introduction: Thirty Years after *Witchcraft, Oracles and Magic*." In *Witchcraft, Confessions and Accusations*, ed. Mary Douglas, xiii–xxxviii. London: Tavistock.

———. 2002 [1966]. *Purity and Danger*. New York: Routledge.

Drayton, Richard. 2000. *Nature's Government: Science, Imperial Britain, and the "Improvement" of the World*. New Haven, CT: Yale University Press.

Dubow, Saul. 1995. *Scientific Racism in Modern South Africa*. Cambridge: Cambridge University Press.

Dunaway, Wilma D. 2014. "Introduction." In *Gendered Commodity Chains*, ed. Wilma Dunaway, 1–24. Stanford, CA: Stanford University Press.

Durkheim, Émile. 1982. *The Rules of the Sociological Method and Selected Texts on Sociology and Its Method*. New York: Macmillan.

du Toit, Andries. 1993. "The Micro-Politics of Paternalism: The Discourses of Management and Resistance on South African Fruit and Wine Farms." *Journal of Southern African Studies* 19, no. 2, 314–36.

du Toit, Andries, and David Neves. 2014. "The Government of Poverty and the Arts of Survival: Mobile and Recombinant Strategies at the Margins of the South African Economy." *Journal of Peasant Studies* 41, no. 5, 833–53.

Dyer, Richard. 1997. *White*. New York: Routledge.

Employment Conditions Commission. 2013. "Report of the Employment Conditions Commision to the Minister of Labour on the Farm Worker Sector, South Africa." http://www.labour.gov.za/DOL/downloads/legislation/sectoral-determinations/basic-conditions-of-employment/Farm%20worker%20report%202011%20final.doc.

Erasmus, Zimitri, and Edgar Pieterse. 1999. "Conceptualising Coloured Indenties in the Western Cape Province of South Africa." In *National Identity and Democracy in Africa*, ed. Mai Palmberg, 167–87. Cape Town: Human Resources Research Council and Mayibuye Centre.

Evans-Pritchard, E. E. 1969. *The Nuer: A Description of the Modes of Livelihood and Political Institutions of a Nilotic People*. London: Oxford University Press.

Ewert, Joachim, and Andries du Toit. 2004. "A Deepening Divide in the Countryside: Restructuring and Rural Livelihoods in the South African Wine Industry." Unpublished paper presented at the Sociology of Work Unit, University of Witwatersrand, and National Labour and Economic Development Institute, June 24–26.

Fanon, Frantz. 2004 [1965]. *The Wretched of the Earth*. New York: Grove.

Feldman, Ilana, and Mariam Tickin, eds. 2010. *In the Name of Humanity: The Government of Threat and Care*. Durham, NC: Duke University Press.

Ferguson, James. 2007. "Formalities of Poverty: Thinking about Social Assistance in Neoliberal South Africa." *African Studies Review* 50, no. 2, 71–86.

———. 2010. "The Uses of Neoliberalism." *Antipode* 41, no. 1, 166–84.

Fischer, Edward F., and Peter Benson. 2006. *Broccoli and Desire: Global Connections and Maya Struggles in Postwar Guatemala*. Stanford, CA: Stanford University Press.

Forster, Rowan. 2013. "Rooibos: The Name to Defend." *Biz Community*, March 19. http://www.bizcommunity.com/Article/196/547/90954.html.

Foucault, Michel. 2000. "Omnes et singulatim: Towards a Critique of Political Reason." In *Power: Essential Works of Foucault, 1954–1984*, ed. James D. Faubion, 298–325. New York: New Press.

———. 2007. *Security, Territory, Population: Lectures at the Collège de France, 1977–1978*. Basingstoke, UK: Palgrave Macmillan.

———. 2008 [2004]. *The Birth of Biopolitics*. New York: Palgrave Macmillan.

Frankenberg, Ruth. 1993. *White Women, Race Matters: The Social Construction of Whiteness*. Minneapolis: University of Minnesota Press.

Freidberg, Susanne. 2009. *Fresh: A Perishable History*. Cambridge, MA: Harvard University Press.

Fuentes, Agustin. 2006. "The Humanity of Animals and the Animality of Humans: A View from Biological Anthropology Inspired by J. M. Coetzee's *Elizabeth Costello*." *American Anthropologist* 108, no. 1, 124–32.

Gausset, Quentin, Justin Kenrick, and Robert Gibb. 2011. "Indigeneity and Autochthony: A Couple of False Twins?" *Social Anthropology* 19, no. 2, 135–42.

Genis, Amelia. 2011. "Rooibostee-aanleg skep nuwe geleenthede." *Landbouweekblad*, May 27, 84.

Geschiere, Peter. 2009. *The Perils of Belonging: Autochthony, Citizenship, and Exclusion in Africa and Europe*. Chicago: University of Chicago Press.

———. 2011. "Autochthony, Citizenship, and Exclusion—Paradoxes in the Politics of Belonging in Africa and Europe." *Indiana Journal of Global Legal Studies* 18, no. 1, 321–39.

Gluckman, Max. 1963. "Gossip and Scandal." *Current Anthropology* 4:307–16.

Gordon, Robert. 1992. *The Bushman Myth: The Making of a Namibian Underclass*. Boulder, CO: Westview.

Graham, Laura R., and H. Glenn Penny. 2014. "Performing Indigeneity: Emergent Identity, Self-Determination, and Sovereignty." In *Performing Indigeneity: Global Histories and Contemporary Experiences*, ed. Laura R. Graham, 1–31. Lincoln: University of Nebraska Press.

Guenebault, J. H. 1837. *Natural History of the Negro Race*. Charleston, SC: D. J. Dowling.

Guthman, Julie. 2009. "Unveiling the Unveiling: Commodity Chains, Commodity Fetishism, and the 'Value' of Voluntary, Ethical Food Labels." In *Frontiers of Commodity Chain Research*, ed. Jennifer Bair, 190–206. Stanford, CA: Stanford University Press.

Guthrie-Smith, Herbert. 2011 [1921]. *Tutira: The Story of a New Zealand Sheep Station*. Cambridge: Cambridge University Press.

Hansen, Thomas Blom, and Finn Stepputat. 2005. "Introduction." In *Sovereign Bodies: Citizens, Migrants, and States in the Postcolonial World*, ed. Thomas Blom Hansen and Finn Stepputat, 1–36. Princeton, NJ: Princeton University Press.

Haraway, Donna J. 2008. *When Species Meet*. Minneapolis: University of Minnesota Press.

Hart, Gillian. 2002. *Disabling Globalization: Places of Power in Post-Apartheid South Africa*. Berkeley: University of California Press.

———. 2007. "The Provocation of Neoliberalism: Contesting the Nation and Liberation after Apartheid." *Antipode* 40, no. 4, 678–705.

Haviland, John. 1977. *Gossip, Reputation, and Knowledge in Zinacantan*. Chicago: University of Chicago Press.

Hawkins, Heidi J., Rhoda Malgas, and Estelle Biénabe. 2011. "Ecotypes of Wild Rooibos (Aspalathus linearis [Burm. F] Dahlg., Fabaceae) Are Ecologically Distinct." *South African Journal of Botany* 77, no. 2, 360–70.

Heatherington, Tracey. 2012. "From Ecocide to Genetic Rescue: Can Technoscience Save the Wild?" In *The Anthropology of Extinction: Essays on Culture and Species Death*, ed. Genese Marie Sodikoff, 39–66. Bloomington: Indiana University Press.

Hegel, Georg. 1977 [1807]. *The Phenomenology of Spirit*. Oxford: Clarendon.

Helmreich, Stefan. 2009. *Alien Ocean: Anthropological Voyages in Microbial Seas*. Berkeley: University of California Press.

Hickel, Jason. 2014. "'Xenophobia' in South Africa: Order, Chaos, and the Moral Economy of Witchcraft." *Cultural Anthropology* 29, no. 1, 103–27.

Hodder, Ian. 2012. *Entangled: An Archaeology of the Relationships between Humans and Things*. Malden, MA: John Wiley and Sons.

Hodgson, Dorothy. 2002. "Introduction: Comparative Perspectives on the Indigenous Rights Movement in Africa and the Americas." *American Anthropologist* 104, no. 4, 1037–49.

———. 2011. *Being Maasai, Becoming Indigenous: Postcolonial Politics in a Neoliberal World*. Bloomington: Indiana University Press.

Hughes, David McDermott. 2010. *Whiteness in Zimbabwe: Race, Landscape, and the Problem of Belonging*. New York: Palgrave Macmillan.

Hung, Po-Yi. 2014. "Frontiers as Dilemma: The Incompatible Desires for Tea Production in Southwest China." *Area* 46, no. 4, 369–76.

Igoe, Jim. 2006. "Becoming Indigenous Peoples: Difference, Inequality, and the Globalization of East African Identity Politics." *African Affairs* 105, no. 420, 399–420.

Information Service of South Africa. 1972. *Progress through Separate Development: South Africa in Peaceful Transition*. New York: Information Service of South Africa.

International Labour Organization and African Commission on Human and Peoples' Rights. 2009. *Country Report of the Research Project by the International Labour Organization and the African Commission on Human and Peoples' Rights on the Constitutional and Legislative Protection of the Rights of Indigenous Peoples: South Africa*. Geneva: International Labour Organization.

Isichei, Elizabeth. 1995. *A History of Christianity in Africa, from Antiquity to Present*. Lawrenceville, NJ: Africa World Press.

Ives, Sarah. 2007. "Performing National Space: Television in Post-Apartheid South Africa." *ACME* 74, no. 3, 245–55.

———. 2014a. "Farming the South African 'Bush': Ecologies of Belonging and Exclusion in Rooibos Tea." *American Ethnologist* 41, no. 4, 698–713.

———. 2014b. "Uprooting 'Indigeneity' in South Africa's Western Cape: The Plant That Moves." *American Anthropologist* 116, no. 2, 310–23.

Jensen, Steffen. 2008. *Gangs, Politics and Dignity in Cape Town*. Chicago: University of Chicago Press.

Kagwanja, Peter. 2008. "Introduction: Uncertain Democracy—Elite Fragmentation and the Disintegration of the 'Nationalist Consensus' in South Africa." In *State of the Nation: South Africa 2008*, ed. Peter Kagwanja and Kwandiwe Kondlo. Pretoria: HSRC Press.

Keahey, Jennifer. 2013. "Emerging Markets, Sustainable Methods: Political Economy Empowerment in South Africa's Rooibos Tea Sector." Ph.D. diss., Colorado State University, Fort Collins.

Keahey, Jennifer, and Douglas L. Murray. 2017. "The Promise and Perils of Market-based Sustainability." *Sociology of Development* 3, no. 2, 143–62.

King, Sipho. 2015. "Rooibos Farmers: 'Empowerment Isn't Our Cup of Tea.'" *South African Mail and Guardian*, February 6. http://mg.co.za/article/2015–02–05-rooibos-farmers-empowerment-isnt-our-cup-of-tea.

Kirksey, Eben S., and Stefan Helmreich. 2010. "The Emergence of Multispecies Ethnography." *Cultural Anthropology* 25, no. 4, 545–76.

Kohn, Eduardo. 2007. "How Dogs Dream: Amazonian Natures and the Politics of Transspecies Engagement." *American Ethnologist* 34, no. 1, 3–24.

Kosek, Jake. 2010. "Ecologies of Empire: On the New Uses of the Honeybee." *Cultural Anthropology* 25, no. 4, 650–78.

———. 2011. "The Natures of the Beast: On the New Uses of the Honeybee." In *Global Political Ecology*, ed. Richard Peet, Paul Robbins, and Michael Watts, 226–53. London: Routledge.

Kuper, Adam. 2003. "The Return of the Native." *Current Anthropology* 44, no. 3, 389–402.

Lahiff, Edward. 2005. "From 'Willing Seller, Willing Buyer' to a People-Driven Land Reform." *Program for Land and Agrarian Studies Policy Brief* 17:1–4.

Lan, David. 1985. *Guns and Rain: Guerrillas and Spirit Mediums in Zimbabwe*. Berkeley: University of California Press.

Lane, Paul. 1996. "Breaking the Mould? Exhibiting Khoisan in Southern African Museums." *Anthropology Today* 12, no. 5, 3–10.

Langham-Carter, R. R. 1993. *Clanwilliam: The Town, the District, St. John's Church*. Rondebosch, South Africa: Diocesan College Press.

Larsen, Soren, and Jay Johnson. 2012. "Toward an Open Sense of Place: Phenomenology, Affinity, and the Question of Being." *Annals of the Association of American Geographers* 103, no. 2, 632–46.

Latour, Bruno. 2004 [1999]. *Politics of Nature: How to Bring the Sciences into Democracy*. Cambridge, MA: Harvard University Press.

———. 2008. "'It's Development, Stupid!' Or: How to Modernize Modernization." In *Postenvironmentalism*, ed. James Proctor, 1–13. Boston: MIT Press.

Lawuyi, Olatunde. 1998. "Persecution in the Name of Tradition in Contemporary South Africa." *Dialectal Anthropology* 23, no. 1, 83–95.

Le Clerc, Georges Louis. 1749. *Buffon's Natural History: General and Particular*. Charleston SC: BiblioBazaar.

Lee, Richard Borshay. 2006. "Twenty-First Century Indigenism." *Anthropological Theory* 6, no. 4, 455–79.

Legassick, Martin. 1980. "The Frontier Tradition in South African Historiography." In *Economy and Society in Pre-Industrial South Africa*, ed. Shula Marks and Anthony Atmore, 44–79. London: Longman.

Li, Tania Murray. 2000. "Articulating Indigenous Identity in Indonesia: Resource Politics and the Tribal Slot." *Comparative Studies in Society and History* 42, no. 1, 149–79.

Lötter, Daleen. 2015. "Potential Implications of Climate Change for Rooibos (*A. linearis*) Production and Distribution in the Greater Cederberg Region, South Africa." Ph.D. diss., University of Cape Town.

Lötter, Daleen, and David Maitre. 2014. "Modelling the Distribution of *Aspalathus linearis* (Rooibos Tea): Implications of Climate Change for Livelihoods Dependent on Both Cultivation and Harvesting from the Wild." *Ecology and Evolution* 4, no. 8, 1209–21.

Malgas, Rhoda, and Noel Oettle. 2007. *The Sustainable Harvest of Wild Rooibos*. Environmental Monitoring Group Trust.

Malinowski, Bronislaw. 1922. *Argonauts of the Western Pacific: An Account of Native Enterprise and Adventure in the Archipelagos of Melanesian New Guinea*. London: Routledge and Kegan Paul.

Malkki, Liisa. 1992. "National Geographic: The Rooting of Peoples and the Territorialization of National Identity among Scholars and Refugees." *Cultural Anthropology* 7, no. 1, 24–44.

———. 1995. *Purity and Exile: Violence, Memory, and National Cosmology among Hutu Refugees in Tanzania*. Chicago: University of Chicago Press.

Marx, Karl. 1988 [1927]. *The Economic and Philosophical Manuscripts of 1844*. Amherst, MA: Prometheus.

———. 1990 [1887]. *Capital, Volume 1*. London: Penguin.

Massumi, Brian. 2002. *Parables for the Virtual: Movement, Affect, Sensation*. Durham, NC: Duke University Press.

Matless, David. 2001. "Bodies Made of Grass Made of Earth Made of Bodies: Organicism, Diet and National Health in Mid-Twentieth-Century England." *Journal of Historical Geography* 27, no. 3, 355–76.

Mauss, Marcel. 1990. *The Gift: Forms and Functions of Exchange in Archaic Societies*. London: Routledge.

Mbembe, Achille. 2001. *On the Postcolony*. Berkeley: University of California Press.

Mendum, Ruth. 2009. "Subjectivity and Plant Domestication: Decoding the Agency of Vegetable Food Crops." *Subjectivity* 28: 316–33.

Meskell, Lynn. 2004. *Object Worlds in Ancient Egypt: Material Biographies Past and Present*. Oxford: Berg.

———. 2012. *The Nature of Heritage*. Malden, MA: Wiley-Blackwell.

Mezzadra, Sandro, and Brett Neilson. 2012. "Between Inclusion and Exclusion: On the Topology of Global Space and Borders." *Theory, Culture and Society* 29, nos. 4–5, 58–75.

Miller, Daniel. 2008. *The Comfort of Things*. Cambridge: Polity.

Mintz, Sidney. 1974. *Worker in the Cane: A Puerto Rican Life History*. New York: W. W. Norton.

———. 1986. *Sweetness and Power: The Place of Sugar in Modern History*. New York: Penguin.

Mirowski, Philip. 1989. *More Heat Than Light: Economics as Social Physics, Physics as Nature's Economics*. Cambridge: Cambridge University Press.

Mitchell, Laura. 2008. *Belongings: Property, Family, and Identity in Colonial South Africa (An Exploration of Frontiers, 1725–c. 1830)*. New York: Columbia University Press.

Mitchell, Peter, and Gavin Whitelaw. 2005. "The Archaeology of Southernmost Africa c. 2000 BP to the Early 1800s: A Review of Recent Research. *Journal of African History* 46, no. 2, 209–41.

Moodie, T. Dunbar. 1975. *The Rise of Afrikanerdom: Power, Apartheid, and the Afrikaner Civil Religion*. Berkeley: University of California Press.

Moore, Donald S., Anand Pandian, and Jake Kosek. 2003. "Terrains of Power and Practice." In *Race, Nature, and the Politics of Difference*, ed. Donald S. Moore, Anand Pandian, and Jake Kosek, 1–70. Durham, NC: Duke University Press.

Morton, Julia F. 1983. "Rooibos Tea, Aspalathus linearis, a Caffeineless, Low-Tannin Beverage." *Economic Botany* 37, no. 2, 164–73.

Mrozowski, Stephen A. 1999. "Colonization and Commodification of Nature." *International Journal of Historical Archaeology* 3, no. 3, 153–66.

Mukerji, Chandra. 2005. "Dominion, Demonstration, and Domination: Religious Doctrine, Territorial Politics, and French Plant Collection." In *Colonial Botany: Science, Commerce, and Politics in the Early Modern World*, ed. Londa L. Schiebinger and Claudia Swan, 19–33. Philadelphia: University of Pennsylvania Press.

Munakamwe, Janet, and Zaheera Jinnah. 2015. "A Bitter Harvest: Migrant Workers in the Commercial Agricultural Sector in South Africa." Migrating for Work Consortium Policy Brief no. 9 African Centre for Migration and Society, University of the Witwatersrand, Johannesburg.

Nattrass, Nicoli. 1991. "Controversies about Capitalism and Apartheid in South Africa: An Economic Perspective." *Journal of South African Studies* 17, no. 4, 654–77.

Ndongeni, Vuyolwethu. 2012. "Magical Properties of Rooibos." *Herald* (Port Elizabeth, South Africa), May 2, 2012.

Neumann, Roderick P. 1998. *Imposing Wilderness: Struggles over Livelihood and Nature Preservation in Africa*. Berkeley: University of California Press.

Neves, David, and Andries du Toit. 2013. "Rural Livelihoods in South Africa: Complexity, Vulnerability and Differentiation." *Journal of Agrarian Change* 13, no. 1, 93–115.

Ntsebeza, Lungisile. 2005. "Land Tenure Reform in South Africa: A Focus on the Moravian Church Land in the Western Cape." In *Competing Jurisdictions: Settling Land Claims in Africa and Madagascar*, ed. Sandra Evers, Marja Spierenburg, and Harry Wels, 55–77. Leiden: Brill Academic.

Nyamnjoh, Francis J. 2006. *Insiders and Outsiders: Citizenship and Xenophobia in Contemporary Southern Africa*. London: Zed.

Oettle, Noel. 2012. *Adaptation with a Human Face: Lessons Learned from an Ongoing*

Adaptation and Learning Process. Suid Bokkeveld, South Africa: Environmental Monitoring Group.

Offe, Claude. 1997. "Towards a New Equilibrium of Citizens' Rights and Economic Resources?" In *Social Cohesion and the Globalising Economy: What Does the Future Hold?*, 81–108. Paris: OECD.

Olsen, Jonathan. 1999. *Nature and Nationalism: Right-Wing Ecology and the Politics of Identity in Contemporary Germany.* New York: St. Martin's Press.

Ortner, Sherry. 1974. "Is Female to Male as Nature Is to Culture?" In *Woman, Culture, and Society*, ed. Michelle Zimbalist Rosaldo and Louis Lamphere, 68–87. Stanford, CA: Stanford University Press.

Paine, Robert. 1967. "What Is Gossip About? An Alternative Hypothesis." *Man* 2, no. 2, 278–85.

Palitza, Kristin. 2011. "Climate Change: Making a Hot Cup of Rooibos Tea Unaffordable." Inter Press Services. http://www.ipsnews.net/news/regional-categories/africa.

Pandian, Anand. 2008. "Pastoral Power in the Postcolony: On the Biopolitics of the Criminal Animal in South India." *Cultural Anthropology* 23, no. 1, 85–117.

Parkington, John. 2003. "Eland and Therianthropes in Southern African Rock Art: When Is a Person an Animal?" *African Archaeological Review* 20, no. 3, 135–47.

Paxson, Heather. 2010. "Locating Value in Artisan Cheese: Reverse Engineering *Terroir* for New World Landscapes." *American Anthropologist* 112, no. 3, 444–57.

Peet, Richard. 2002. "Ideology, Discourse, and the Geography of Hegemony: From Socialist to Neoliberal Development in Postapartheid South Africa." *Antipode* 34, no. 1, 54–84.

Peet, Richard, Paul Robbins, and Michael Watts. 2011. "Global Nature." In *Global Political Ecology*, ed. Richard Peet, Paul Robbins and Michael Watts, 1–48. London: Routledge.

Penn, Nigel. 2005. *The Forgotten Frontier: Colonist and Khoisan on the Cape's Northern Frontier in the 18th Century.* Cape Town: Double Storey.

Pierotti, Raymond, and Daniel Wildcat. 2000. "Traditional Ecological Knowledge: The Third Alternative." *Ecological Applications* 10, no. 5, 1333–40.

Pooley, Simon. 2010. "Pressed Flowers: Notions of Indigenous Alien Vegetation in South Africa's Western Cape, c. 1902–1945." *Journal of Southern African Studies* 36, no. 3, 599–619.

———. 2012. "Recovering the Lost History of Fire in South Africa's Fynbos." *Environmental History* 17, no. 1, 55–83.

Pretorius, Gerhard. N.d. "Rooibos Biodiversity Initiative (RBI): Biodiversity Best Practice Guidelines for the Sustainable Production of Rooibos." http://www.cepf.net /Documents/rooibosguidelines.pdf.

Pretorius, Gerhard, Victor Harley, and Lisa Ryser. 2011. *Handbook for Implementing Rooibos Sustainability Standards.* South African Rooibos Council. http://www .conservation.org/global/ci_south_africa/publications/Documents/handbook -implementing-rooibos-sustainability-standards.pdf.

Raimondo, D., L. Von Staden, W. Foden, J. E. Victor, N. A. Helme, R. C. Turner, D. A. Kamundi, and P. A. Manyama, eds. 2009. *Red List of South African Plants.* Strelitzia 25. Pretoria: South African National Biodiversity Institute.

Ritvo, Harriet. 1987. *The Animal Estate: The English and Other Creatures in the Victorian Age*. Cambridge, MA: Harvard University Press.

Robbins, Paul. 2004. "Comparing Invasive Networks: Cultural and Political Biographies of Invasive Species." *Geographical Review* 94, no. 2,139–56.

Robins, Steven L. 2008. *From Revolution to Rights in South Africa: Social Movements, NGOs and Popular Politics after Apartheid*. Pietermaritzburg: University of KwaZulu-Natal Press.

Rodman, Margaret. 1992. "Empowering Place: Multilocality and Multivocality. American Anthropologist" 94, no. 3, 640–56.

Rosnow, Ralph L., and Gary A. Fine. 1976. *Rumor and Gossip: The Social Psychology of Hearsay*. New York: Elsevier.

Rose, Deborah, Thom van Dooren, Matthew Chrulew, Stuart Cooke, Matthew Kearnes and Emily O'Gorman. 2012. "Thinking through the Environment, Unsettling the Humanities." *Environmental Humanities* 1, no. 1, 1–5.

Rose, Nikolas. 1999. *Powers of Freedom: Reframing Political Thought*. Cambridge: Cambridge University Press.

Ross, Fiona. 2010. *Raw Life, New Hope: Decency, Housing and Everyday Life in a Post-Apartheid Community*. Cape Town: UCT Press.

Rudnyckyj, Daromir. 2010. *Spiritual Economies: Islam, Globalization, and the Afterlife of Development*. Ithaca, NY: Cornell University Press.

Ruiters, Michelle. 2009. "Collaboration, Assimilation and Contestation: Emerging Constructions of Coloured Identity in Post-Apartheid South Africa." In *Burdened by Race: Coloured Identities in Southern Africa*, ed. Mohamed Adhikari, 104–33. Cape Town: UCT Press.

Rutherford, Blair, and Lincoln Addison. 2007. "Zimbabwean Farm Workers in Northern South Africa." *Review of African Political Economy* 34, no. 114, 619–35.

Sahlins, Marshall. 2011. "What Kinship Is (Part One)." *Journal of the Royal Anthropological Institute* 17, no. 1, 2–19.

Salo, Elaine. 2003. "Negotiating Gender and Personhood in the New South Africa: Adolescent Women and Gangsters in Manenberg Township on the Cape Flats." *European Journal of Cultural Studies* 6, no. 3, 345–65.

Sandra Kruger and Associates. 2009. *Rooibos Socio-Economic Study*, public version. Pniel, SA: Ministry of Agriculture, Nature, and Food Quality.

Scheiner, Samuel. 1993. "Genetics and Evolution of Phenotypic Plasticity." *Annual Review of Ecology and Systematics* 24:35–68.

Schiebinger, Londa L., and Claudia Swan. 2005. "Introduction." In *Colonial Botany: Science, Commerce, and Politics in the Early Modern World*, ed. Londa L. Schiebinger and Claudia Swan, 1–18. Philadelphia: University of Pennsylvania Press.

Sen, Debarati. 2014. "Fair Trade versus Swaccha Vyāpār: Women's Activism and Transnational Justice Regimes in Darjeeling, India." *Feminist Studies* 40, no. 2, 444–72.

Shepherd, Nick. 2002. "Disciplining Archaeology: The Invention of South African Prehistory, 1923–1953." *Kronos* 28:127–45.

Shivambu, Floyd, and Zolani Mkiva. 2011. "ANC Youth League and CONTRALESA Joint Media Statement after a Bi-lateral Meeting." Press release, October 20.

Simpson, Audra, and Andrea Smith. 2014. "Introduction." In *Theorizing Native Studies*, ed. Audra Simpson and Andrea Smith, 1–30. Durham, NC: Duke University Press.

Skade, Thandi. 2012. "Rooibos: It's More Than Just a Tea." *The Star*, January 29. http://www.iol.co.za/scitech/science/news/rooibos-it-s-more-than-just-a-tea-1.1222491#.UYovosp49vo.

Soodyall, Himla. 2008. "Final Report: Living History Project." National Health Laboratory Service and School of Pathology, University of the Witwatersrand, Johannesburg.

Spivak, Gayatri. 2003. *Death of a Discipline*. New York: Columbia University Press.

Stewart, Pamela J., and Andrew Strathern. 2004. *Witchcraft, Sorcery, Rumors and Gossip*. Cambridge: Cambridge University Press.

Stoler, Ann Laura. 2009. *Along the Archival Grain: Epistemic Anxieties and Colonial Common Sense*. Princeton, NJ: Princeton University Press.

Strathern, Marilyn. 1988. *The Gender of the Gift*. Berkeley: University of California Press.

Strauss, Helene. 2009. "'. . . [C]onfused about Being Coloured': Creolization and Coloured Identity in Chris Van Wyk's *Shirley, Goodness and Mercy*." In *Burdened by Race: Coloured Identities in Southern Africa*, ed. Mohamed Adhikari, 23–48. Cape Town: UCT Press.

Subramaniam, Banu. 2001. "The Aliens Have Landed! Reflections on the Rhetoric of Biological Invasions." *Meridians: Feminism, Race, Transnationalism* 2, no. 1, 26–40.

Surplus People Project and Legal Resources Centre. 2000. "An Inventory and Description of the Historical Acquistion of Moravian Church Land." Report compiled for the Moravian Church of South Africa, November. http://www.spp.org.za/reports/moravian.pdf (page discontinued).

Sylvain, Renee. 2002. "'Land, Water, and Truth': San Identity and Global Indigenism." *American Anthropologist* 104, no. 4, 1074–85.

Tambiah, Stanley. 1985. *Culture, Thought, and Social Action: An Anthropological Perspective*. Cambridge, MA: Harvard University Press.

Taussig, Michael. 1980. *The Devil and the Commodity Fetishism in South America*. Chapel Hill: University of North Carolina Press.

Trigger, David S., and Cameo Dalley. 2010. "Negotiating Indigeneity: Culture, Identity, and Politics." *Reviews in Anthropology* 39:46–65.

Trotter, Henry. 2009. "Trauma and Memory: The Impact of Apartheid-Era Forced Removals on Coloured Identity and Cape Town." In *Burdened by Race: Coloured Identities Southern Africa*, ed. Mohamed Adhikari, 49–78. Cape Town: UCT Press.

Tsing, Anna Lowenhaupt. 1995. "Empowering Nature, or: Some Gleanings in Bee Culture." In *Naturalizing Power: Essays in Feminist Cultural Analysis*, ed. Sylvia Yanagisako and Carol Delany, 113–43. New York: Routledge.

———. 2003. "Cultivating the Wild: Honey-Hunting and Forest Management in Southeast Kalimantan." In *Culture and the Question of Rights: Forests, Coasts, and Seas in Southeast Asia*, ed. Charles Zerner, 24–55. Durham, NC: Duke University Press.

———. 2012. "Unruly Edges: Mushrooms as Companion Species." *Environmental Humanities* 1:141–54.

———. 2013. "Sorting Out Commodities: How Capitalist Value Is Made through Gifts." *HAU: Journal of Ethnographic Theory* 3, no. 1, 21–43.

————. 2015. *The Mushroom at the End of the World: On the Possibility of Life in Capitalist Ruins*. Princeton, NJ: Princeton University Press.

Turner, Victor. 1995 [1957]. *Schism and Continuity in African Society*. Oxford: Berg.

Van Den Berg, Johan. 2012. "South Africa: Farmers Must Proactively Manage Crops to Protect Rooibos Industry." AllAfrica, April 23. http://allafrica.com/stories/201204240989.html.

Visser, Margareet, and Stuart Ferrer. 2015. *Farm Workers' Living and Working Conditions in South Africa: Key Trends, Emergent Issues, and Underlying and Structural Problems*. Pretoria: International Labour Organization.

Wacquant, Loïc. 2012. "Three Steps to a Historical Anthropology of Actually Existing Neoliberalism." *Social Anthropology* 20, no. 1, 66–79.

Walker, Cherryl. 2012. "The Distribution of Land in South Africa: An Overview." Institute for Poverty, Land, and Agrarian Studies, University of Western Cape. http://www.plaas.org.za.

Wallerstein, Immanuel. 1974. *The Modern World-System, Volume 1: Capitalist Agriculture and the Origins of the European World-Economy in the Sixteenth Century*. New York: Academic Press.

Watt, John Mitchell, and Maria Gerdina Breyer-Brandwijk. 1932. *The Medicinal and Poisonous Plants of Southern Africa*. Edinburgh: E. and S. Livingstone.

Weber, Max. 1947 [1922]. *The Theory of Social and Economic Organization*, trans. A. M. Henderson and Talcott Parsons. New York: Free Press.

————. 2003 [1905]. *The Protestant Ethic and the Spirit of Capitalism*. New York: Courier Dover.

Wert, Sarah, and Peter Salovey. 2004. "Introduction to the Special Issue on Gossip." *Review of General Psychology* 8, no. 2, 76–77.

West, Paige. 2012. *From Modern Production to Imagined Primitive: The Social World of Coffee from Papua New Guinea*. Durham, NC: Duke University Press.

Western, John. 1996. *Outcast Cape Town*. Berkeley: University of California Press.

————. 2001. "Africa Is Coming to the Cape." *Geographical Review* 91, no. 4, 617–40.

White, Luise. 2000. *Speaking with Vampires: Rumor and History in Colonial Africa*. Berkeley: University of California Press.

Why Go South Africa. 2012. "Southafricanisms: Rooibos Tea." http://www.southafricalogue.com/travel-tips/southafricanisms-rooibos-tea.html.

Wilcox, Michael. 2010. "Marketing Conquest and the Vaninshing Indian: An Indigenous Response to Jared Diamond's *Guns, Germs, and Steel* and *Collapse*." *Journal of Social Archaeology* 10, no. 1, 92–117.

Williams, Raymond. 1961. *The Long Revolution*. London: Chatto and Windus.

————. 1977. *Marxism and Literature*. Oxford: Oxford University Press.

————. 1979. *Politics and Letters: Interviews with the New Left Review*. London: New Left.

Wilmsen, Edwin. 1989. *Land Filled with Flies: A Political Economy of the Kalahari*. Chicago: University of Chicago Press.

Wilson, Michael Lewis. 1986. "Khoisanosis: The Question of Separate Identities for Khoi and San." In *Variation, Culture, and Evolution in African Populations*, ed. Ronald Singer and John K. Lundy, 13–25. Johannesburg: University of Witwatersrand Press.

Wolf, Eric R. 1982. *Europe and the People without History.* Berkeley: University of California Press.

Wolpe, Harold. 1972. "Capitalism and Cheap Labour-Power in South Africa: From Segregation to Apartheid." *Economy and Society* 1, no. 4, 425–56.

Worby, Eric, Shireen Hassim, and Tawana Kupe. 2008. "Introduction." In *Go Home or Die Here: Violence, Xenophobia and the Reinvention of Difference in South Africa*, ed. Shireen Hassim, Tawana Kupe, and Eric Worby, 1–15. Johannesburg: Wits University Press.

Yanagisako, Sylvia, and Carol Delany. 1995. "Naturalizing Power." In *Naturalizing Power: Essays in Feminist Cultural Analysis*, ed. Sylvia Yanagisako and Carol Delaney, 1–21. New York: Routledge.

Ziervogel, G., M. New, E. Archer van Garderen, G. Midgley, A. Taylor, R. Hamann, S. Stuart-Hill, J. Myers, and M. Warburton. 2014. "Climate Change Impacts and Adaptation in South Africa." *WIREs Climate Change*, no. 5, 605–20.

Index

affect: nature and, 80–81; terroir and, 196

"Africa Is Coming to the Western Cape" (Western), 111

Africanization narrative, migrant labor and, 111–12

African National Congress (ANC): migrant politics and, 128–30; postapartheid politics and, 151, 162, 174–76, 179–82, 226n5; South African identity and, 104–6; workers' rights and, 182–86; Youth League of, 55, 62, 166

Afrika, Alida, 165

Afrikaans Protestant Church (AP Kerk), 153–54

Afrikaner culture: "alien" concepts in, 97–101; anthropological view of, 208–9; botany and naturalized belonging in, 75–76; capitalism and, 224n3; climate change and rooibos migration and, 199–200; coloured community and, 34–37, 42–45, 90–93, 102–6; ecological exceptionalism and, 66–68; embodied adaptation in, 203–4; English-Afrikaans tensions and, 169–71; ethnographic ethics in research on, 26–28; history of rooibos in, 142–43, 149–54; indigeneity in, 54–57, 61–64, 94–95; isolationism of, 101–6; labor relations in, 174–76; land ownership in, 53–55, 94–95, 146–47, 222n14;

migrant labor and, 98–101, 110–12, 123–28, 131; mixed race heritage in, 222n16; national identity and, 103–6; pathological belonging and, 38–40; politics and, 128–30; postapartheid land ownership transition and, 179–82; racialized characterizations of, 74–75; religious aspects of rooibos in, 83–89; rooibos cultivation and, 4–8; rooibos in, 54–57, 79–83, 142–43; white-white identity politics and, 57–61

Agamben, Giorgio, 117

alcoholism, racial attitudes concerning, 116–20, 127–28

Alexander, Benny. *See* Khoisan X

aliens and alienation: Afrikaner concept of, 97–101; citrus cultivation and, 121–23; indigeneity and, 132–33; land tenure and, 130–31; plant imperialism and, 106–10; precarity in rooibos industry and, 175–76

All Pay system, 116–20, 225n5

alterity, of non-Afrikaners, 102–6

Alywin, Nicole, 193–95

Anderson, Kay, 75–76

Anglican Church, 84

Anglo-Boer War, 57–61

Anthropocene epoch, climate change and, 205–6

anthropocentrism, human/nonhuman binary and, 223n1
anxiety: embodied adaptation and, 203–4; in postapartheid era, 178–79, 207–9
apartheid era: archaeology and history during, 57; churches during, 159; coloured identity and, 34–37; coloured land ownership during, 186–88; ethnic homeland creation during, 96–101; indigeneity and, 30–32; migrant labor and legacy of, 113–15; racial classifications during, 35–37; rooibos industry during, 147–49
Appadurai, Arjun, 2, 4, 30–32
Ashton, Glenn, 168–69
aspalathin compound, 12, 69–72
autochthonous belonging: for Afrikaners, 94–95; migrant labor and, 111–12; plant imperialism and, 109–10

Bantustan system, 96–101
Barchiesi, Franco, 15, 183
Barnard, Alan, 47, 72
Bauman, Zygmunt, 118, 121
Beck, Ulrich, 110
Beinart, William, 107–10
Benjamin, Walter, 190
Bennett, Jean, 81
Bensen, Peter, 194–95
Besky, Sarah, 22–23
biodiversity, rooibos cultivation and, 122–23
biopolitics, 67
Black Economic Empowerment program, 166–69, 214
Boddy, Janice, 28, 139
botany, race and, 74–76, 94–95
Bravo, Michael T., 222n4
Breytenbach, Breyten, 94–95
British South Africans: Afrikaner views of, 57–61, 102–6; Caledon Code and, 145–46; embodied adaptation and,

203–4; English-Afrikaans tensions and, 169–71; farming by, 88
Browne, Thomas (Sir), 68
Buffon's Natural History: General and Particular (Le Clerc), 74
Bush ecology, rooibos and, 66–68
Bushman culture: colonization and erasure of, 40–44, 54–57; ecological exceptionalism and, 66–68; language concerning, 217n3; nonhuman racial classification of, 74–75; white naturalized belonging and erasure of, 75–76. *See also* Khoisan identity
Bushman Relics Act of 1911, 74

Caledon Code, 145–46
Cape Floristic Kingdom, 63–64; ecosystem of, 12
Capital, Volume One (Marx), 22
capitalism: Afrikaner view of, 149–54, 155–57; agriculture and, 148–49, 220n18; ecosystems and, 224n3; politics and, 161–64; rooibos cultivation and, 7–8, 21–23
Carruthers, Jane, 65
cartography of rooibos cultivation, 23–26
Cason, Chris, 1
Cederberg Fees, 223n20
Cederberg region: climate change and rooibos migration from, 199–200; demographics of, 34–37; fire in, 210–11; history of rooibos and, 144–46; politics in, 162–64; rooibos cultivation in, 1–2, 14–17
Cerwonka, Allaine, 45, 61, 130
charismatic belonging, indigeneity and, 63–64
Chatterjee, Piya, 13
Childs, John Brown, 19–20
Christianity: in Afrikaner culture, 55, 222n14; rooibos cultivation and, 83–89
citrus cultivation, 121–23
Citrusdal, 121–23
civil religion, Afrikaner's concept of, 55

Clanwilliam: coloured community in, 49–53; land tenure reform in, 41–44; rooibos cultivation in, 1–2, 23–26; tourism in, 60–61; Wildflower Festival in, 173

Clanwilliam cedar tree, 107–10

Clark, Nigel, 108–9, 133

class politics: elections and, 162–64; romantic nationalism narrative and, 170–71; rooibos consumption and, 147–49

Clifford, James, 16

Climate and Development Knowledge Network, 205

climate change: culture and, 12; rooibos cultivation and, 16–17, 200–203, 227n6; southward migration of rooibos and, 197–200

Coetzee, J. M., 53, 77, 87, 110, 178–79

Collins, Jane, 22–23

colonization: capitalism and, 224n3; classification of indigeneity and, 224n3; coloured identity and, 33–37; history of rooibos and, 13–17, 141–43; invasive species and, 96–101; migrant labor and, 125–28; national identity in resistance to, 98–101; social history of, 10–12; white farming and, 225n6

coloured community: Afrikaner view of, 34–37, 42–45, 90–93, 102–6; class politics and, 169–71; climate change and rooibos migration and, 199–200; diversity within, 221n5; ecological exceptionalism and, 66–68; embodied adaptation in, 203–4; erasure in rooibos cultivation of, 89–93; farming terminology in, 218n5; fluidity in rooibos region, 35–37; government subsidies and, 164–69; indigeneity and, 18–21, 30–32, 44–48, 61–64; labor relations in, 174–76; land ownership and, 186–88, 214–16; limits of research on, 219n12; migrant labor as threat to, 98–101, 110–15, 117–20; mis-

sionaries and, 159–61; organic farming by, 224n3; pathological belonging of, 37–40, 94–95; placelessness and forced nomadism and, 40–44; politics in, 34–37, 128–30, 149–54; postapartheid rooibos regulation and, 149–54; poverty and, 32–33; rooibos cultivation and, 3–5, 40–44, 90–93; spirituality in, 85–89; terminology of, 221n1; workers' rights and, 183–86

Comaroff, Jean, 102–3, 106, 132–33, 140, 215

Comaroff, John, 102–3, 106, 132–33, 215

commodities and commodification: climate change and, 200–203; culture and, 8–9; gender issues in research on, 220n16; history of rooibos and, 141–43; indigeneity and, 30–32; localization strategies and, 188–91; of nature, 224n3; precarity in rooibos industry and, 175–76; rooibos cultivation history and, 136–38, 220n17; workers' rights and, 183–86

"commodity ecumene," Appadurai's concept of, 2, 4

Congress of Traditional Leaders of South Africa (CONTRALESA), 62

Conservation International, 122–23

consumption of rooibos: class politics and, 147–49; as domestication of exotic, 13–17; double-fetish concept and, 229n18; gender dynamics of, 68–72; indigeneity and, 3–4

Cook, Ian, 220n18

Coombe, Rosemary J., 193–95

cooperative tea plantations, 5–6

cosmology: history of rooibos and, 9–12, 141–43; politics in rooibos industry and, 134–38; rooibos history and, 25, 138–41

Crang, Philip, 220n18

Crapanzano, Vincent, 178–79

criminality, migrant labor linked to, 98–101, 112–15, 125–26, 128–30

onization and, 11–12; farm size and, 127–28; geographical indications and, 193–96; human intervention in, 70–72; invasive species and, 24–25, 96–101; pathological belonging and, 77–83; plant imperialism and, 107–10; race and, 7–8; rooibos cultivation and, 3–6, 24–25, 77–83

embodied adaptation, 203–4

emotions, nature and, 80–81

"endemic," in indigeneity discourse, 218n7

Enlightenment philosophy, social and natural world in, 101, 205–6, 227n8

entanglement, precarity in rooibos industry and, 175–76

ethics, of rooibos cultivation, 80–83

"ethnic entrepreneurship," 44

ethnic homeland policies, apartheid-era creation of, 96–101

ethnicity: history of rooibos and, 142–43; indigeneity and, 220n14

ethnography: ethics of, 26–28; limits of research on coloured community, 219n12

Evangelical churches, 84

exotic: black migrants as examples of, 97–101; rooibos consumption as domestication of, 13–17

fair trade certification, 214

Fanon, Frantz, 74

farming: Afrikaner identification with, 57–61, 94–95, 146–47, 218n5, 222n14; climate change impact on, 200–203; globalization and, 169–71, 213–16; government subsidies for, 147–49, 164–69; labor unrest and, 173–76; localization strategies in, 189–91; politics of terminology concerning, 137–38, 217n5; postapartheid land ownership transition and, 179–82; workers' rights and, 182–86

Ferguson, James, 136, 165

Ferrer, Stuart, 155, 224n4

fertility, stereotypes of blacks and, 117–20

first-arrival narratives: in Afrikaner culture, 55–57, 61; xenophobia and, 105–6

Fischer, Edward, 194–95

flavonoids in rooibos, 69–72

forced nomadism, coloured identity and, 41–44

Foucault, Michel, 67, 90–91

France, trademark of rooibos attempted by, 210–16

Freedom Charter (1955), 39–40

Freedom Front Plus Party, 56–57

Frozen Ark, 86

fynbos biome: citrus cultivation and disruption of, 121–23; climate change and, 198–200; plant imperialism and, 107–10; rooibos cultivation and, 11–12, 21–23, 65–68, 79–83, 132–33; white naturalized belonging and, 75–76

Genadendal Accord, 225n4

gender: in commodity analyses, 220n16; gossip and rumor and, 139; migrant labor and, 112–15; rooibos consumption and, 68–72

genealogy, in Afrikaner culture, 55

Genesis, book of, 86–87

geographical indications (GIs): governance of plants and people and, 193–96; precarity in rooibos industry and, 176

Geschiere, Peter, 125

Gibaudan flavor company, 14

Gilomee, Hermann, 54

GINI Index, 14–15, 219n9

Ginsberg, Benjamin, 11–12, 14, 142

globalization: government subsidies and, 165–69; indigeneity and, 30–32; rooibos cultivation and, 3–9, 13–17, 136–38, 169–71, 207–9; xenophobia and, 130–31

Gluckman, Max, 138

government subsidies, of rooibos production, 147–49, 164–69

labor brokers: migrant labor and, 113–15; missionaries as, 159

labor relations: mining strikes and unrest, 173–76; permanent vs. migrant rooibos workers, 22–23, 116–20; racialized hierarchy in rooibos production and, 126–28; rooibos cultivation and, 22–23, 116–20; workers' rights and, 182–86

Labor Relations Act, 114

Lahiff, Edward, 56

Lan, David, 111–12

land ownership: Afrikaner's concepts of, 53–55, 94–95, 146–47, 222n14; alienation and, 130–31; barriers for coloured locals to, 40–44; birthright to land claims and, 39–40; colonization and, 11–12; coloured community and, 186–88, 227n5; ethnic homeland policy and, 96–101; geographical indications and, 193–96; history of rooibos and, 145–46; indigeneity and, 20–21, 48, 130–31, 187–88; missionary societies and, 225n4; postapartheid policies and, 36–37, 179–82; restitution vs. redistribution and, 226n4; rooibos cultivation and, 5–7, 25–26; "willing buyer, willing seller" model of, 55–56; workers linked to, 116–20; xenophobia and, 104–6

Land Tenure Security Act, 41–44

language: labor issues and, 182–86; South African politics and banality of, 217n3

Lantern Festival, 47–48

Larsen, Soren, 216

Latour, Bruno, 70, 85

Lawuyi, Olatunde, 62

Le Clerc, Georges Louis, 74

Legal Resource Centre, 222n12, 225n4

Lévi-Strauss, Claude, 143

Li, Tania Murray, 17–18, 47, 220n13

Linnaeus, Carl, 74

Living Landscape Project, 34–37, 47–48

localization strategy, precarity in rooibos industry and, 176, 188–91

Lonmin mine, violence at, 173–76

Maasai, indigenous identity of, 18

Mail and Guardian newspaper, 164–66

Malema, Julius, 55–56, 166–67, 179–82

Malgas, Rhoda, 205–6

Malkki, Liisa, 95, 101, 130–31, 140, 143, 167

Mandela, Nelson, 25, 222n16

mapping technology, rooibos production and, 194–96

Marketing Act (1937), 148

marketing of rooibos: climate change and, 200–203; cultural marketing strategies and, 174–76, 191–93; health claims and, 225n4; localization strategies, 189–91; national unity imagery and, 76, 103–6

Marx, Karl, 22–23, 175–76, 183–86

masculinity, stereotypes of blacks and, 117–20

Massumi, Brian, 81

materiality, human/nonhuman binary, 223n1

Mauss, Marcel, 9

Mbeki, Thabo, 224n1

media coverage of rooibos, 13–17

Mendum, Ruth, 68, 71

Meskell, Lynn, 20, 27, 173, 193

Middleton, Karen, 107–10

migrant labor: "alien" framing of, 97–101, 224n4; coloured community and, 98–101, 110–15, 117–20, 132–33; cultural difference and, 123–28; ecosystems and, 24–25; farmers' attitudes concerning, 116–20; informal settlements of, 112–15, 117–20; as invasive threat, 98–101, 110–12; politics and, 128–30; stereotypes of black strength and, 117–20, 123–28; strikes and unrest and, 174–76

Mintz, Sidney, 8–9

Mirowski, Philip, 100
missionaries: Afrikaner culture and, 222n14; Khoisan and, 158–61; racial divisions and, 225n4
mixed race community, terminology of, 221n1
morality, rooibos cultivation and, 80–83
Moravian Church, 84, 159, 224n3, 225n4
Mrozowski, Stephen, 224n3
Mulder, Pieter, 56
"mutuality of being," 189
mythico-histories, cosmologies and, 140

narratives: of coloured identity, 34–37; marketing of rooibos and, 191–93; of postapartheid rooibos industry, 151–54; resistance and, 155–57; romantic nationalism narrative, 170–71; rooibos history and, 25, 134–38, 212–16
National Party, 129, 151
nation-states, invasive species concept and, 99–101
Natives Land Act (1913), 36–37, 221n10
neoliberalism: government subsidies and, 164–69; labor unrest and, 174–76; land ownership and, 187–88; rooibos cultivation and, 3–9, 13–17, 136–38; spirituality and, 160–61
network theory, agricultural production and, 220n18
Neves, David, 95
Nkwinti, Gugile, 221n10
Noble Savage concept, white naturalized belonging and, 75–76
nongovernmental organizations (NGOs), identity politics and, 34–37, 47–48
Ntsebeza, Lungisile, 225n4
Nyamnjoh, Francis, 113, 132–33

Offe, Claus, 15
organic farming, 224n3

Pan-Africanist Party of Azania (PAC), 44, 162

Pandian, Anand, 72, 90–91
"passing" in apartheid era, 35–37
pathological belonging: in Afrikaner culture, 102–6; charismatic belonging and, 63–64; coloured identity and, 90–93; erasure of Bushmen culture and, 72–75; indigeneity and, 37–40; migrant labor and, 98–101, 110–12, 125–28; politics in rooibos industry and, 134–38; precarity in rooibos industry and, 173–76; workers' rights and, 183–86; xenophobia and, 130–31
Paxon, Heather, 196
Penn, Nigel, 144–46
Penny, Glenn, 223n18
plant imperialism: geographical indications and, 193–96; rooibos cultivation and, 106–10
politics: capitalism and, 161–64; migrant labor and, 128–30; in rooibos industry, 134–72; workers' rights and, 182–86
Pooley, Simon, 109, 121–22
Port Jackson trees, invasiveness of, 121–23, 131–33
positioning, identity and, 220n13
postapartheid era: capitalism in, 161–64; economic stagnation during, 178–79; globalization and, 169–71; government subsidies and, 164–69; land ownership transition and, 96–101, 179–82; migrant labor and, 126–28; nation-states and, 99; racial attitudes and, 36–37, 116–20; rooibos historical narrative and, 149–54, 172; South African discourse on, 15–17; strikes and labor unrest in, 173–76
postcolonialism: commodity scholarship and, 220n18; invasive characterizations in, 98–101; rooibos as representation of, 13–17
poverty, coloured identity and, 32–37
precarity: localization strategies and, 176, 188–91; rooibos industry and, 175–76; in South Africa, 15–17

United Nations Special Rapporteur, 56
United Nations Working Group on Indigenous Populations, 56

value-add policy: farmers' embrace of, 152–54; localization strategies and, 189–91
Van Riebeeck, Jan, 33, 56
veldskoene trade, 159
violent crime, in South Africa, 14–15
Visser, Margareet, 155, 224n4

wage structure in rooibos production, 127–28, 163–64, 173–76
Waiting: The Whites of South Africa (Crapanzano), 178–79
Waiting for the Barbarians (Coetzee), 178–79
Wallerstein, Immanuel, 220n18
Weber, Max, 63–64, 224n3
Wert, Sarah, 138
West, Paige, 21, 22–23, 191–92
Western, John, 44, 111
White, Luise, 138–39
white nationalism, postapartheid politics and, 37
whiteness, indigeneity and, 18–21
White Paper on South African Land Policy, 55–56
white-white identity politics, 57–61; autochthony and, 109–10; botany and naturalized belonging and, 75–76;

plant imperialism and, 109; workers' rights and, 183–86
White Writing (Coetzee), 87
Wiedouw Tea, 31–32
Wilcocks Commission of 1937, 35–37
Wilcox, Michael, 55
Williams, Raymond, 178–79
"willing buyer, willing seller" land market model, 55, 186–88
Wolf, Eric, 185–86
Working for Water program, 107–10
World Bank, 187
World Heritage Site, fynbos ecosystem as, 133
Wretched of the Earth (Fanon), 74
Wupperthal Moravian Church, 40–44, 159, 222n14, 225n2

xenophobia: foreignness ideology and, 102–6; globalization and, 130–31; migrant labor and, 98–101, 112–15, 117–20; in postapartheid South Africa, 99–101, 224n1; racial politics and, 128–30

Yanagisako, Sylvia, 17, 32, 34

Zimbabwe: migrant labor from, 112–15; unrest in, 99–101
zoology, racial violence in context of, 74–75
Zuma, Jacob, 56, 104, 226n5

www.ingramcontent.com/pod-product-compliance
Lightning Source LLC
Chambersburg PA
CBHW050344270326
41926CB00016B/3600